KIT GUNS
& *HOBBY GUNSMITHING*

Publisher
Paul T. Ballard, Ph.D.

Executive Editor
Alan F. Lundin

Managing Editor
William L. Janning

Associate Editor
C. Robin Renfroe

Exotic Weapons Editor
Gary E. Reisenwitz

Copy Editor
Lisa J. Brown

Graphics
David Van Etten

Mechanical Design
Michael P. D'Elia

Chief Photographer
Simon E. Smith

Assistant to the Publisher
Joyce A. Booher

Circulation
Donna J. Ballard

Telecommunications Consultant
Edward Bratka

CONTENTS

Blackpowder Kits

Modern Kits

Exotica

Gunsmithing Tips

the Directory—*your source for kit gun information*

WARNING!

This publication contains material on weapons which are regulated by the Federal Bureau of Alcohol, Tobacco and Firearms. Severe penalties, up to a $10,000 fine, and/or a jail sentence of up to 10 years may result if these regulations are not strictly observed. Refer to ATF Form 1 for details. You must also observe all applicable state and local regulations for your area regarding the possession or use of firearms. Check with your local authorities before proceeding with any project.

All firearms are intrinsically dangerous and can cause death or serious injury if improperly handled. Proceed with extreme caution when constructing or working with any firearm. If in doubt, consult a professional gunsmith. *KIT GUNS & HOBBY GUNSMITHING* and Balund, Inc. assume no liability for the willful or negligent misuse or illegal use of the material contained in this publication.

the CVA Shotgun Kit

by Glen Webster

Connecticut Valley Arms has recently introduced a blackpowder shotgun kit which should appeal to just about any shooter. This new shotgun is one of only a few shotgun kits available to the blackpowder (or for that matter, even smokeless powder) enthusiast. CVA's entry is truly magnificent — a fine addition to any gun collection.

The CVA shotgun kit comes complete with a detailed set of instructions on: (1) how to assemble and finish the kit; and (2) how to safely shoot the shotgun after it has been finished. The kit arrives packed in a styrofoam box which separates and protects all of the major pieces.

The metal components were very well finished: no file, milling or casting marks were found on any exposed part. The stock was about 99% inletted and almost completely shaped to the final contours. The stock, unlike the finished CVA shotgun, is not checkered. This only makes sense, since any checkering done before the stock is fully finished would probably be ruined.

The Kit

The 12-gauge, smooth-bore barrels measure 28-5/8" from bore to tang and are configured as a side-by-side double. The breech is hooked for easy take-down. No mention is made in the finishing instructions against hot-bluing the barrels, so we presume that they have not been soft-soldered. My inspection of the barrels indicates that they may have been silver-soldered or brazed together. A brass bead front sight is provided, but not installed by the factory.

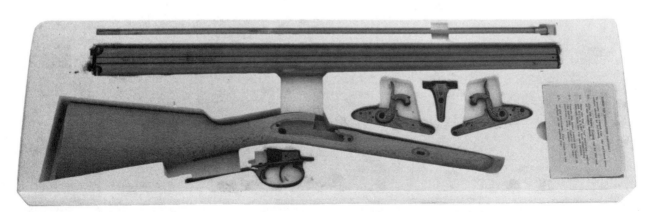

The CVA Shotgun Kit.

The barrels of the CVA Shotgun are configured as a side-by-side double, measuring 28-5/8" from bore to tang. The breech is hooked for easy takedown. The finish on the barrels is the nicest I have ever seen on a blackpowder kit.

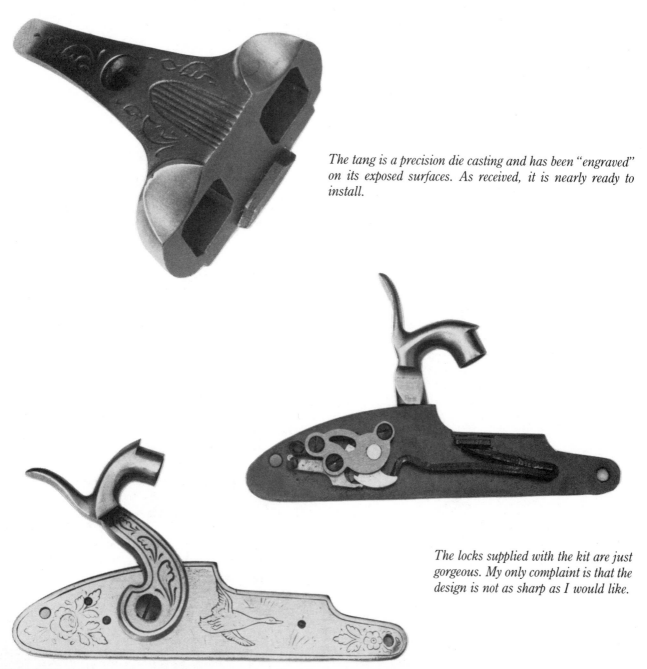

The tang is a precision die casting and has been "engraved" on its exposed surfaces. As received, it is nearly ready to install.

The locks supplied with the kit are just gorgeous. My only complaint is that the design is not as sharp as I would like.

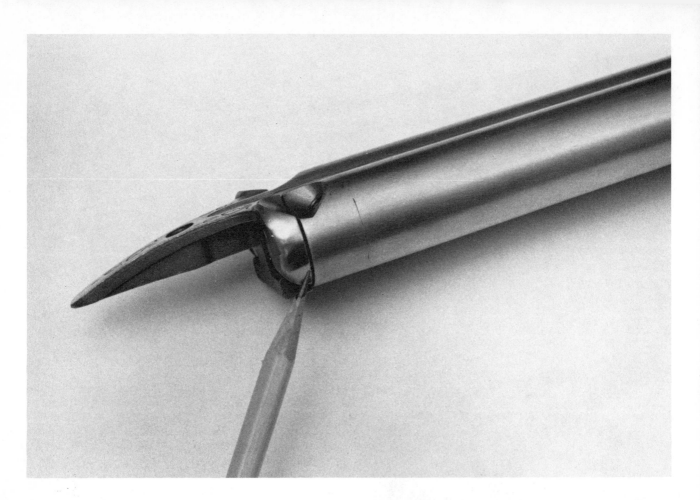

The tang and barrel had to be fitted. Ideally, there should be no visible gap between the two.

The tang is a die casting which has been polished and *engraved* on the exposed portions. The finish on the tang is very good (for a kit), and the tang is very nearly ready to install. I am somewhat reluctant to describe the designs on the tang (and most of the other metal parts) as engraving. It is not. It is attractive and it is definitely the best that I have seen on a blackpowder kit, regardless of price, but it is not engraving. What it appears to be, at least in the case of the tang, is a design incorporated into the die which was then cast into the tang. I plan to use these designs as a starting point, and will deepen and refine them before I call this kit finished.

The locks are a joy to behold. They are well finished, but will require the same ministrations to the *engraving* as described above. The locks feature a screw-adjustable sear engagement, a fly and a V-type mainspring. All of the internal parts of the lock appear to be very well made and I see no reason for the kit builder to consider working on any part of the locks, except to occasionally replace a worn or damaged part. I would like to qualify that, however, in that the hammer will have to be removed in order to touch up the engraving and to restore the finish that Spanish craftsmen had originally applied, but which has been subsequently damaged by in-process handling. As the final inspector, I want these pieces to be the very best possible before I install them.

The triggers leave some to be desired, at least on first inspection. The internal fits are extremely loose, and in my experience, this leads to marginal trigger pulls. For-

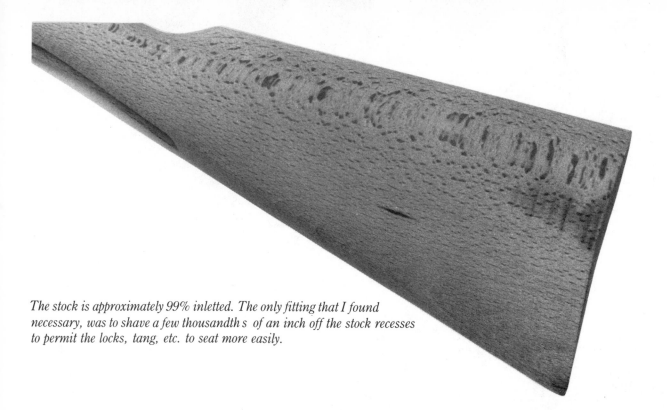

The stock is approximately 99% inletted. The only fitting that I found necessary, was to shave a few thousandths of an inch off the stock recesses to permit the locks, tang, etc. to seat more easily.

tunately, it appears that the sloppy fit in the triggers can be corrected by installing a brass washer on the trigger pivot pins.

The trigger guard is an artful construct. The trigger guard has obviously been formed from sheet steel, but CVA has managed to add a small flourish just behind the rear trigger that must have been welded in place. However, I cannot see any evidence of a join mark. The trigger guard has also been engraved with a fairly intricate design.

The stock supplied by CVA is approximately 99% inletted. Basically, everything fits where it should, but the fit is extremely tight. I plan to shave off a few thousandths of an inch around most of the inletted parts before I install them permanently. CVA advertises their stock as being "select" hardwood. I don't know what that is, so I will describe what I see in the kit. The stock is made from a fairly-light colored wood, similar to white oak or maple. The wood is moderately dense (the pre-shaped stock weighs 2.7 pounds) and hard, but it is easy to cut with a sharp knife. There is no figure to speak of in the wood and there are some fairly large cells which are very evident due to the way the stock blank was sawn. Naturally, I

would rather have some sort of exhibition grade stock, but the economic realities of producing an affordable kit prohibit such touches.

Building the CVA Shotgun

The first task faced in building this kit is to inlet and seat the right- and left-hand locks. CVA recommends that the kit builder trace the outline of the lock onto the stock and then cut away the excess material with a sharp knife or chisel. Since both of my locks fit into the stock (at least partially) I merely shaved a slight amount of material around the periphery of the lock recess and then set the locks into place.

The barrel and tang were next to be fitted. The tang was placed on the barrel hooks and the gap between the barrel and tang was inspected. The ideal is to have no visible gap here. With a fine file, the rear of the barrels and the barrel hooks were de-burred. This allowed the tang to fit flush to the barrels. I also found it necessary to do some blending of the contours between the tang and barrel to obtain a pleasing assembly. This was accomplished with a Dremel tool and a 1/2" sanding drum.

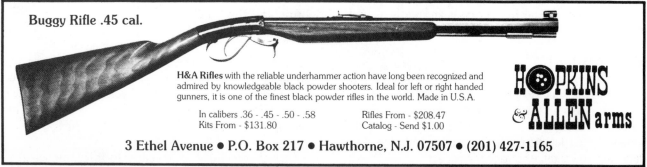

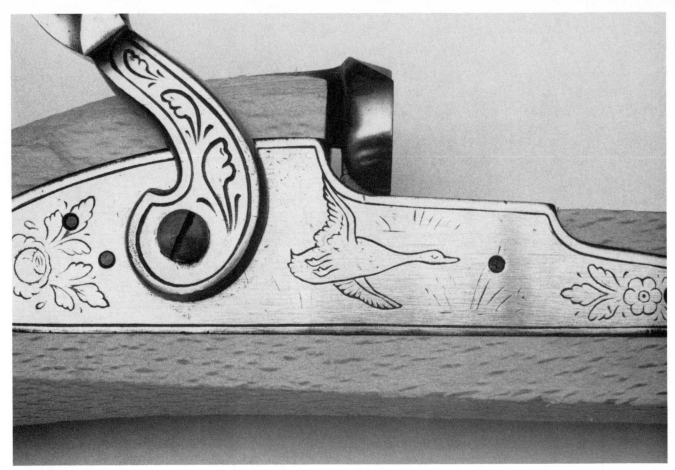

The tang and locks interfered with each other slightly. This was corrected by removing a small amount of material from the backside of the lock plate.

Like the lockwork, the tang could be readily set into the stock. It also was a very tight fit and some wood had to be shaved in order to obtain an acceptable fit. The locks interfered with the tang, and so I had to grind some material from the underside of the lock plate to allow the tang to seat fully into the stock. This only required a few minutes to accomplish.

Next, the wedge plates were inserted into their recesses in the stock and four pilot holes were drilled into the stock with a 1/16" drill. The four flat-head screws were then installed, completing the installation.

The trigger assembly had to be modified to remove the looseness noted earlier. I stopped by the local hardware store and picked up a couple of no. 6 brass washers which I installed inside the trigger housing. The trigger guard had to be screwed onto the trigger before either could be installed into the stock. The trigger guard and trigger fit easily into their respective recesses and were securely fastened using the screws provided.

Metal Finishing

The barrel, tang, locks, trigger and trigger guard are the most nicely finished parts that I have seen on a black-powder kit in many years. Despite the obvious care that somebody had put into finishing these parts, the inevitable dings due to handling managed to appear.

Most of these dings were easily removed by rubbing the effected part with 320-grit emery paper. Some areas, especially on the barrel, required a few strokes with a fine file. One area that required some serious ministrations with a file, however, was the rear of the barrel assembly where CVA stamped their name. Once this was cleaned up, the barrel and other metal parts were ready for bluing or plating.

I chose to have the barrel blued, rather than browned, because I prefer the appearance of modern bluing to browning. The advertisements for the CVA Shotgun show the locks (and possibly the trigger guard) in the white. I found this to be very attractive and rather than trust the vagaries of nature to maintain their appearance over time, I decided to have the locks and trigger guard electroless nickel plated. The trigger assembly, tang, and all the other assorted bits and pieces were blued, along with the barrel.

Finishing the Stock

The stock had to be sanded, using medium-coarse garnet paper stapled to a wood block, to remove the ripples produced by the shaper knives. The stock also had to be sanded flush to the inletted metalwork. Tape was applied to the exposed metal pieces to prevent them from being damaged by the garnet paper during the sanding process.

Once the stock had been reduced to its final proportions,

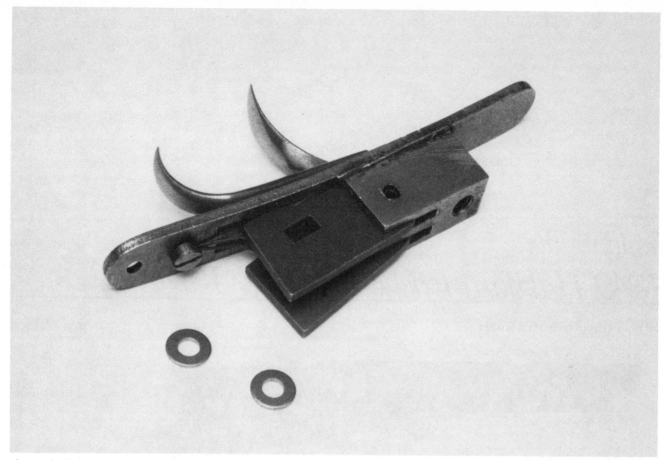

As received, the trigger assembly was very loose. The side-to-side play was removed by installing two brass washers inside the trigger housing.

successively finer grades of garnet paper were utilized until an acceptably smooth finish was obtained. A transparent walnut stain was applied to the stock and wiped about with a clean rag until the color seemed about right. Next, a liberal coating of linseed oil was applied to the stock and allowed to dry.

The linseed oil treatment was repeated several times, rubbing the stock between coats with 0000 steel wool, until an even, satiny finish was obtained.

Final Assembly

Once the stock had been finished, it was only necessary to assemble the various pieces.

First, the locks had to be re-installed into their recesses and the retaining screws assembled through the left lock. Next, the tang was placed into the stock, followed by the trigger and trigger guard. Then, the tang screw was inserted and drawn up tight, securing the tang and trigger assembly to the stock.

The wedge plates were installed and fastened to the stock with the four screws supplied. The thimbles were attached to the barrel assembly using the small flathead screws provided with the kit. Next the brass bead sight was installed onto the barrel. The sight only required that it be screwed in with a pair of padded pliers to its pre-

drilled and tapped hole.

Finally, the barrel assembly was installed onto the stock. First, the breech was hooked into the tang. Then, the barrel was set down into the stock and the barrel wedge installed. The final step in the assembly was to insert the ramrod and the two stainless steel nipples.

Conclusion

I am not a shotgunner. I am not even a blackpowder enthusiast. Since I am now the owner of a beautiful blackpowder shotgun, I plan to do something about the previous two deficiencies.

The CVA Shotgun Kit is very easy to assemble and the instructions are detailed and easy to follow. Both the novice and experienced kit builder will enjoy assembling this kit.

building the
1849 Hartford Pocket Revolver Kit

with a little help from a friend

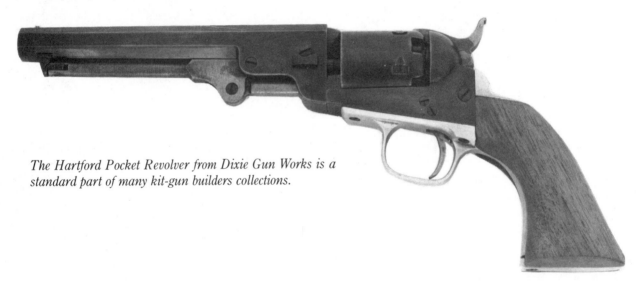

The Hartford Pocket Revolver from Dixie Gun Works is a standard part of many kit-gun builders collections.

by Charles W. Janning

Editor's note: If you thought that all you needed to build a kit gun was an abundance of talent, time, and tools then read on. This author makes the point that a flexible conscience, an over-active imagination and a little help from history can be just as useful.

Like a beautiful woman, any handgun with a frontier-style grip makes a powerful first impression. Its intrinsic qualities may as yet be undetermined but its appearance invites further consideration. That, basically, was my thinking when I saw the 1849 Hartford Pocket Cap and Ball Revolver from Dixie Gun Works for the first time.

I had never finished a gun from a kit and, a short while ago, I didn't even know that they made kit guns. In fact, I didn't even know that much about cap and ball firearms. When the editors of KG&HG asked me to build this kit, I explained to them that my knowledge of cap and ball revolvers was limited mostly to western movies—the ones

from the earlier period which, frankly, as a kid, I didn't even care much about. My favorite movies were from the later period which featured modern cartridge-type ammunition along with Gary Cooper, John Wayne, John Payne, Forrest Tucker, Randolph Scott, Dale Robertson, and an absolutely gorgeous bunch of female stars whose names and other attributes I'm sure you will remember if you're in my age category which is not yet half a century. Such was my almost zero knowledge of cap and ball guns. I did, however, remember that John Payne was in more cap and ball movies than the others and it was this recollection that prompted me to accept the challenge of the editors. Such are the impeccable credentials with which I present myself to you the readers of this august publication.

About the author: Charles W. Janning, an attorney, received his A.B. degree from Harvard, his LL.B. from Case Western Reserve and is a member of the Bar of Ohio. He did post graduate work in pistols and guns with the Federal Bureau of Investigation where he served as a Special Agent for three years.

The kit comes assembled although most of the parts are still quite rough. The metal parts, while blued, still have many machining marks and the grip is only roughly fitted.

Now, it's not my intention to bore you unnecessarily (some boredom is necessary) but I should tell you a few other things about myself since this article is intended primarily for the beginner. I am familiar with guns, have fired quite a few — but never a cap and ball — and I lean toward the handgun. I never did have enough coordination or patience for long guns. It's enough trouble trying to get one hand and arm to do what you want without having to worry about the two hands and arms it takes to shoot a rifle or a shotgun. As you can see, I'm a very simple fellow. (This is basically the same reason I played defensive tackle on the high school football team: no coordination needed and everything was very simple — just don't let anyone come through that eight-foot hole.)

There, now you have all of my qualifications for the job, except perhaps, for one other. I am also a carpenter. "Who gives a ?" you say. "That's about as related to kit guns as being a notary public." (I'm also a notary public.) Well carpenter work does give you a lot of experience in working with your hands and tools, and I didn't want you to get the impression I'm one of those smooth-pawed slickers who never got his hands dirty before.

So much for experience, but what about attitude? Do you have to be an absolute precision-loving, Swiss-watch-making, perfectionist to be a kit gun finisher? If so, then they picked the wrong guy when they handed this thing to old CWJ. In addition to a regular job, I have other hobbies and outside interests, and I just didn't have the time to fool around with this gun all summer long. Besides, they gave me a one month deadline to finish the gun as

The first thing I did to the kit was to disassemble it. This was easy and only took a few minutes.

"I shouldn't think that you could do it properly in thirty years," replied Arch. "You don't even have any of the proper tools."

well as this literary masterpiece. Please don't think that I'm sloppy, but I do have a definite attitude toward getting things done in a reasonable amount of time. However, we all have within us certain conflicts. Sometimes, another self is submerged deep inside us and we feel its pressure against our conscience. Thus, in my case, there was the constant conflict between the predominating "get the job done" versus "lets do this thing right and have it displayed in the Smithsonian." With that explanation out of the way, I must introduce you to the companion who collaborated with me throughout this project.

He appeared on my workbench late the first night when I began the draw-filing operation. He was a wrinkled old guy about ten inches high, all togged up in a three-cornered hat, a white lacey shirt with big ballooned sleeves, and a worn leather apron. He introduced himself as Archibald Picayune Fusseybiddle, Grand Master of all Master Gunsmiths, and Supreme High Priest of the Insufferable Order of Nitpickers. (I'll call him Arch.) He explained that he came from the "dark and rather small and neglected chamber which is my conscience" and proclaimed that he was here to make sure that I didn't botch-up this very worthy firearm. I politely indicated that it was swell to have him, but that he should stay the hell out of the way because *Big Charlie* only has thirty days to wrap this up.

"I shouldn't think that you could do it properly in thirty years" he replied. "You don't even have any of the proper tools."

"What do you call this stuff, Arch? I've got two old files, six pieces of only slightly used emery paper, and my trusty old electric drill that hardly ever shorts-out any more since I wrapped it in electrical tape."

"I call that junk!" replied Arch, who then proceeded to lecture me on the need to lay-in a full range of only the finest in metalcrafting tools.

"Tell you what Arch; I'll buy a couple of new files if you promise not to talk too much. I've got work to do."

So the next day, I went down to my local hardware store and bought four new files — well actually three files and a rasp. They were an 8″ flat file, one that was a 6″ triangular, and a 6″ round. (The rasp would later be used on the wood grip.) That night, Arch said that the 16 bucks that they cost me was "a pittance" and he also thought that the $17 bench vice that I was using on the project was "not fit to hold the manured shoes of a Tory plough horse!" I ignored him.

Disassembly

The gun comes assembled. Disassembly is simple. It takes about eight minutes to remove approximately one dozen screws and the thing is in pieces. ("No doubt forever," commented Arch.) The barrel and frame are blued but the metal is pretty rough. The cylinder is also blued and has a much smoother finish. The trigger guard and

The barrel is the only piece that can be draw filed. Putting the file tang to the left presents the cutting teeth to the direction of the draw.

backstrap are brass or some other alloy and are also pretty rough. The loading lever, plunger, hammer, and trigger are case hardened steel which was a tad rusty. The grip was a good quality hardwood — I didn't know what kind — that would need a lot of finishing.

The very brief instructions in Italian and English don't really provide much insight into what you're getting into, but they do contain a good illustrated parts breakdown that was helpful when I reassembled the gun about a month later. The Italian part of the instructions were not very useful to me since I don't even understand English very well. (Arch says that he speaks 27 languages.) It is interesting, however, to contrast the English words with the corresponding Italian. Not to be smug, but English is a good bit more efficient. For instance, the Italian for *barrel stud* is *Ergot de levier de chargement.*

Draw Filing

The only piece that can and must be draw filed is the barrel or *cannon* as the Italians put it. Remember the barrel has eight sides. The top side has the front sight soft-soldered into it and the bottom side is obstructed toward the front by the *Ergot de levier de chargement,* i.e., the barrel stud which I later came to call the *pain in the as-serini.* Because of these protuberances you do not have a clean file shot at two of the eight sides. In these situations when I'm doing something for the first time I always do what seems to be the easiest thing first. So, I mounted the barrel in the vice with one of the totally unobstructed sides up. I used a couple of scrap pieces of hardboard in

the vice jaws to keep from chewing up the metal.

I then put my 8″ flat file on the barrel with the tang to the left since this presents the cutting teeth of the file to the direction of the draw. Starting at the muzzle end, I slowly drew the file to me being careful to keep the file flat on the metal so that the edges forming the octagon shape would not be disturbed. I don't know how many times Arch told me to be careful not to *break* the barrel edges in order that the finished product would appear authentic. I went along with him on this because if you bugger-up the edges it really would look a mess. I was amazed that the metal sheared-off so easily, taking with it portions of the factory bluing.

It occurred to me that the reason for the factory bluing was not only to prevent rust, but also to let me know, when the bluing was all gone, that I had filed off enough metal. Therefore, the bluing was my gauge. After about two dozen strokes the metal was completely shiny and much smoother.

The immediate and clear effect of the filing was so satisfying that I had to resist the temptation to continue. But, Arch reminded me that there was really no point in filing the thing into a pile of dust on the garage floor. So, I then took my smaller, finer, triangular file and hit it a few more times and pronounced draw filing finished for that side. Arch said that I was a "blundering incompetent; it should be draw-filed lightly with seventeen different, increasingly finer files to get the caliber of work that I'm used to doing." "Sorry Arch," said I. "I haven't got a fortnight to draw file

Above: I laid emery paper on a flat surface and finished the barrel by rubbing it back and forth in the long direction while proceeding to successively finer grades of paper.

Right: The curved surfaces of the barrel were finished with the sanding wheel first, and then the emery paper to get a smooth finish.

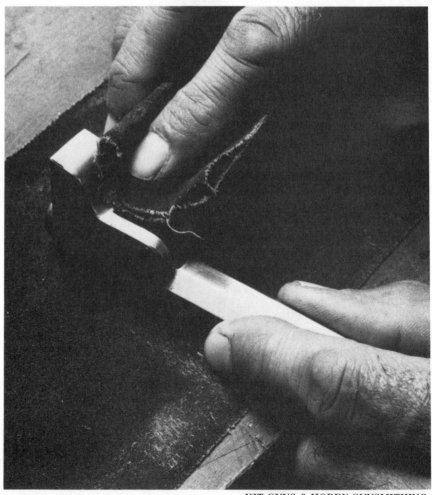

one side. I've only got two fortnights to finish the whole damn thing." (I was cleverly testing him to see if he knew what a fortnight was. He did of course. He knows everything.)

By this time I had one side in pretty good shape — now for the others. Next, I selected another unobstructed side and finished it in the same manner as the first. Then I decided to go for one of the tough ones and mounted the top side with the soft-soldered front sight in the vice. I proceeded with my 8″ flat file behind the sight and toward me away from the muzzle, i.e., the long clear shot. This of course was no problem but it left an unfinished spot next to the sight on my side and also on the front portion of the barrel which extended about one-half inch from the sight forward. There is no scientific answer to the problem of finishing close around the sight unless you know how to take it out and put it back in without destroying it in the process and I didn't. My technique was to use the large file for a few short strokes to take off the worst and then work around the sight with the small file to take off what was left. I ended-up getting off most of the factory bluing, but it really wasn't very pretty and I noticed that I left a couple of file marks that were a little more noticeable than I care to admit. Arch noticed them too and called me a "butcher." "Don't worry, old pal," I said. "All of that will come off in the next process," I promised with more bravado than confidence, hoping that emery paper would make me an honest man.

By now, you have probably guessed that the bottom side with its Ergot de levier de chargement embedded near the muzzle presented a similar problem. With predictable predictability (otherwise known as a lack of imagination) I attacked this area with the same highly-skilled and refined techniques as before: short strokes first with the big file and then the smaller one. I must confess that this seemed a bit of hit-or-miss risky, and I didn't enjoy it either because my mind kept flashing pictures of terrible, unfixable gouges. However, I managed to end up after quite a bit of labor with most of the factory bluing gone and no really bad file marks. "There, that looks pretty good," I told Arch a little meekly. "Only to a blind man on a bucking bronco in a sand storm," replied the garrulous gnome. (Where did he pick up that carpenter talk, I wondered?) And then, he delivered the coup de grace. "By the way, my spike driving, wood butchering, sun stroked friend, did it ever occur to your resin soaked mind that you could have removed the Ergot de levier de chargement by merely taping it out with a small hammer and a brass drift, thus providing an unobstructed surface for filing?" Silently I thought "!", and my lips moved over clenched teeth but there was no sound.

Emery and Sanding

This story moves right along to the next phase of work because of my decision that any minor problems with the draw filing could be corrected by a good rub with emery paper and a sanding wheel. I decided not to knock out the

High spots on the dome at the back of the frame were attacked first with the sanding wheel. This was especially effective against the casting marks which appeared at the front of the dome.

barrel stud as Arch had so diplomatically (and belatedly) suggested because a second look told me the filing job was actually not bad with only one faintly visible file mark. Secondly, there were other curved areas of the barrel where filing was not possible. These, of course, were the sharply curved portions to the rear of the barrel assembly where the barrel connects to the frame. My thinking was that if I had to do it all with emery paper and sanding in that curved area, I might as well finish up around the barrel stud in the same manner. Also, I was kind of chicken about taking a hammer to the barrel stud—who knows, I might have busted something.

I think I neglected to tell you earlier about one additional purchase. At the local hardware store I bought a small sanding wheel for my old electric drill. It's a cylindrically-shaped thing about one-half inch in diameter and one-half inch high with a one inch long shank that fits in the drill. Over this, fits a cylindrically-shaped piece of sandpaper. I also bought four pieces of sandpaper. They don't seem to have any identification on them, so I can only tell you that two were fine and the other two were not-so-fine. My other supplies for this phase of the operation were eight pieces of emery paper which I had on hand — didn't have to buy them, thank God!

The emery phase was to be another first for me. I had never put emery paper to metal before for the express purpose of making it very smooth like the finish on my factory-built Ruger single action revolver. Therefore, I proceeded with my customary caution and started on one

of the unobstructed barrel sides first; the same one on which I started the draw filing operation. Here again, one should take caution not to bugger the sharp corners of the barrel, and for all I knew, the emery paper might disintegrate the barrel like balsa wood under a jack hammer. So, I took the coarsest paper and put it flat down on the work bench, held it with my left hand, and very carefully rubbed the surface of the barrel back and forth with my right hand. The barrel was rubbed in the long direction along the length of the barrel. After about 45 seconds of this, I looked at the barrel and observed that things were proceeding nicely but not fast enough. Losing my initial inhibitions, I repeated the process much more vigorously for another couple of minutes. The result seemed to be all that the coarse paper would do so I proceeded on with the next finer grade of paper. When I had completed the process with multiple grades of paper I seemed to detect a small smile of approval from Arch as he observed the finished side, and I was on the verge of thinking that this was too easy.

My overconfidence grew as I finished the remaining flat and unobstructed sides of the barrel but deep down I knew hard times were ahead — up close to the front sight and the barrel stud. I was right. There is nothing very scientific about working around these areas with the emery paper — just a lot of finger and thumb-numbing work as best you can with the various grades of paper. Working these small areas took as much time and more labor than all of the flat areas put together.

Finally, the frame was finished with emery paper to erase the marks left by the previous operations.

The final area of the barrel was the underside with its two sets of sharp curves. The curvature seemed to be rather close to that of my sanding wheel so I mounted the barrel in my vice once again and attacked it with the coarse wheel attached to the old electric drill. The trick here is to hold the drill level so that you sand the entire area without grinding-in any new grooves that were not intended by the gun's designer. When wielding these magnificent power tools you really must resist the temptation to be original (or sloppy as Arch put it). While not intending to do so, I did do something a little bit original while bearing-down on the inside of the barrel where the sanding wheel is just a tad bigger than the curve. You can guess the rest—I ground out a little bit more than just the factory bluing and created an original *CWJ* where the designer of this flawless masterpiece had not put one. Now, I must admit that most of my original creations are instant successes and wind up selling for hundreds of thousands of dollars, but I really didn't think that this one would make the Louvre in Paris so I did what any honest person would do. I covered it up by grinding-out a little more on both the front and back edges of the groove to make it appear less noticeable. Luckily, the cover-up was successful and the unintended original creation was nearly invisible as even Arch would attest: "At least in so far as a blind man on a bucking bronco in a sand storm is concerned," he repeated with increasing regularity.

I knew that the frame, upon which no draw filing could be done because of its lack of unobstructed flat surfaces, would have to be totally finished with the sanding wheel and emery paper. The lower flat surfaces of the frame were quite rough and it was obvious that the only effective tool that I had for this was the coarser paper on the sanding wheel. This was nothing to be timid about because a lot of grinding lay ahead. I did the flat surfaces freehand with the wheel, holding the frame with my left hand and applying quite a bit of force with the drill in my right. After about ten minutes of grinding, both flat portions of the frame appeared clean. Next, I switched to the finest paper I had for the wheel and again went over the flat surfaces working close to the dome-like structure at the back of the frame. However, the wheel would not entirely smooth and clean the metal along the crease where the dome meets the flat surfaces. I knew that the crease could only be finished by hand work.

Then I attacked the dome itself with the fine paper. The coarse paper was not necessary because the dome was a good bit smoother than the flat surfaces. I had misgivings about using the cylindrical wheel on the opposite curves of the dome, but I managed to clean off the factory bluing without creating any more *originals*. The light touch here was definitely in order.

I had now done all that I was going to do to the frame with electricity and the rest was up to muscle. Arch condescended that I was uncharacteristically patient during all of this. I admit that on the frame I did more *piddling* than any other part, i.e., on several occasions I thought I was finished only to see some other flaw and start again. I think that during this encounter with the frame Arch

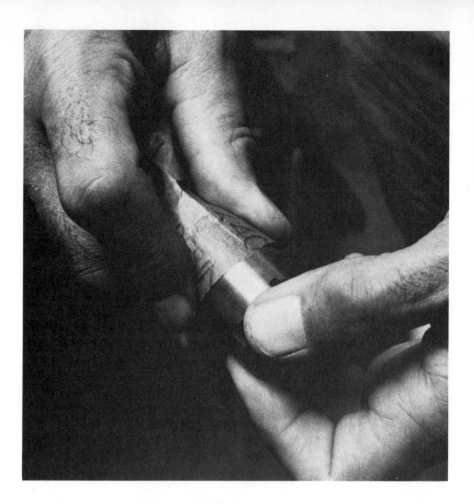

The cylinder turned out to be easier than I expected. I didn't have to do much more to it than remove the factory bluing with the emery paper.

began to see a ray of hope for me.

The last chapter of the emery paper saga is not much of a story at all. The cylinder came out of the factory in very smooth condition. I believe this was done with merciful intent by the manufacturer who must have understood that no hammer mechanic like me could finish so round and intricate an object without some very serious equipment and experience. I also suspect that not a little self interest was involved since they no doubt desire that their guns end up looking pretty good for the purpose of further sales. Whatever their motives, I was most grateful that the only thing the cylinder required was enough emery work to remove the bluing. I did this by merely turning the cylinder briskly with my right hand inside a circle of emery paper held in the left hand. The cylinder took no more than 20 minutes. Totally without fear of contradiction (my hand is now over Arch's mouth) I can tell you that there is absolutely no point in doing anything about the small and intricate crevices at the rear of the cylinder in the area of the nipples. Preying into these numerous small orifices would have taken the rest of the century for no observable result except to prevent the occasional, itinerant, microscopic germ from residing in one of those tiny places.

On the Brass Parts and Other Matters of Equal Felicity Not Requiring Great Skill

If you ever read Cervantes' great masterpiece, *Don Quixote*, you know he had a tendency to use extremely long and flowery titles. They always struck me as being mildly humorous and definitely classy. Thinking that this piece could do with a little class, I threw in the one above. I hope you will forgive me for this minor indulgence.

From Don Quixote we move to the mundane world of the brass parts: the backstrap and the trigger guard. If you're a beginner, and not too confident of your ability, I would suggest you start with the brass parts as a test of your probability of being able to finish the kit. To put it another way, if you can't do the brass parts you're in big trouble. The brass is very soft and easy to work even though the parts are quite rough to start.

My procedure was as follows: First, I knocked off the roughest edges with the small file. Next, I used the sanding wheel on the drill with the rough paper first and then the fine. After this, I went down the list of emery paper from the medium to the fine. The final step was polishing with a cloth polishing wheel inserted in the electric drill. During all of this you must be careful not to take off too much metal or you will undersize the parts where they are supposed to match up with the steel, e.g., where the trigger guard attaches to the frame.

Working the brass required quite a lot of use from my old electric drill and that's a story in itself. The drill is about 20 years old and has helped to build two houses. Over its long and hard life it has been severely tested by

16

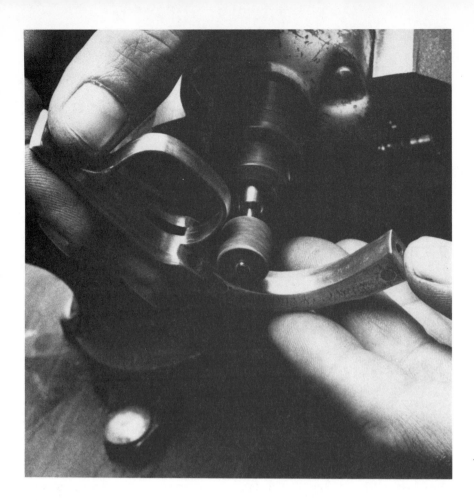

I was glad I saved the brass for last. It was easy to work and by this time I felt that I was getting pretty good at metal finishing. The brass only served to boost my confidence.

many of the opponents that it was required to face such as 3″ plumbing holes in ¾″ plywood and the countless holes it was forced to bore in concrete with a dull masonry bit. All of this has left the poor machine in a state of near collapse. Its history of abuse has been so extensive that when turned on it makes a terrible screeching sound that causes my dog to immediately head for cover. It also produces lots of blue sparks along with a peculiar electric odor and it has a tendency to get quite hot almost instantly. The tendency to over-heat may be related to the fact that in the past it has many times been driven under heavy load to the point of getting so hot that I needed welding gloves to hold on to it. My trusty old drill is a source of constant amusement to friends who think I'm just too cheap to buy a new one. Mere lucre, however, is not the real reason I keep it. It's been with me for so long, through so much, and so many hard times that it's become an old pal I can't bear to part with, even though it is somewhat of a fire hazard. I confess all of this only to demonstrate that my finishing operations were not conducted in the world's most modern machine shop.

Another thought struck me while working on the brass. As I recall from grammar school history, Paul Revere was a silversmith. It's now clear to me why he had so much time to fool around with politics and such — working with soft metal must have been one of the easiest of the trades in those days.

The subhead at the beginning of this section promised

you *Other Matters of Equal Felicity* and that of course means the wooden grip. It also comes very rough in the kit but working such a small piece of wood is like falling off a small log. All it takes is a few seconds of work with the rasp and then three grades of sandpaper from medium to fine. When it was smooth I finished it with two coats of tung oil which gave it a fairly dark appearance. You might want to consider a lighter finish especially if the metal is to be darkly blued. A thousand stains of different colors are available. It also occurred to me that a urethane finish over the stain might look good, however, I realize that the *authenticators* would certainly reject this idea.

Bluing

Having got the thing in reasonably good shape I now had to consider bluing. Hot bluing seemed to be out of the question because the front sight is soft-soldered into the barrel and I was told that the hot bluing process would probably melt the solder and the sight would fall out in the bluing tank. The other alternative was cold bluing. Some of my *expert* friends told me that it was difficult to get a consistent finish with cold bluing, which amounts to little more than painting the parts with a paste or fluid and letting the finish react with the metal.

Faced with these obstacles, which to a novice like me seemed insurmountable, I let my mind loose to discover something surefire, easy, and not necessarily orthodox. I think that because I always liked shiny guns I hit upon the

Since I call myself a carpenter, working with the wooden grip was no challenge at all. It's nice to be back in your own element and in no time I had a well-fitting and finished grip.

idea of nickel plating. Nonsense, said the experts, that wouldn't be authentic! Maybe so, but it sure would please *my* eye hanging on *my* wall and I'm the only one that it really has to please. Then I remembered what General Patton is supposed to have said about pearl-handled guns: "They are only carried by pimps and other undesirables." I figured that he would probably feel the same about nickel plate. Daring to question one as authoritative as General Patton on these matters, I decided to have it nickel-plated anyway and tell people that it was once carried by a Pony Express rider who moonlighted as a pimp in New Orleans. That idea really settled the question for me so I immediately contacted a local plating shop for price and other details. The other details were easy — just have it nice and smooth — but the price was another matter. It would cost from $30 to $50 for the job.

That fact kind of cooled my enthusiasm for the pimp in New Orleans and I decided that the traditionalists were right after all. I just couldn't betray the memory of all of those sturdy pioneers who founded this country with blue guns. It was final then, I would finish the gun with a special brand of blue called "Much Less Costly Than Nickel Plating Blue" or MLCTNP Blue for short.

One trip later to my local sporting goods store revealed that they were all out of MLCTNP Blue so I settled for the other brand they carried which was *Old Time Blue and Finish Kit* from Connecticut Valley Arms, Inc. With this kit you get a stain and finish for the wooden parts as well as a degreaser and bluing solution for the metal. I had already finished the grip so the stain and finish remained

unused. The directions for the metal bluing process were simple, short, and adequate. They call for washing the metal parts in detergent and hot water which I did religiously in the downstairs sink for about five minutes. After drying with a clean rag, you apply the degreaser twice, rubbing the hell out of it each time with another rag and all the while being careful not to touch it with your bare hands and get grease on it again. This is easier to do if you stick a wooden dowel pin in the bore of the barrel and grasp the other parts of the metal with the degreasing rag.

Now you're ready to put the blue to it. This is really the critical step, but it turned out to be a fairly easy task. With a cotton swab I put the bluing stuff on, trying to cover it evenly and in long uninterrupted strokes. As it went on, the metal turned almost the shade of MLCTNP Blue that I was shooting for. After covering the whole barrel, it looked a bit blotchy but not too bad. At this point, the instructions say to wash it with water and then rub it with fine steel wool. I did those things but I found that the steel wool seemed to take off too much color, especially around the sharp edges.

After the first application, I found that I had a fairly even color with only a few light spots here and there. I decided to give it another coat with the bluing solution, once again as heavy and even as possible. After this, I washed it and while I was drying the part I noticed that the coarse rag I was using seemed to be helping to spread the color around on the part. The rag seemed to be smoothing-out the finish without rubbing it off. The rag was actually doing what the steel wool was supposed to do but doing it better. It's possible that the steel wool I used wasn't fine enough.

A third application of blue and another hard rub with the rag seemed to do the trick. Not a factory bluing job, but a passably good job to be sure. And from what the experts told me, it must be a darn sight better than what they were able to achieve with their bluing kits. I was really cocky now and I blued the remaining two parts, the cylinder and the frame, in no time. The result was a bluing job that easily rivaled the one on my factory-built Colt Woodsman automatic.

In total, the whole process of bluing all three parts, the barrel, cylinder, and frame, took about three hours. But remember, this was first time beginner time. Now that I've got experience, a veteran if you please, I think I could do the whole job in an hour-and-a-half flat.

Reassembly

All of the parts were now ready for reassembly which I figured should be about a ten minute job if you were familiar with the gun. There's really not many parts and nothing is tricky about the process. As it was, I had not taken the time to mark any of the screws as to where they came from and it had been several weeks since I disassembled the gun. Therefore, it took me about forty five minutes of fooling around to put the whole thing back together.

Conclusion

So now it was finished and I looked at it and I looked at Arch and I said that I was satisfied. "I did my best in a reasonable amount of time and I plan to make a small plaque for it and hang it in my office and all of my friends who see it will think that it's a damn fine job." Instead of the smart retort I expected, Arch was silent and seemed to be deep in thought. In a few moments, he said softly and without animosity: "I suppose that *your* friends wouldn't see what *my* friends would see. We do move in different circles, you know. After all, you're not even a member of the Order of Nitpickers."

Then he added, "How much time do you think that you have into it?"

"About eight two-hour evenings and one four-hour Saturday morning," I replied, "and I could cut that by about a third on the next one now that I have some experience."

"I suppose that there is some benefit in not taking too

long to finish," Arch admitted quietly and mostly to himself. "Perhaps I could have used you back during the war."

"What war?"

"The war with England, dunderhead. You have heard of the Revolutionary War of 1776 haven't you? It was in all the papers!" he bellowed.

"Oh, that war. Why don't you tell me about it old patch box breath."

Once again, the bluster seemed to drain from Arch's voice as he explained: "Well, it was like this. You see, I had a contract with the Continental Congress to supply a thousand muskets to General George Washington's army. I don't suppose I should tell you this," he said with a look of resignation, "but it didn't work out too well."

"What happened?"

"Well, the contract called for delivery of the thousand muskets in one year but I only got one of them finished and they terminated my contract for default."

I suppressed a smile as he continued.

"But the thing that really hurt was when George Washington himself told me, after looking at the one magnificently finished musket, that he didn't give a pinch of snuff about the fine engraving and beautiful woodwork because he had more than one Hessian to fight and he needed a thousand muskets. After that, they wouldn't give me any more government contracts and a nasty rumor circulated that I was a security risk and soft on Tories."

Needless to say, I was deeply touched by this obviously painful confession so I leveled with him and told him that although we didn't see eye-to-eye on a few matters, that his looking over my shoulder throughout this project kept me on the ball and made for a pretty good balance between time and quality. The little fellow seemed to appreciate that, and as he turned to reenter the dark confines of my conscience, he looked back over his shoulder and said: "You'd better get rid of that old electric drill before you burn down the whole Commonwealth!"

The only other sound was the crash of the trash can on the bare concrete floor as it reeled from the impact of *Old Sparky* the electric drill, deftly placed dead center by an astoundingly accurate six-foot hook shot. It was launched by its ungrateful owner who is now too fussy to have such junk cluttering the garage.

the Ethan Allen Pepperbox Kit

the Publisher's Wife Builds Her First Gun

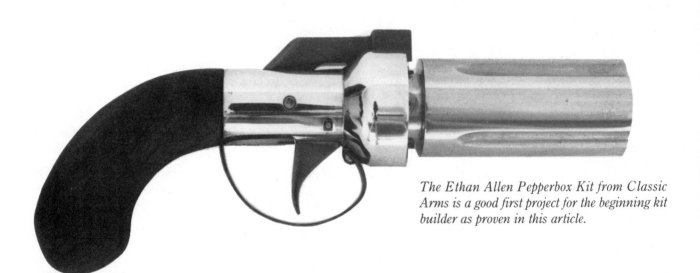

The Ethan Allen Pepperbox Kit from Classic Arms is a good first project for the beginning kit builder as proven in this article.

by Donna J. Ballard

One day when my husband Paul, and his staff were organizing their material for the directory section of this publication, I noticed that they were making notations regarding "difficulty of assembly". Such comments as "easy", "moderately easy" or "difficult" to assemble were added to each directory listing. I asked, "Who will be determining if these kits are easy to assemble?" "We will," Paul said. "But you already know how to do this," I countered. "It seems to me you need the opinion of a real novice; a neophyte in the world of guns; someone who has never assembled a model airplane or tinkered with an old jalopy;

someone who doesn't even know how to check the air in the tires of her car; someone who, in high school, scored a 2 percent in *mechanical ability* on an aptitude test. If someone like this could assemble a kit gun, then it really must be easy to assemble. In short, you need me!"

They exchanged disbelieving looks. "Do you really think you could build one?" Paul asked. My husband is familiar with my shortcomings, not the least of which is lack of patience. "What kind of gun would you want to build?" he inquired. "Oh, something little and cute that fits in my hand nicely and doesn't weigh a ton," I replied. At the word

Left: The first thing that I did after unpacking the kit was to compare the parts to the parts list on the instruction sheet. Notice all the confusing pictures on the box. Anyone could make a mistake and pick the wrong gun.

Below: The Ethan Allen Pepperbox Kit just as it comes from Classic Arms. The shrink-wrapped package is difficult to unpack but makes it impossible to have a part rattle around and get lost.

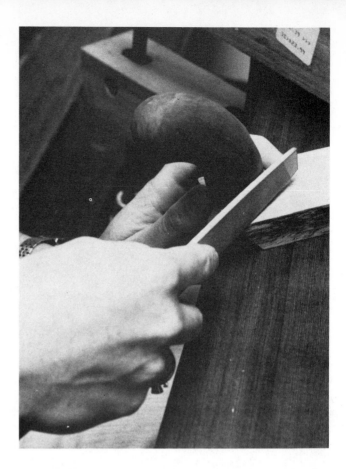

Paul screwed the grip to a piece of wood so that I could clamp it to a workbench. This makes it much easier to file and sand the grip.

cute, I received an exasperated look and a smirk. "We'll think about it," they said.

Several weeks later, the Ethan Allen Pepperbox kit arrived. This looked like my kind of gun. It was fairly small, light in weight, and I thought it was cute. The cover of the box pictures several guns, and as I sat eyeing my components, I zeroed in on the wrong picture. I kept trying to match what I had in the box with this picture and was coming up empty. I mentioned to Paul that the picture of the finished gun didn't seem to completely match the parts in the box. He said, "Sure it does. I can see that from here!" (He was sitting ten feet away on the other side of the room.) "You're looking at the wrong picture!" OOPS! (Talk about a novice.) His face acquired that disgusted, 'Oh, God, this will never work' look...

Now, after that inauspicious beginning, we're off!

About The Kit

The American pepperboxes were manufactured from the 1830s to the 1860s by several companies (one of which was Ethan Allen) in varying calibers and with various barrel lengths and grip styles. They were the first double-action revolvers produced in this country. The Ethan Allen Pepperbox reproduction by Classic Arms is a four-shot, .36-caliber, muzzle-loading gun with a three and one-eighth inch barrel that must be hand rotated to the next position after firing. The gun measures nine inches in length, weighs about two pounds, and is slightly muzzle-heavy.

Now there are gun kits and then there are gun kits. Some come pre-assembled and the builder finishes the wood and metal parts to his or her liking. Others come in a myriad of big and little pieces; i.e., disassembled. The Ethan Allen Pepperbox comes disassembled; the twenty-seven parts are laid neatly and separately in the box and then covered with plastic which is heat-shrunk around them to prevent any piece from getting lost. The tiny pieces are all placed in a small box to keep them together. The wood grip is roughly hewn into the basic grip shape and the metal parts arrive just as they come off the lathe (or whatever they come from), which means they are unfinished. Depending on how beautiful you want your gun to look, you'll need to do some finishing work on most of the metal pieces as well as the wood grip. The amount of time this takes will vary considerably depending on your taste and the equipment you use.

I wanted a nice finish on my gun: highly polished and maybe even blued. I decided at the outset that I would finish the pieces as far as possible before I began to assemble the gun so that once I started to build it, it would go together fairly quickly.

The kit instructions indicate that the following supplies are needed to assemble and finish the gun: coarse file, fine file, emery paper in 180, 240, and 400 grit, brass polish, screwdriver, hammer and pin punch. I would add three others: an electric finishing sander, a polishing wheel, and a vice. The instructions are clear and are accompanied by several very detailed and easy-to-read diagrams of the gun

This is a close-up view of the receiver end of the grip. Notice that the rightmost hole has been filled with wood putty.

with all the parts numbered and identified by position. The first step is to finish the wood (walnut, I think) grip.

Woodwork

The grip is attached to the receiver, and excess wood is marked for removal so that the contours of the grip will fit smoothly with the brass receiver. The grip is then removed and finished with a coarse file, a fine file, and then progressively finer types of sandpaper. It is reattached to the receiver to check the fit, and then removed and stained or oiled while the rest of the gun is worked on. It took me about four hours to file and sand the grip. I finished it with boiled linseed oil.

I noticed that, when attached to the receiver, the grip curved slightly to the left when held in the hand. At first, I thought the grip had been cut and drilled incorrectly, but later decided that the grip was designed for a right-handed person. It fit comfortably in the right hand and awkwardly in the left.

The grip has a circular hole, 6mm wide and 11mm deep, drilled into it to receive the hammer-spring retainer and to fit around the end of the trigger guard, which fits in a notch between the grip and the receiver. This hole is much larger than it needs to be (the hammer-spring retainer is 3mm wide and indents 11mm) and extends almost to the surface of the grip, which is also unnecessary. If the grip is filed flat enough to evenly match the contours of the receiver, a paper-thin strip of wood is left which can break through to the interior bore hole with ordinary handling.

To avoid the overly thin wall, I rounded the grip some at this point; but, thanks to my husband, I know how to fix this problem should it occur.

Paul thought the grip should fit flush to the receiver, so he filed the grip flat in my absence, and then proceeded to chip a hole several millimeters wide when replacing the trigger guard. To fix this, we filled the entire chamber with wood putty, seated the retainer and trigger guard while the putty was still damp, and then removed the retainer and trigger guard and allowed the putty to dry. Once dry, this part of the grip was refinished. Again, I suggest that you check the position of the drilled hole before working on the grip and fill it with wood putty, if necessary, *before* you begin to finish the grip. It will make it more sturdy.

Metalwork

The next step involved the metal parts. The hammer, trigger and nipples had small burrs that needed to be removed with a fine file. This was easy and took only ten or fifteen minutes. Most of the metal pieces also had gouges or scratches; however, these were another story. The barrel was uniformly covered with fine lathe marks that were quite deep. I found that removing the scratches by hand with the materials recommended took a very long time, by my standards. A coarse file scratched the barrel and a medium file didn't quite do the job. (Or, I wasn't able to exert enough pressure.) Using the file to work around the barrel in the direction of the circumferential ridge marks had a tendency to break the edges of the barrel flutes.

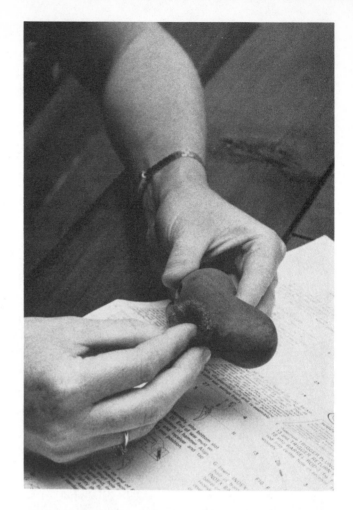

Right: After the linseed oil dried, I had to rub it down with fine steel wool.

Below Left: The instructions said to clean the parts thoroughly in a suitable cleaning solvent and (Below Right) to dry thoroughly and oil.

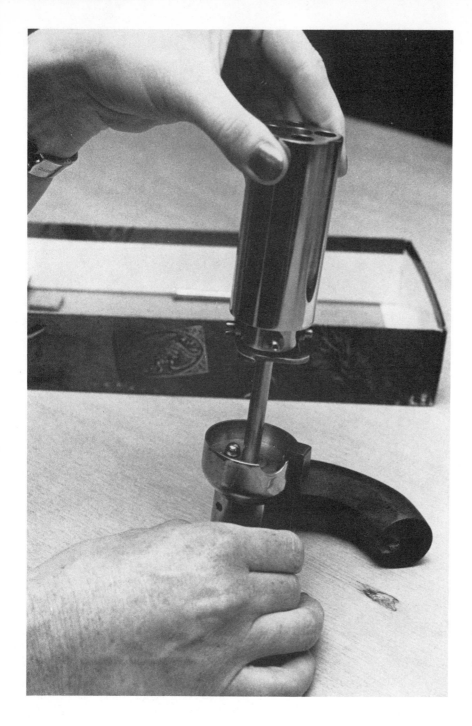

The barrel slides down the barrel rod and is held in place with a screw and washer. Notice the ball near the bottom of the barrel rod. You have to make sure that the ball doesn't move while you are installing the barrel.

Filing the barrel lengthwise, across the ridge marks, preserved the fluted edges, but care had to be taken not put flat spots in the round barrel contours. Gripping the barrel in a vise allowed me to apply more pressure and exert more control over the file.

An electric sander is a good substitute for lack of muscle, and I ended up using one for most of the metal work, with the following emery papers in succession: extra coarse, coarse, medium, fine, 240, 320, and 400 grit. This part of the job took ten to twelve hours and would have taken longer by hand. The shapes of the trigger and hammer made them very difficult to hold and sand, but this enabled me to make a fascinating observation. Sandpaper is good for removing fingernails and extra coarse sandpaper is good for removing skin.

While I was working on this part of the project, I got a lot of *help* and *advice* from the rest of the family. My mother called, and I told her I was building my first gun. She offered an opinion on the subject in general: "Guns, UGH!" Huey, one of our cats, laid down on whatever I wanted to lay my hands on at the moment, and Paul gave me some unsolicited pointers. "You should be using a polishing wheel." (I *should* be doing the laundry.) "But we don't have a polishing wheel," I replied. (Minor detail.) Ladies, if you plan to do much kit gun building, I suggest you invest in a polishing wheel. I also suggest that you work on your gun while your husband is out of the house.

After some negotiation, we purchased the aforementioned polishing wheel. (Ahem!) What a Godsend! It put a beautiful shine on both the brass and steel parts. After

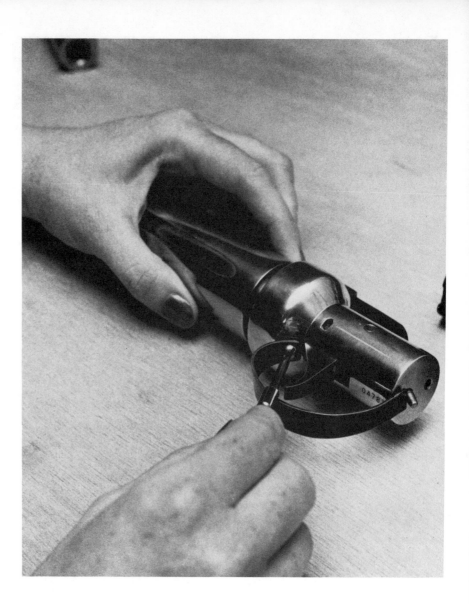

The trigger guard is attached with one screw and clips into a hole in the receiver at the other end. The grip attaches to the rightmost end of the receiver.

the sanding and polishing were finished, I decided to clean up the parts before assembly. I washed them in the sink with detergent and water. I'm not sure this was the "suitable cleaning solvent" the manufacturer had in mind, but it seemed to work well. I dried the hard-to-reach parts with a hair dryer and cotton swabs and wiped the barrel interior with Hoppe's No. 9 solvent to prevent rust.

Finishing

I decided to blue the hammer and trigger. For those of you who don't know what bluing is, allow me to clarify. Bluing is a procedure whereby you take the shiny steel piece you have spent hours polishing to a mirror-like finish so that your gun (and your husband) will love you, and cover it with a foul smelling liquid or paste that makes the metal blue-black and tarnished in appearance like the silver tableware you hate to polish. This is considered attractive. I used Birchwood Casey Perma Blue and applied it with a cotton swab. The color wasn't quite as dark as I wanted and was not quite uniform. Perhaps the fact that both of these pieces are heat-treated (hardened) steel accounts for this.

Paul suggested that I have the barrel nickel plated to achieve the chrome-like finish shown on the gun pictured on the kit box. He said we could get the necessary ingredients and the *recipe*, and cook the stuff on my stove, or we could send the barrel to a commercial plating shop. I've seen Paul's workshop, so I opted to send it out.

Assembly

Now I was ready to assemble the gun. First, the hammer spring is placed on the hammer-spring retainer and fitted into the receiver. The hammer is placed on top of the retainer and the fit is checked. Then the hammer is pushed down against the spring and locked into position with the hammer pin. The spring is very hard to compress and hold while inserting the pin. To be honest, I wasn't strong enough, and Paul had to help. A youngster assembling this kit will need a little help in terms of muscle. The pin fits very snugly and once started, you can't see if the receiving hole in the hammer is still in position.

Next is the trigger assembly. The sear plunger and sear spring are inserted into a hole in the trigger. The sear is

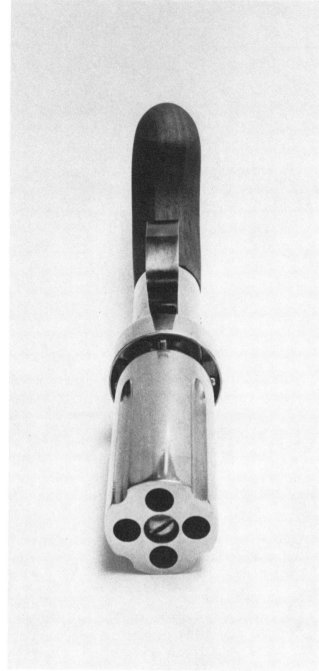

Notice the slight curve in the Pepperbox grip; a definite advantage for right-handed shooters.

positioned above and held in place with the sear pin. The sear didn't swing freely enough, and I had to remove the sear plunger and file a little off the bottom of it to shorten it slightly. This did the trick. The trigger assembly is positioned so that the sear engages a groove in the bottom of the hammer. Holding the assembly in this position, you tap the trigger pin into place to fasten the trigger to the receiver. My kit came with two trigger pins, but you only need one. At this point, one can work the hammer up and down and fit the receiver to the wood grip to see if the hole bored into the grip is deep enough to receive the hammer spring retainer when the gun is fired. Since I had filled this hole with putty, my grip needed some adjustment.

The cam plate is placed on the end of the barrel and secured with the cam-plate pin which I pressed into place with my vise. (Don't laugh; it worked very well.) The plate doesn't sit quite flat on top of the barrel, but tilts at a slight angle. As far as I can tell, this doesn't make any difference. Next, the instructions say to insert three standard nipples and a test nipple into the barrel. The purpose of the test nipple is for dry firing which can damage the ends of the nipples and cause misfiring. To determine which nipple is the *red test nipple*, hold each of the five nipples with the tiny opening toward you. Inside the rim of one of them will be a very faint, tiny, rust-red stripe around the opening. After one or two test firings the color was gone, so I suggest you place a dab of red nail polish or paint on it before use so you don't damage more than one nipple by dry firing.

Next, place the trigger-plunger spring, followed by the trigger-return plunger into the barrel rod. Then screw the rod into the receiver. I received a barrel rod that already had a spring in it, and until I discovered this, I couldn't understand why the spring would not seat itself in the hole in the rod. The index-ball spring is placed in the receiver, topped by the index ball and then the barrel is placed on the barrel rod and rotated until the index ball lodges in one of the indentations in the cam plate. The barrel rod is fixed in place by a washer and screw at the muzzle-end of the barrel. Lastly, the trigger guard and grip are reattached and the kit is complete. Assembly takes about thirty minutes. When the gun is fired, the trigger stays pulled-back and slack in the post-fire position until the barrel is hand-rotated counterclockwise to the next firing position. This procedure automatically repositions the trigger.

All in all, I found the Pepperbox fun to work on and easy to assemble. Now that I'm finished, I think it's...cute.

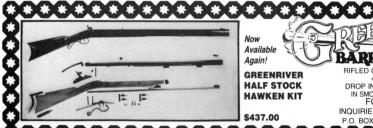

the Lyman Plains Pistol Kit

by Jim Reed

The Lyman Plains Pistol is an authentic reproduction of a popular early 1800s firearm.

The Lyman Products Plains Pistol is a reproduction of the pistols carried by the western pioneers and fur trappers, circa 1830. The Plains Pistol combines faithful Hawken styling with modern embellishments, such as coil spring lockwork.

I obtained a .50 caliber Plains Pistol and eagerly anticipated sallying forth into the field with Plains Pistol tucked into my belt.

Upon arrival, I unpacked the Plains Pistol and looked it over carefully. The Plains Pistol preserves the original Hawken styling with its half-stocked barrel and its gracefully sweeping lines. In contrast to the Great Plains Rifle that they also sell, Lyman chose to utilize a brass trigger guard on the Plains Pistol. I wondered what the motivation was for this difference. Whatever the reasons for the minor style change, I was thoroughly pleased with the pistol on first inspection.

After arranging all the pieces and verifying that nothing was missing, I sat down and read the instructions to get a feel for the kit. The instructions were clear and detailed, possibly the best I have seen. Next, I took a closer look at the various components.

Barrel

The $^{15}/_{16}''$ octagonal barrel is a full nine inches from muzzle to tang. The .50 caliber bore is broach rifled one turn in $30''$ and measures $.520''$ across the grooves and exactly $.500''$ across the lands. The barrel has a hooked breech takedown which works very nicely. A very substantial wedge hoop is soldered to the bottom of the barrel. A steel barrel rib, with a steel thimble permanently attached, is secured to the underside of the barrel by two screws. A small leaf spring in the rib assembly retains the ramrod.

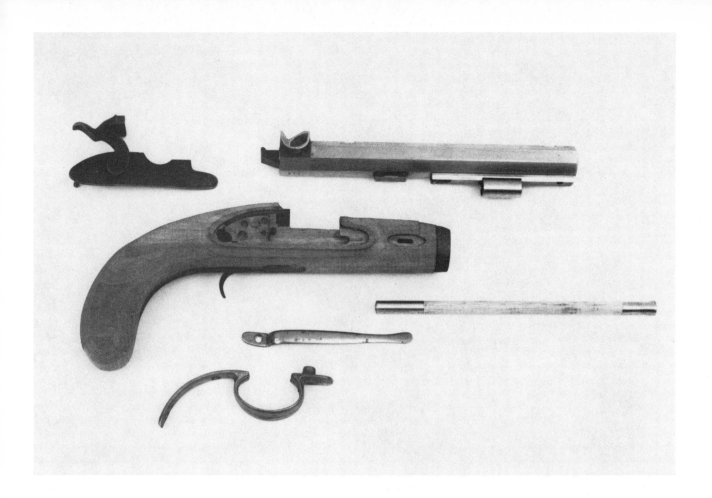

Above: Plains Pistol as it comes from Lyman. Note the hooked breech permitting easy take-down. The part just above the trigger guard is an optional belt hook.

Right: The breech should be blackened to fit it to the tang. A candle is a convenient way to do this.

Lockwork and Trigger

The color case hardened lockwork utilizes a coil mainspring, as well as a coil sear spring. The trigger is preloaded via a leaf spring against the sear. This very effectively eliminates annoying rattles and excessive free travel of the trigger before sear engagement.

Ramrod

The ramrod is equipped with brass fittings at either end. A brass cleaning jag is also supplied.

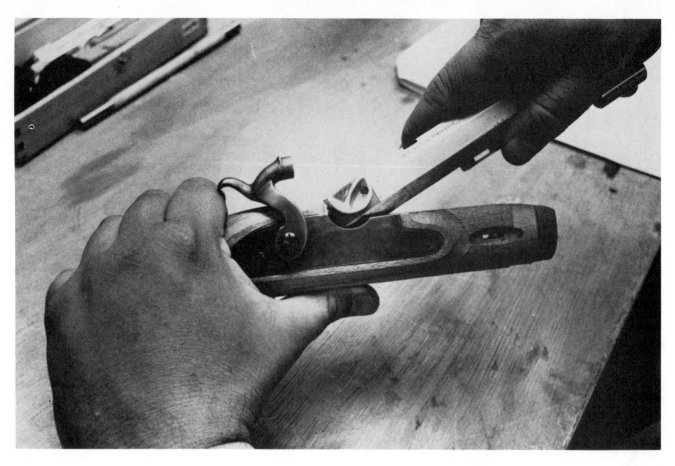

Above: Assemble the barrel to the tang and check it for a proper fit.

Below: Note the areas where the carbon black has been rubbed off. These areas need to be filed slightly in order to obtain a proper fit.

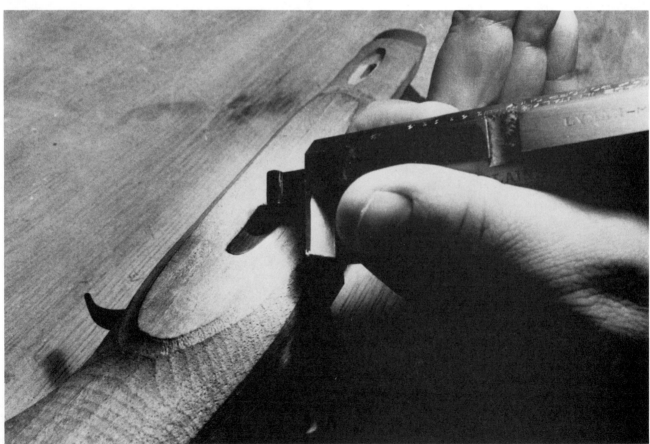

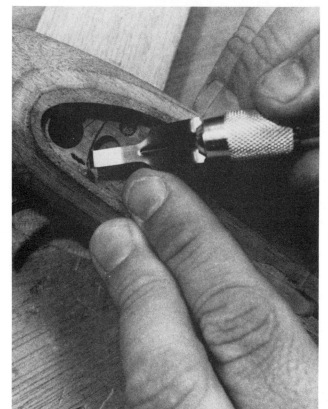

Top Left: The lockwork is blackened with a candle. The idea here is to leave black marks on the high spots in the stock recess.

Top Right: Tap the lockwork into the stock recess. High spots will be indicated by carbon black transferred to the stock.

Left: High spots in the stock recess can be removed with a sharp chisel. Continue the operation until the lockwork seats fully into the stock.

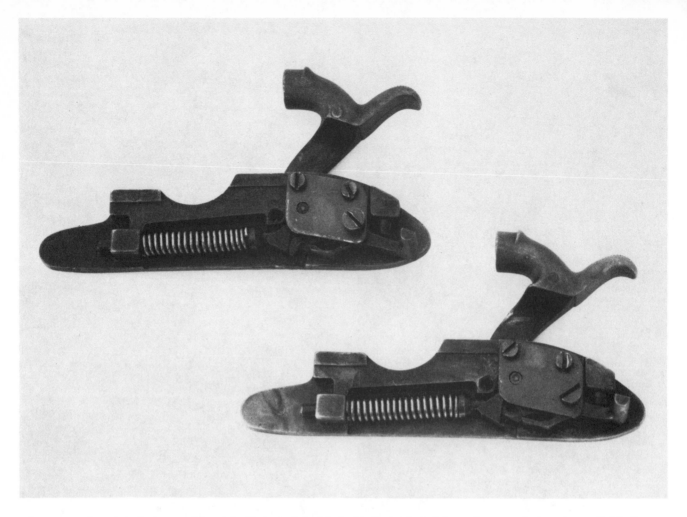

A close-up view of the lock assembly originally included with the kit (bottom) and the replacement lockwork supplied by Lyman (top). Note that the replacement lockwork includes a fly (see text).

Fittings

The trigger guard is a brass casting with a tang extending perhaps two-thirds the length of the grip. The wedge escutcheons are stamped from .050″ steel and are completely finished except for polishing. The forend cap is a steel casting with all critical fitting operations completed by the factory. Two lock screw bushings are provided, one plain and one fashioned into a belt hook; both are steel.

Stock

Lyman conservatively estimates that the stock is 95% inletted. A loose assembly of the various pieces to the stock indicated to me that the stock is more like 99% inletted. The contours of the gun are precut, and only smoothing and blending of the contours are required for final shaping.

The stock is advertised as being walnut. While I have no doubt that the wood is in fact walnut (there are over

40 species of walnut), it is not the American Black walnut (Juglans Nigra) that some kit builders might expect. An experienced kit builder will not be surprised by this. I have only seen a few kits using black walnut and never a fancy or exhibition grade. Not being an expert at identifying woods, I was not able to positively identify the wood in this stock; however, it most closely resembles mahogany in its appearance and properties.

Draw Filing the Barrel

The first step recommended by Lyman is to draw file the barrel. The barrel appeared to have been ground after rough milling. After a few passes with a medium mill file, the barrel looked much better. I had some problems with rounding the areas near the sight dovetails, so after the barrel was cleaned up by the draw filing operation, I placed a piece of medium (approximately 80 grit) emery cloth on a flat surface and drew the barrel across it. This is equivalent to what Lyman describes as draw sanding the barrel, i.e., wrapping a piece of sandpaper around a piece of wood and drawing it across the barrel, but is much faster since the entire barrel is being sanded at the same time. One caution, however; if you wet the emery cloth, as recom-

A sharp gouge is useful to shape the contours around the stock where the lockwork is seated.

mended, be sure to place it on a waterproof surface, as the surface (such as a wood table) will absorb the water and warp, ruining your best efforts.

Fitting the Tang

The next operation recommended by Lyman is to fit the barrel to the tang. This took about five minutes. Only a slight amount of material needed to be removed from the breech plug to achieve a perfect fit.

Inletting the Lock Screw Bushing

There was no need to inlet the lock screw bushing as it already fit well below the surface of the rough stock and appeared level.

Inletting the Lockwork

The lockwork only needed a slight amount of inletting to fully seat into the stock. During this process, I discovered that the lock had an annoying tendency to catch on the half cock notch. I determined that the likely cause of this was a burr in the trigger return spring. A quick call

to Lyman brought a new lockwork which didn't quite fit into my already inletted stock. I decided to swap the offending parts, instead of inletting the new lock, because the new lock contained a fly - a distinct improvement.

With a pair of needle-nose pliers, I removed the mainspring, thereby releasing most of the tension from the lock. Next, it was a simple matter to remove the three screws holding the lock work together. Repeating the operation on the second lock allowed me to freely swap parts. After assembly, the resulting lock fit my stock perfectly and worked perfectly also.

Inletting the Tang and Barrel

Assembly of the Tang/Barrel unit to the stock revealed that the tang needed to be moved rearward about 1/32 of an inch. At first, I was concerned because the lock screw goes through the stock immediately behind the tang. However, my concern vanished after reading the instructions (when all else fails). Material is to be removed from the tang to move the tang and barrel rearward, not from the stock as I had supposed. It took only a few minutes to achieve a good fit between the bolster and the lockwork.

Top: A half-round jeweler's file is helpful in shaping the stock around the lockwork.

Bottom: A strip of garnet paper can be used to shape the gentle contours of the stock by sanding the stock with a shoe-shine motion.

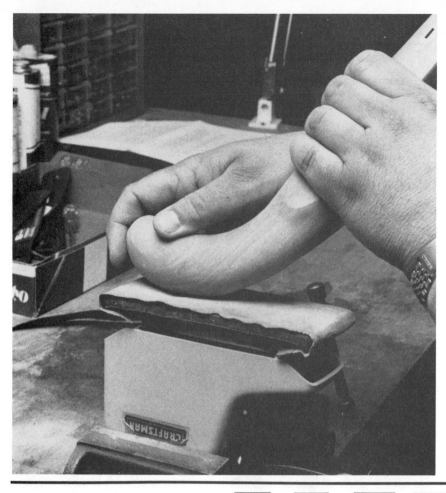

An electric sander can be useful, especially during the final sanding operation. Finishing with 400 grit garnet paper is recommended.

CRAFTSMAN MUZZLE LOADING

KITS

Navy Arms offers two famous Civil War Percussion Revolvers, one from the North, the other South. These, as well as a selection of long rifles including our famous HAWKEN Mark One (shown) are offered as complete construction kits with easy instructions for assembly, proper care and firing.

IMAGINATIVE CONCEPTS THAT SALES ARE BUILT ON!

Send $2.00 for 25th Anniversary Catalog

NAVY ARMS CO.

689 Bergen Blvd.
Ridgefield, NJ 07657

Classic Arms offers a selection of 8 distinctive and historically significant muzzle loading handguns. Each kit is complete with easy assembly instructions, parts list and directions for proper care and use.

FIRST EDITION

35

Before applying a finish to the stock, wipe the entire surface with a damp cloth and then sand lightly again with the 400 grit garnet paper.

Miscellaneous Inletting

The trigger guard and forend cap required no further inletting to permit full seating below the surface of the stock. The barrel wedge escutcheons required only a very slight amount of inletting. This took about 30 seconds to perform.

Shaping the Stock

Except for a few troublesome areas, the shaping of the stock is not particularly difficult, though time consuming. Rough shaping can be achieved with a simple set of tools, such as an Xacto knife set and a medium half round file. A great deal of care has to be taken in the area of the lock-work, however. The contours in this area are relatively severe and the wood surrounding the lock is very thin - greatly exaggerating any mistake. I didn't care for the con-tours of the stock near the forward part of the lock and its matching contour on the other side of the pistol. None of my files could fit into this area, so I had to carefully cut the desired contour with a very sharp gouge.

Final finishing of the stock was accomplished with pro-gressively finer grades of garnet paper, ending with 400 grit. The trouble areas near the lockwork had to be fin-ished by wrapping sandpaper around a small dowel. An electric finishing sander made quick work of most of the stock, however.

Opposite Page: The trigger guard needs to be shaped with a round file, then with a fine half-round file such as a Swiss pattern jeweler's file. Finally, emery paper is used to remove all of the file marks.

Finishing the Stock

The factory finished Plains Pistol has a very dark finish, which, though historically authentic, tends to hide the nat-ural beauty of the wood. I chose, instead, to finish the stock with plain boiled linseed oil. Some care is advisable here. If the linseed oil is not properly prepared (boiled), it will not dry - ever - and you're left with a gooey mess. You may prefer to use a commercial finishing product such as Formby's Tung Oil or a similar product.

After the oil dried, I rubbed the finish with 00 steel wool and then applied a second coat of oil. This was repeated several times until I had achieved a pleasingly warm brown color. A final polishing with 000 steel wool finished the stock operation.

AR/CAR-15 RIFLE KITS

Available now direct from the barrel factory are unassembled AR or CAR-15 semi-automatic rifle kits complete with all new parts except AR lower receiver. You may purchase an SGW lower receiver from your local FFL dealer. Send a copy of this ad with your order and receive a free 30 round clip and black nylon sling.

A. 20″ AR Heavy Match Barrel (1-9 Twist) with all <u>new parts</u> necessary for complete rifle <u>except AR lower receiver</u>. (Includes assault handguards, stand, trapdoor butt stock, FA upper receiver and choice of teardrop forward assist or round head style.)

Kit price $405.00
For 24″ barrel . . . . add $ 5.00
For stainless steel barrel. . . . . add $ 15.00

B. XM (CAR-15) Barrel unit with all <u>new parts</u> necessary for complete rifle <u>except AR lower receiver</u>. (Includes 16″ barrel with permanently attached flash suppressor, FA upper receiver, choice of teardrop forward assist or round head style, and CAR butt stock.)

Kit price $375.00
For stainless steel barrel. . . . . add $ 15.00

<u>ORDERING INSTRUCTIONS</u>: Send money order or cashier's check, personal and business checks must clear first. We will ship COD. Minimum shipping charge is $3.50 and add $1.65 on COD orders. Add sales tax on Washington orders.

SGW

(A Division of Olympic Arms, Inc.)
624 Old Pacific Highway S.E.
Olympia, Washington 98503
(206) 456-3471

Right: The barrel, wedge escutcheons, and forend cap (shown) should be polished by drawing them across a piece of emery cloth laid on a flat surface.

Below: After the barrel has been sanded, a good commercial metal finish can be applied. Lyman specifically recommends against hot bluing or browning due to soft-soldered attachments.

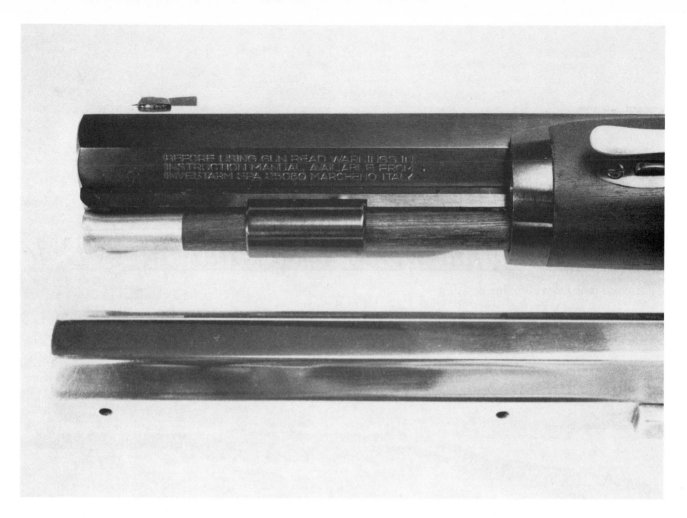

If you don't like messages printed on your barrel (top), buy Lyman's kit version of the Plains Pistol. The barrel in the kit version (bottom) is not so encumbered.

Final Polishing and Browning

The barrel was finished by drawing the barrel over progressively finer grades of emery paper laid flat on a waterproof surface. Final polishing was accomplished with a cloth wheel and metal polish. Although the metal was brought to a mirror-like polish, it was at the expense of all the barrel edges. To many, including myself, broken edges are unprofessional looking, and I now regret taking the quicker route to finishing my kit gun. It is a matter of personal choice, however, as to whether one wants a shiny gun or a gun with sharp edges.

The most difficult part to finish was the trigger guard due to its complicated contours. Fortunately, the trigger guard material is relatively soft (brass) and void of sharp corners to break, so this finishing operation went very quickly.

The barrel, forend cap and barrel wedge escutcheons were finished by using a commercial cold browning solution. Lyman specifically recommends against hot browning (or bluing) the barrel as the ramrod thimble and wedge hoop are soft soldered to the barrel rib and barrel respectively.

Conclusion

I thoroughly enjoyed assembling the Lyman Plains Pistol and found pleasure in its gently sweeping lines. I look forward to taking the Plains Pistol along with the Plains Rifle to the range to try them out side by side.

One final note: As is the trend following several liability suits against some major gun manufacturers, Lyman has chosen to roll print a warning message on the side of the factory finished Plains Pistol. This message is not printed on the kit gun, but rather on the instructions provided with each kit. If roll stamped messages on your gun offend you, as they do me, then the kit version of the Plains Pistol is definitely for you.

the Underhammer Boot Pistol and Buggy Rifle

a matched pair from Hopkins & Allen

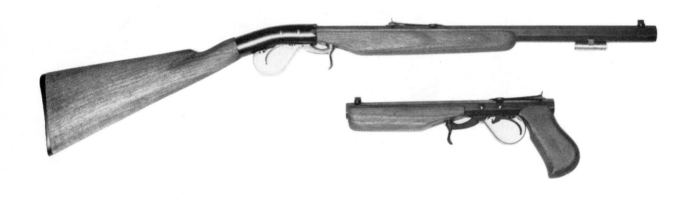

by Alan F. Lundin

Boot pistols and buggy rifles conjure up images of 19th Century society. Indeed, these weapons attained great popularity during this period, particularly the 1830s through the 1850s. The boot pistol, or bootleg pistol, was a term usually applied to a weapon with a slim, smooth design that allowed it to be concealed and worn inside the boot. The underhammer gun, with its hammer, trigger and trigger guard located on the underside of the weapon, was often carried in this manner.

Buggy rifles, also known as _boy's_ rifles, were probably so-named because of their small size which made them convenient to carry in a buggy. They were generally lesser

in size, weight and proportion than standard rifles of a given type. Barrel lengths usually ranged from twelve to twenty-two inches (the Hopkins & Allen Buggy Rifle has a twenty-inch barrel) and often were produced in the underhammer design.

The Hopkins & Allen Underhammer Boot Pistol and Underhammer Buggy Rifle are a unique set of firearms designed with simplicity in mind. The novel lockwork provides a first rate action with an absolute minimum of parts. The locations of the hammer and percussion cap prevent damage to the eyes of the shooter in the event of an accident — a nice safety feature — and also provide a clear line of sight along the top of the barrel.

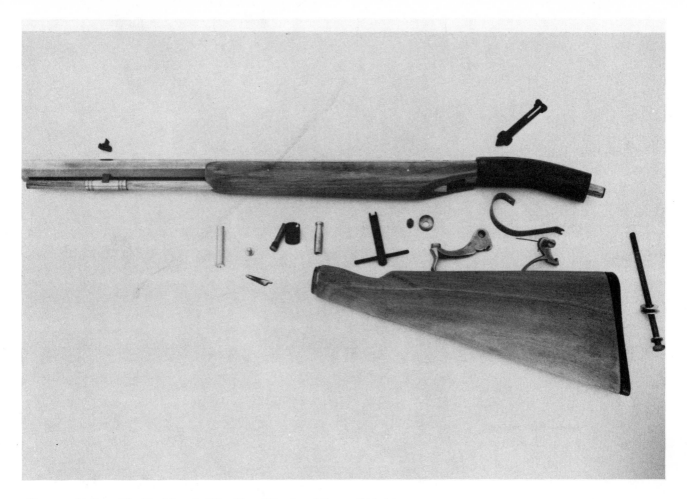

Above and below: The Hopkins & Allen Boot Pistol and Buggy Rifle kits.

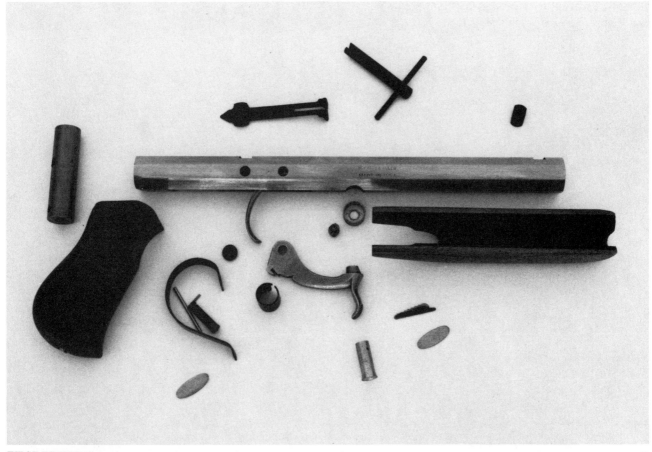

Draw filing requires a solid vise and a good, clean, sharp mill file. Progress is being inspected by the author.

Once all the major nicks and scratches are removed by draw filing the barrel, the surface is further refined by drawing the barrel back and forth over a sheet of emery cloth laid on a flat surface.

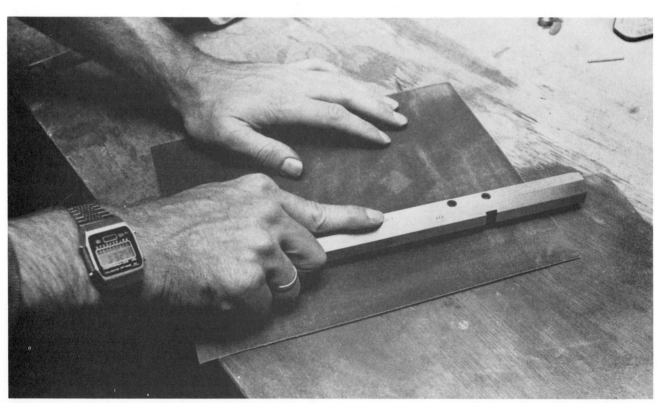

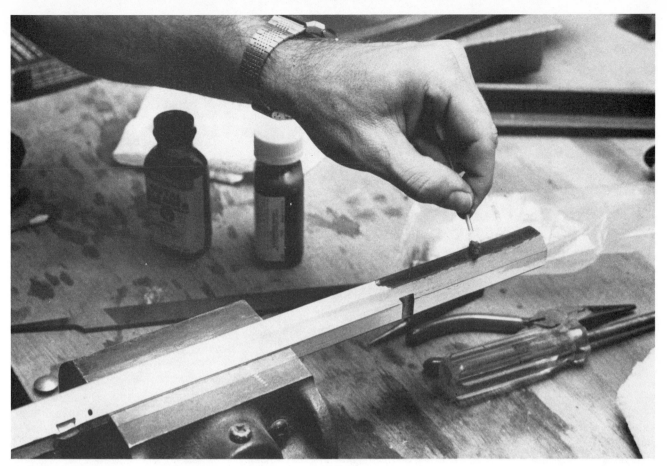

A commercial touch-up blue solution was applied to the barrel as a check for scratches which might not show up while the barrel was in-the-white. Later, this finish would be removed and replaced by a professional hot-bluing finish.

The Kits

Both kits were complete and pre-fitted. It would have been possible to assemble the kits and have a working set of guns immediately, but their appearance would have been unacceptable to me. The barrels on both guns were quite rough, having occasional gouges of fair depth. The stocks were pre-finished, but clearly would profit by some touching-up. Like nearly all kits of this type, most of the time spent in building the kit goes into the finishing operations rather than the actual assembly.

The first step, given in the one-page instruction sheet included with the kit, cautioned the reader to check the enclosed parts against the parts list. The parts list was accompanied by an exploded-view drawing, which labeled each item with a part number which could be cross referenced to the parts list. This was easy enough, and most of the parts were quickly identified. Apparently, however, there must be two versions of the buggy rifle, since some of the decorative parts included in the list did not come with my kit. These parts were: a patch box, a trigger-guard extension, and what looks like a brass butt plate.

Assembly

The instructions made no mention of finishing either the metal parts or the stock pieces. I was really baffled

by this, since the barrels on both the buggy rifle and the boot pistol seriously needed finishing. Naturally, each barrel had milling and grinding marks that were relatively easy to smooth out; however, each barrel also came complete with pits and gouges that appeared to be at least .005″ deep. Some of these defects looked like casting marks, but each barrel also had marks that looked like the results of an overly tightened, toothed vise. The depth of these marks would obviously determine the amount of steel to be removed, and how much time would be required to rough-finish the barrels. Inspecting the barrel further, I saw that most, if not all, of the stamped inscriptions would be lost when the necessary metal was removed.

Since I've never been able to do a good job of draw filing in the past, I began with some reservation. My technique, by the way, was greatly improved after talking with a friend who is more knowledgeable than I about metal working. He informed me that a file has a cutting direction; the teeth are not symmetrical, but are angled to cut efficiently in one direction only. It's odd, but even after all the years I've been using a file, I never knew that files should be drawn in one direction only. This, of course, means that there is no point in trying to cut in both directions at once. He also explained that draw filing requires that the file be held roughly perpendicular to the direction of motion.

After learning these draw-filing fundamentals, the only

With a sharp triangular file, the front sight dovetail was fitted to the front sight. I never took more than two swipes with the file without checking the fit of the sight in its dovetail. It is very time consuming, but it has been my experience that to do otherwise is to court disaster.

> "a file has a cutting direction; the teeth are not symmetrical, but are angled to cut efficiently in one direction only."

trick left was to keep the file level and remove a uniform thickness from the surface being worked. Both barrels were octagonal with 0.4″ flats, so it was fairly easy to get the file to lay flat. It is important to apply downward pressure with the thumbs or index fingers directly over the barrel without tipping the file to one side or the other. The fingers of each hand are then curved around, and behind, the file so that it can be drawn easily. The file should be drawn over the entire length of the barrel in one stroke, so that an even layer of metal is removed with each stroke.

The barrel must be gripped firmly in a vise so that the barrel will remain stationary. This is especially true of long barrels. Kit builders should consider using two vises when assembling a long-barreled gun. It is not only important to draw the file smoothly over the entire length, but it is also important to draw the file with a constant downward pressure. At the barrel ends, the resultant torque will be fairly high — probably high enough to cause the barrel to rotate in the vise. The vise should be padded, to cause as little damage to the barrel surfaces as possible, particularly to the surfaces that have already been filed. The 20″ barrel on the buggy rifle that I worked on, was short enough so that one vise was just marginally adequate.

Discontinuities in the surface also cause snags in the draw-filing process. Usually, this occurred at dovetail notches. It is difficult to draw the file smoothly over a dovetail notch without rounding or damaging the edges. So, what do you do? I'm not sure of the best answer, but I tried two things: (1) use of a wider file that allows the file to more easily bridge the gap, and (2) treating the length of the barrel as two or more surfaces; i.e., drawing the file from one end of the barrel to the first dovetail as though it were one surface; from the first dovetail to the second as the next surface; and so on. Normally, of course, you wouldn't want to break a barrel into smaller, shorter surfaces if there are no gaps or other breaks in the surface.

With all these things in mind, I clamped the pistol barrel in a vise and began. The short pistol barrel (only 12″ long) was, if not easy, at least straightforward. After about four hours of work on the flat surfaces, the barrel began to look pretty good. It is always surprising to me that filing can leave as fine a finish as it does. That's nice, because that means less sanding.

In the process of draw filing the boot pistol, I learned one important lesson. It is necessary to clean and chalk the file after almost every stroke; otherwise, the file quickly becomes filled with shavings, which slow the cutting action. Even worse, sometimes a rather nasty scratch will appear down the length of the barrel due to a metal chip that becomes lodged in the file's teeth. I soon decided that it was well worth my time to clean the file frequently.

Draw filing the rifle barrel progressed in a manner identical to the pistol except that it had four dovetails instead of two. The first step was to remove the receiver (which was quite distinct from the barrel), the ramrod ferrule from the underside, and a dummy plug that filled an unused dovetail under the forestock. The dovetails, by the way, further complicated the process somewhat. I used my ring fingers to stabilize my draw filing action by sliding them along the sides of the barrel. After only a few passes of the file, the dovetail edges became razor sharp, and I suffered some sizeable gouges in my fingernails and lost a few drops of blood in the process.

After filing all eight surfaces, until all the nicks, pits, tool marks, etc., were removed, I decided to work on filing the ends. I quickly found that I had made a minor tactical error in the order in which I had finished the barrel surfaces. I found that I was more likely to round an edge while working on the ends. If I had waited to file the flats until after I had worked on the ends, I would have had more room to make up for mistakes and slips. Next time I'll be ready. As it turned out, I was careful enough so that I had no problems with those edges.

The rear end of each barrel was simply a flat surface perpendicular to the barrel axis. The front end of each barrel, however, had a combination of rounded and flat surfaces that, while looking better than a simple flat surface (such as on the rear of the barrel) requires a more sophisticated finishing technique. It seemed to me that the best way to finish the barrel fronts would be with a lathe, file and emery paper. I, as most of you, don't have access to a lathe. Therefore, I shaped the front of the barrel as best as I could with coarse emery paper until all the major tool marks were removed.

The last complication was to finish the off-center conical grind at the rear of the pistol barrel. I began to remove the coarse marks on the tapered portion with a file. At first, the surface looked rather choppy from a poor filing technique, but after a little work I learned to draw the file while swinging the file around so that it was always tangential to the surface. A little work and this section looked ready for emery paper.

The filing operation left the metal surface looking fairly

good, so I started with 240-grit emery paper. Sanding the ends again was fairly difficult. It was hard to sand evenly and perpendicularly to the barrel axis. *Notice, this time I got the order correct.* After finishing the ends (more through patience than technique), I attacked the flats.

The flats were, in concept, easy. Simply lay a sheet of emery cloth on a flat surface and carefully slide the barrel back and forth so that as much of the barrel contacts the emery cloth as possible at any given time. Ostensibly, this enables the kitgun builder to finish the maximum amount of metal in the least amount of time.

Well, it went almost that smoothly. The emery cloth slid and crumpled some, but by holding it close to where the barrel contacted it and by lightening up on the downward pressure, most of the problems disappeared. I graduated to 340 grit emery cloth, then 400 grit, repeating each process with the new grit size. Finally, the barrel surfaces were ready to blue. I could have sanded with 600-grit cloth or even polished the surfaces to a bright polish, but the 400-grit cloth provides the slight matte finish that I prefer. I was not equipped to undertake a bluing operation, so I paid $20 to have a local gunsmith drop the barrels in his bluing tank.

Although I like a slightly matte-blue finish, I prefer my brass parts to be highly polished. The only brass parts included with my two kit guns were: the flash shields, the forestock pins, the ramrod ends and two decorative brass inlays for the pistol forestock. The brass-finishing operation was fast and easy. Each part got a quick going-over with fine emery cloth to get rid of any rough marks. This operation, though a little awkward at times, went quickly. This was partly due to the lack of bad marks and partly due to the quick removal of material when working on brass.

I found that it was fairly easy to round the sharp edges of the brass parts, so I again laid the emery cloth against a flat surface and worked the parts against the cloth with my fingers. This was very effective in controlling the sanding operation and preserving the sharp edges. I only *free-handed* when I felt there would be a leverage advantage or when the part was in no danger of being improperly rounded. After a quick sanding, each part was polished with a buffing wheel.

A buffing wheel requires liberal use of brass polishing compound and produces a highly polished surface in a very short time. The only difficult aspect of polishing is to keep hold of the part being polished. The polishing wheel has a tendency to grab and fling the part across the room. Obviously, this could be dangerous, so I had to keep a solid grip, and I didn't try to polish too much at one time.

The installation of the sights was next. Both the front and rear sights of each gun were dovetailed. This meant that each sight had to be tediously fitted into the appropriate dovetail notch. My experience in the past with dov-

The forestock holding pins on both the Boot Pistol and the Buggy Rifle were a little oversized to permit them to be filed flush to the forestock.

etail fitting has usually proved disastrous. It seemed that as I carefully took off a little metal, I suddenly went from a fit much too tight to a fit much too loose. In the past, therefore, I made heavy use of shims.

Armed with the caution of experience, I bought the sharpest, finest triangular file I could find. This time, I decided to proceed very slowly and try to avoid an accidental over-adjustment. The main rule that I *set in stone* before I started was: *never, under any circumstance, take more than two swipes with the file without checking the fit!* This meant I would have to continually repeat the process of popping the sight out, picking up the file, making one or two light passes of the file, setting down the file, picking up the sight, fitting it into the dovetail, lightly hammering the sight into place and visually checking the fit and the progress made. This process took about ten-times longer than it took in the past, but it worked.

The next step for each gun was to install the flash shield and nipple. This involved inserting the nipple through the flash shield and screwing the threaded end into the barrel. The threading on both the nipple and the barrel was clean enough that I was able to hand twist the nipple almost all the way in. Hopkins & Allen includes a nipple wrench to aid in the nipple installation. This was a nice touch that they didn't even include in the parts list.

The pistol required that a plug be inserted into the rear end of the barrel to provide a base for the pistol grip and the mainspring screw. This plug was a thick metal rod of .75″ diameter that was cut to a 2.70″ length and drilled and tapped for the hand grip and the mainspring-holding screw.

The rear end of the barrel had previously been drilled to the outside dimensions of the plug so the fit was good and no machining was required. The manufacturer cut the plug a little long so that it protruded a few thousandths-of-an-inch beyond the end of the barrel. The cut was fairly rough and it would have looked quite rustic without finishing.

To remove the metal, I simply inserted the end cap into the back of the barrel, screwed the grip bolt and the mainspring screw into place and clamped the barrel in a vise with the rear end up. I then carefully filed away most of the excess metal, taking great pains to keep the file perpendicular to the barrel axis. After taking off enough metal to make the plug flush with the rear edge of the barrel, I continued finishing with emery cloth backed against a short two-by-four block of wood to keep the surface flat. I finished the end by gradually working down to 400-grit emery cloth to match the remainder of the barrel.

The trigger group was next on the list to be installed. The hammer and trigger must be fitted so that the trigger's engaging nose fits into the half-cock and full-cock notches in the hammer. According to the instructions enclosed with the kits, the half-cock notch normally requires opening so that the engaging nose can drop into the notch. This of course is designed to catch the hammer should it drop accidentally. The full-cock notch must usually be deepened in order to reliably hold the trigger. This step must be done with a great deal of care so that the trigger is held securely, but not so deeply that the trigger becomes *creepy*.

The trigger group installation was quite simple. The instructions suggested that the receiver slot be de-burred if necessary for smooth operation of the action. Neither of my kits required de-burring. The trigger group consists of the hammer, trigger, trigger spring, two cross pins and two cross-pin screws.

I first placed the trigger spring inside the slot cut in the trigger. This allowed the cross pin to slide through the cross-pin hole drilled into the trigger. I then removed the screw that held the plug in place within the barrel and pushed the grip attachment screw through the pre-drilled hole in the pistol grip and inserted the longer screw into the plug. The attachment screw was tightened until the grip rested firmly against the barrel stock.

The buggy rifle required that the plastic butt plate be removed so that the stock-bolt hole could be accessed. The stock bolt was inserted through the pre-drilled hole in the rifle stock and the rifle's stock was installed onto the end of the receiver. The stock bolt was then tightened until the stock was firmly in place.

Each gun came with a forestock although the assembly instructions made no mention of a forestock in the case of the boot pistol. Fortunately, forestock installation is extremely straightforward. The forestocks on each gun came pre-shaped and sanded and they required only some oil or varnish. I used linseed oil, since I like the natural look it provides. Each forestock was designed to attach to the barrel by means of holding pins. The barrels with each gun came complete with predrilled holes that matched the pre-drilled holes in the the forestocks.

Installation of the forestocks required only minor alignment and insertion of the brass holding pins. The pistol forestock required only one holding pin and the rifle required two. The only snag that I encountered was a slight misalignment of the pre-drilled holes in the rifle barrel and forestock. It was necessary to bend the holding pins slightly before they could be fully inserted. The holding pins on each gun were a little longer than the width of the forestock. This required a little filing in order to make the pins flush with the sides of the forestock.

Both the pistol and the rifle came with a ramrod and two brass ramrod tips. The pistol assembly instructions made no mention of the required installation steps, however this presented no problem for me. The rifle's instructions first directed the kit builder to install the ramrod ferrule to the barrel. A small error was noted here.

Apparently, a design change has occurred that has not been reflected in the instructions. The instruction sheet specified that the ferrules were to be attached by means of two 4-40 machine screws. On the rifle kit that I received, the ferrule came pre-attached to the barrel by means of a dovetail slot. I personally prefer the dovetail arrangement and was glad that my kits came that way. Since the ferrule had been removed from the barrel during the draw-filing stage, I simply returned it to its dovetail.

Although both instruction sheets included a ramrod in the parts list, no mention was made of the work required to make it functional. The ramrod, in each case, was a hardwood dowel. Each came complete with two brass tips. There was a problem though. The tips were separate, not attached, and could not be simply glued or pinned into place. The brass tip's outside diameter was the same as the wooden dowel's, so one could not fit the tip over the ramrod. The dowel required some lathe work at the ends. Unfortunately, I didn't have access to a lathe. My approach was not the best solution, but about the only thing I could think of.

I put one end of the dowel into a drill and had my wife slowly turn the dowel with the drill, while I used a file to take wood off the free end. It worked, but I wouldn't recommend it. Find a lathe if at all possible, or go to a local shop and buy a pre-assembled ramrod. After I fitted the tips to the dowel I stained the dowel to match the forestock and glued the brass tips into place.

Final Observations

The Hopkins & Allen Underhammer Boot Pistol and Buggy Rifle set were very simple in design. I particularly liked the simplicity of the underhammer lockwork. The lockwork part count was very low, consisting of only a hammer, trigger, trigger spring and mainspring. I thought the use of the mainspring as a trigger guard to be very clever. The simple barrel/receiver design also required a minimum of parts. In short, I like the design.

My only criticism of these kits is not the guns, but the assembly instructions. One page cannot provide more than just the sketchiest outline of how to assemble and finish a gun. The kits were simple enough, however, so that a person reasonably familiar with guns, could probably assemble them with no instructions at all. (This is the way that most of the kits that we have seen are sold. Ed.)

In summary, the kits were very easy to put together and the finishing work was easy and well within the capabilities of even a novice gun builder. It does take time to do a really fine job, but if I didn't want to put in the time I could have purchased the factory finished guns instead. Overall, I believe the Hopkins & Allen Underhammer Boot Pistol and Buggy Rifle to provide an excellent value to the kit-gun builder and would recommend them, without hesitation, to someone looking to build an underhammer-type weapon.

the 1858 New Model Remington Kit

a Stainless Steel Classic from Euroarms of America

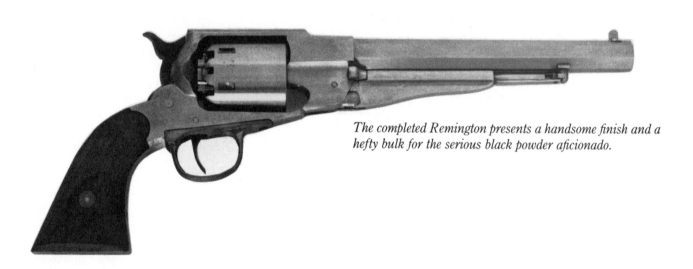

The completed Remington presents a handsome finish and a hefty bulk for the serious black powder aficionado.

by Les Keller

In my opinion, stainless steel is the ultimate gun material for the casual black powder shooter. Its corrosion resistant finish is tolerant of the aggressively hygroscopic residue resulting from an afternoon's shoot. Many a black-powder enthusiast has found his or her gun's innards eaten away because they neglected to clean their gun promptly after a shooting session.

Kit gun builders also find stainless steel attractive because it can be left *in the white* without fear of rust or criticism. Since stainless steel requires neither bluing nor browning to protect it, the kit builder saves both time and money. It also allows the kit builder to modify a weapon without refinishing it. Finally, since the finish is no longer a treatment applied to the surface of the metal, gone forever are the worries about holster-wear ruining the finish.

When I saw that Euroarms of America was offering a replica of the Remington 1858 New Model Revolver in stainless steel, I immediately placed an order. It arrived a few days later, and I discovered that my excitement was well founded.

The kit comes packed in a styrofoam box with compartments for individual components and a separate tray for all of the smaller parts. The smaller parts are keyed to an exploded-view diagram of the gun provided in the instructions. This is accomplished by numbering the parts with a cellophane overlay. These numbers correspond to numbers on the diagram in the instructions. This is such a nice touch that I wish Euroarms had numbered the styrofoam tray itself, instead of the overlay, since the numbers disappear when the cellophane is removed. The only solution I can offer is to cut the parts out of the packaging with an X-acto knife, leaving the cellophane (and numbers)

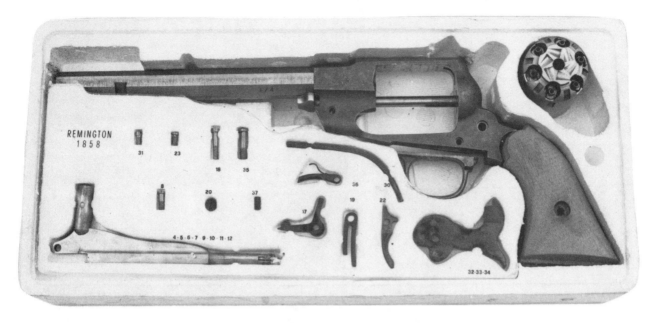

The Remington kit comes packed in a styrofoam box with all of the parts contained in separate compartments. Smaller parts are keyed by number to an exploded-view diagram packed with the kit.

surrounding the tray intact.

First Observations

After reading the instructions several times, to get some idea as to the steps involved in assembling the Remington, I took a closer look at the kit gun parts themselves.

The barrel was rough, with milling marks plainly visible. It was screwed in tightly to the frame and had to be removed for filing and sanding. The front sight and loadinglever retainer were installed by the factory and also had to be removed before the barrel could be finished.

The frame is cast stainless steel and had to be filed and carefully sanding to obtain an acceptable finish. The inside of the frame showed evidence of machining and required some filing to remove burrs and other superfluous material.

The cylinder was moderately rough on the circumference, with tool marks clearly evident. However, the chambers and cylinder face were in good condition. Euroarms is obviously conscious of the capabilities and equipment limitations of the average kit builder.

The rammer would not fit into the frame as delivered, so the hole in the frame had to be enlarged. The rammer hole, incidentally, looked very rough - as though the drill worked up a burr which gouged the inside of the hole.

The grips were fashioned from some indistinct wood and required fitting to mate with the frame. I plan to purchase some exotic grip material, such as ebony, at the next gunshow and make some new grips.

The front sight and loading-lever retainer had to be driven out of the barrel before the barrel could be finished.

Right: The frame is cast stainless steel and required finishing on all of its exterior surfaces. Shown is part of the frame after a few passes with a file. Note the low spots indicated by the darker reflections.

Below: The grips were fashioned from some indistinct wood. As may be seen here, the grips required a fair amount of filing and sanding to fit them to the frame.

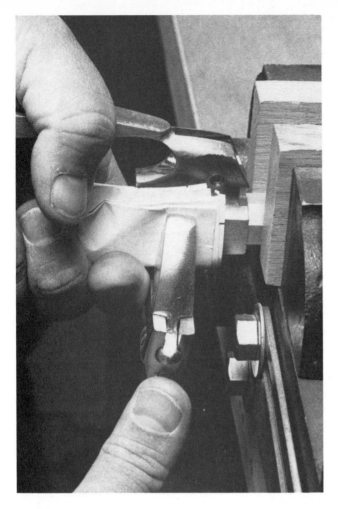

The barrel had to be removed in order to draw file and polish the surface. I used a vise and a well-padded wrench to remove the barrel. Caution is advised here. You don't want to distort the frame.

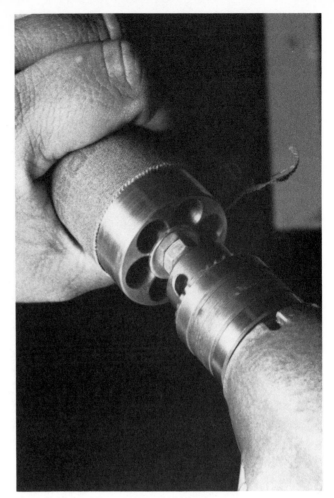

The outside of the cylinder was fairly rough. I fashioned a makeshift lathe to polish the cylinder. I had no problems controlling the low-powered and low-speed drill and was able to achieve a beautiful finish in just a few minutes.

Having checked over most of the major components of the New Model Remington, I was ready to assemble the kit.

Barrel

The first step for the assembly of the 1858 New Model Remington was to fit the barrel to the frame. Usually, it is necessary to remove a small amount of material from the front face of the frame where the barrel makes contact. This is necessary so that the barrel can be rotated properly (front sight pointed straight up) when the barrel is screwed in tightly. As it happened, my gun did not require any further fitting: the barrel fit perfectly, right out of the box.

If your gun requires the barrel to be fitted, *go at it slowly!* It is relatively simple to remove material from the frame, but it is nearly impossible for the hobbiest to put it back.

After the barrel had been fitted to the frame, I removed it from the frame and detached the front sight and loading-lever retainer. Clamping the barrel in a wood-faced vice

allowed me to draw-file the rough-milled finish. *(If you're unfamiliar with the draw-filing process, be sure to see the other articles in this issue which discuss draw-filing basics. Ed.)* This operation went very quickly, and after about an hour, I was ready to sand the barrel.

If you tack a piece of fine emery paper to a flat table, you can polish an entire side of the barrel by gripping the barrel firmly with the finger tips and drawing it lightly across the emery paper. Care should be exercised to insure that the flats of the barrel remain flat on the surface of the emery paper. This technique for polishing flat surfaces is far superior to polishing with a piece of emery paper wrapped around a block of wood or your fingers because the entire surface of the barrel is in contact with the emery paper during most of the stroke. It also assures that the barrel flats are truly flat, both along the barrel axis and across it. One caution, however; it is imperative that your work surface be as flat as possible because the piece that you are working on will assume the contours of your work surface. If you wish to wet the emery paper, be sure to work on a waterproof surface. The surplus

Above: The rammer hole was very rough and was too small in diameter to permit the rammer to pass freely. After carefully enlarging the hole with a 7/16" drill, I fashioned a polishing tool out of a length of 1/4" bolt and reamed the hole until the rammer did not bind.

Right: Burrs and casting marks had to removed from the inside of the frame to allow the lockwork to function properly. This process went rapidly as there was no need for a great deal of care; the file marks wouldn't show and all the burrs and such were easy to identify.

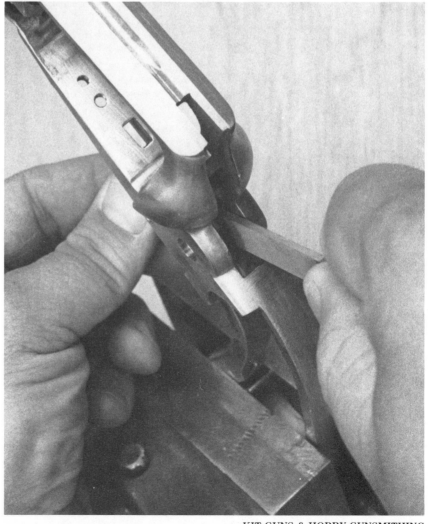

Above Left: These are the Remington's lockwork components pictured in their correct relationship to each other.

Above Right: To check the function of the lockwork, it is convenient to substitute finger pressure for spring pressure. The fitting of the lockwork is a time-consuming task and requires that the lockwork be removed from the frame many times.

A close-up view of the bolt, showing where metal has to be removed to obtain correct function.

water will cause a stain in your work surface; water absorbed into the work surface will cause it to swell and become distorted.

Cylinder

The cylinder showed much evidence of being turned in a lathe. In order to remove the tool marks from the cylinder, I found it necessary to improvise another tool. I obtained a ¼″ x 3″ carriage bolt from the local hardware store plus a couple of washers and a nut. Inserting the carriage bolt through the axis of the cylinder and securing it firmly with the second washer and nut, I then chucked the assembly into a portable electric drill. I wrapped a length of emery paper around the cylinder and then spun the cylinder with the electric drill in my right hand while holding the emery paper in my left. Soon the cylinder looked as though it had been polished in a lathe.

I polished the face of the cylinder in exactly the same manner as I had finished the barrel, by stroking the cylinder across a piece of emery cloth tacked to a flat surface. In just a few minutes, the cylinder face looked perfect.

Assembly Of The Action

As received, the rammer would not fit through its hole in the frame. As noted above, the rammer hole was very rough and needed some work to clean it up. The rammer itself is approximately .435″ at its widest dimension and

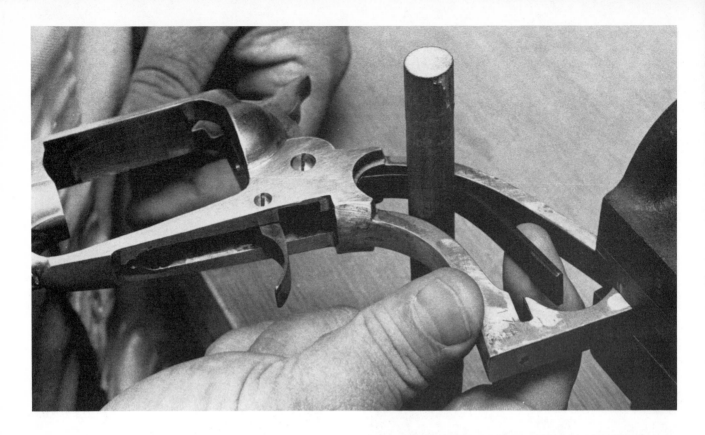

Above: In order to install the mainspring, it was convenient to use a small wooden dowel to increase the arch of the spring.

Right: A nickel was almost a perfect fit in the frame recess.

Below: The nickel permitted the rough contour of the recess to be marked on the grip.

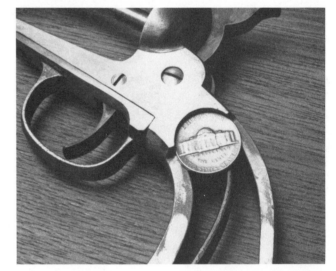

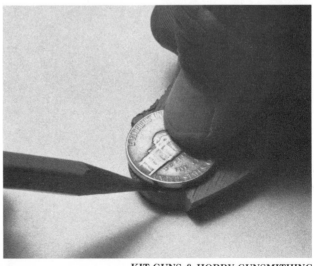

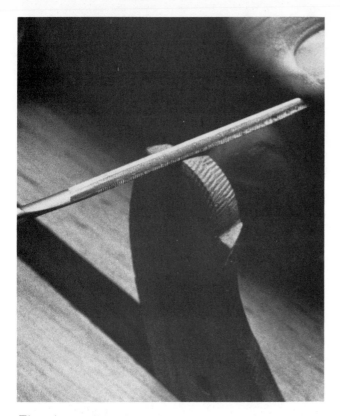

The grip was filed with a fine file —

until it fit perfectly in the frame recess.

requires approximately a ⁷⁄₁₆″ hole in the frame for clearance. Ideally, a ⁷⁄₁₆″ reamer could be run through the hole. I don't own one, so I tried a ⁷⁄₁₆″ drill. By working very slowly (and trying not to panic when the drill jammed) I was able to get a clean hole through the frame without spending an hour with a round file trying to make a bigger round hole. *This technique is not recommended for the weak-of-heart or if you have shaky hands. If in doubt, buy a reamer or use a file.* I finished up the rammer hole by slotting a ¼″ steel rod (¼ - 20 bolt with the head cut off) about 1″ down from the end and wrapping about 3″ of emery cloth around the rod. After chucking the rod into a portable hand drill, I was able to ream the hole until the rammer moved freely through the hole into the cylinder. Trophy tip: Do not use this device in a high speed tool, such as a Moto-tool. When the emery cloth unwinds, the imbalance makes it extremely dangerous for you and anyone around you.

Hammer, Hand And Spring

The inside of the frame required some filing to provide clearance for the hammer and cocking mechanism. First, it was necessary to remove all obvious burrs and casting marks from the frame recesses. After those were eliminated, the hammer was smoked and assembled to the frame. Areas in the frame which picked up black were then filed-down with a fine file until the hammer worked with no interference.

The hand was assembled to the hammer and the assembly inserted into the frame through the hammer re-

cess. At first, the assembly would not fit into the frame. Additional filing of the hammer recess to remove casting marks freed-up the hammer, and the assembly of the hand and the hammer to the frame was completed easily.

Next, it was necessary to check the operation of the hand. This is an extremely important step and must be done before the gun can be fired. The hand's function is to rotate the cylinder until it lines up with the hammer and the bore of the gun. If the cylinder does not rotate far enough, the bolt will not engage the cylinder cut, and the cylinder will not be properly aligned with the barrel, creating a very unsafe condition.

To check proper function, slowly cock the hammer and observe the rotation of the cylinder. Sometime before the hammer reaches full cock, the cylinder will stop rotating, and the nipple should be exactly centered in the hammer cutout. The axis of the uppermost chamber will be exactly centered on the axis of the barrel. This must be checked again after the bolt is assembled to assure proper operation of the gun.

Bolt

The cylinder bolt must be hand-fitted to the hammer to permit proper operation. The bolt's function is to lock-up the cylinder during the firing process. As the hammer is cocked, the bolt pulls away from the cylinder, retracting into the frame. The cylinder rotates to the next firing position. Then the bolt pops up, out of the frame, and engages the cylinder cut. Finally, the hammer reaches full

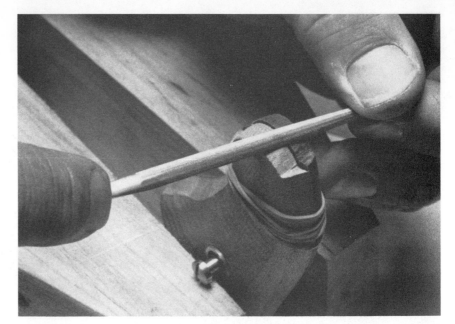

The second grip half was roughed out using the first grip as a pattern. The filing was stopped just short of matching the two grip halves in case the two sides of the frame did not match exactly.

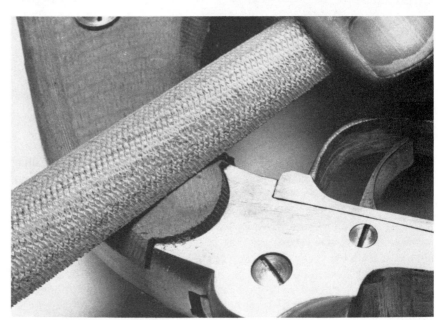

After the grips fit into the frame recess, the rough contours of the grip were filed. Care was necessary not to scratch the frame with the file.

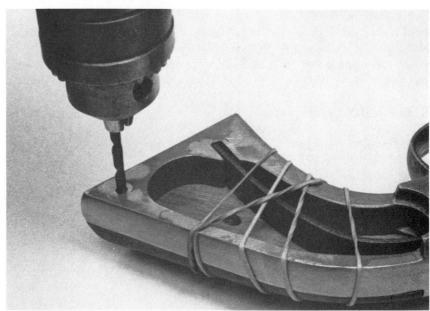

A hole for the grip-alignment pin was drilled by clamping the grips to the frame and using the hole in the frame as a guide.

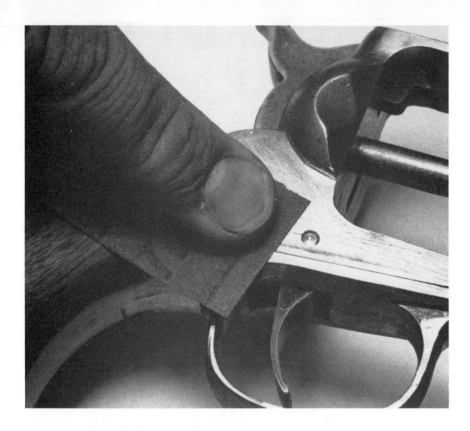

The grips were finished with successively finer grades of garnet paper.

cock. Actually, the way most revolvers are tuned at the factory, the bolt pops up slightly before the cylinder stops rotating, which provides a margin of safety in case the gun is slightly mis-timed.

On my gun, a fair amount of material had to be removed from the bolt tab. I found it was easiest to fit the bolt if I left all the parts out of the gun, except for the hammer, the trigger, and the bolt. Substituting finger pressure on the bolt and trigger for the trigger spring, I slowly cocked the hammer. I observed that the bolt drew into the frame just as the hammer started to be cocked. I then observed when the bolt popped up from the frame to engage the cylinder. Ideally, this should occur slightly before the hammer reaches full cock. As my gun came from the factory, the bolt would not pop back up at all at full cock. Material had to be filed off the bolt tab until proper function was achieved. Keep the file square and only remove a very slight amount at a time. Always remember that it is far easier to remove material than to add it.

Check Timing

Now I was ready to check the gun for proper timing. I assembled the hammer, trigger, hand, bolt, and trigger spring together in the frame. I then installed the cylinder, cylinder pin, and mainspring. I cocked the hammer slowly and observed that: (1) the bolt retracted into the frame; (2) the cylinder rotated almost to the next firing position; (3) the bolt popped up from the frame, contacting the cylinder; (4) the cylinder continued to rotate into firing position; (5) the bolt clicked into place in the cylinder cut; and (6) the hammer engaged the full cock notch, in that order. No binding or drag should be or was felt.

Grips

The grips fit into a semicircular recess at the top of the grip frame. I discovered that the diameter of the recess was nearly identical to the diameter of a US nickel. (Limited legal tender notwithstanding, it's still useful for something besides feeding parking meters.) I therefore used a nickel to provide the approximate outline of the frame recess and filed the top of the grip to this outline. Once the rough outline of the recess was established, it was necessary to blacken the frame recess with a candle and install the grip onto the frame. When the grip is removed from the frame, high spots made visible by soot transferred to the wood can be removed. This process is repeated until the grip fits perfectly into the recess.

To fit the other half of the grip, it is advisable to first remove the half already fitted to the frame, screw the two grip halves together (using the screw provided) and trace the outline of the fitted onto the unfitted grip. File the unfitted grip but stop a little short of filing the wood down to the mark just in case the two halves of the frame are slightly different. Fit the second grip as before, except frequently check to be sure that both grip halves fit into the frame recess simultaneously. This is necessary because the grips must fit into the frame with the additional constraint that they must also fit together.

Once the grips fit into the frame properly, they can be shaped to the contours of the frame. This is accomplished very quickly using a medium half-round file. There is no particular *best way* to contour the grips; everybody has different hands, but do be careful not to scratch up the grip frame too badly with the half-round file. Scratching

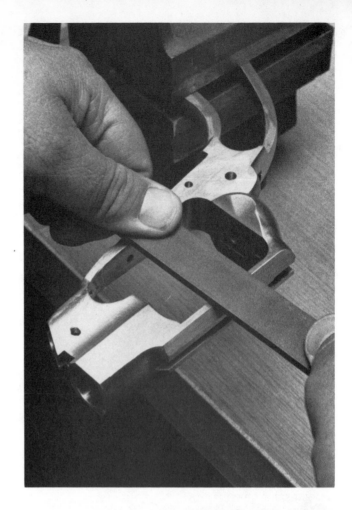

The flat surfaces of the frame were draw filed, leaving a very nice finish.

the grip now will only mean more work later when the grip frame is filed down.

When the grip is properly filed down into the desired contours, it is necessary to sand with the grain using successively finer grades of garnet paper - usually between 240 and 400 grit. Sand until no sanding marks are evident. After sanding, the grips are ready for staining, sealing, and oiling or varnishing.

I prefer a minimum of stain on my wood projects and I am particularly wary of various opaque stains available on the market. Usually, such stains are used to cover up an inexpensive wood and hopefully, make it resemble a more expensive or desirable wood such as walnut. In my opinion you might as well paint the wood. Stain should be used to emphasize the beauty of the wood by bringing up the grain and possibly altering its color.

Sealer is used to prevent the stain and subsequent finishes from exaggerating the porosity of the wood. For example, oak, an otherwise desirable wood for some applications (though rarely guns) usually requires a sealer to prevent its pores from dominating the appearance of the finish.

Concave surfaces were finished using a ½" sanding drum and a high-speed die grinder.

Complex and small surfaces were finished by whatever means seemed to work best.

I chose to finish the grips with Birchwood Casey's Maple Wood Stain and then followed with their True Oil gunstock finish. Unless you have some experience finishing wood, I suggest that you simply pick up a finishing kit at your local gunshop and follow its directions. This is probably the easiest and most satisfying part of kit gun building; it is for me.

Frame

The frame required a fair amount of filing. It arrived with most of the exterior surfaces just as cast. In addition, as I discovered when fitting the action, some of the interior surfaces needed dressing with a file to remove casting marks or machining burrs. The interior surfaces could be filed acceptably smooth in just a few minutes, especially since appearance was a secondary consideration. The exterior surfaces required a great deal of time for the gun to be properly finished.

The flat surfaces of the frame, i.e., the top, parts of the sides, and the grip frame were filed using a flat-mill file. Except for the grip frame, which was filed primarily to provide a flat mounting surface for the grips, the frame was filed until no low spots (evidenced by the dull cast finish) remained.

The concave contours of the frame were not filed, but rather sanded using a ½″ diameter sanding drum and a hand-held die grinder, which is basically a bigger version of a Dremel Moto tool. The Dremel tool would work just fine, but I don't own one.

The convex contours of the frame were finished by various means, depending on the condition of the surface and the difficulty of finding a suitable tool to work with. As an example, the areas around the breech face had to be sanded with medium grit emery cloth wrapped around my finger.

The final finishing of the frame was accomplished, as was the barrel, by repeating each operation with successively finer grades of emery paper. When I reached 320 grit emery paper, I carefully followed the contours of the gun. This left the stainless steel exterior of the gun with a brushed look which I find very pleasing.

Sight Installation

The final step to the completion of the revolver was the installation of the front sight and the loading-lever retainer. It is suggested in the instructions supplied by Euroarms, that the sight be staked in place after the gun has been test fired. Euroarms cautions the novice kit builder to have his new gun checked thoroughly by a competent gunsmith before taking it to the range. This is very important and shouldn't be expensive. A mis-timed revolver is potentially very hazardous to yourself and fellow shooters. Good shooting!

the CVA Philadelphia Derringer Kit

by Alfonso Torres

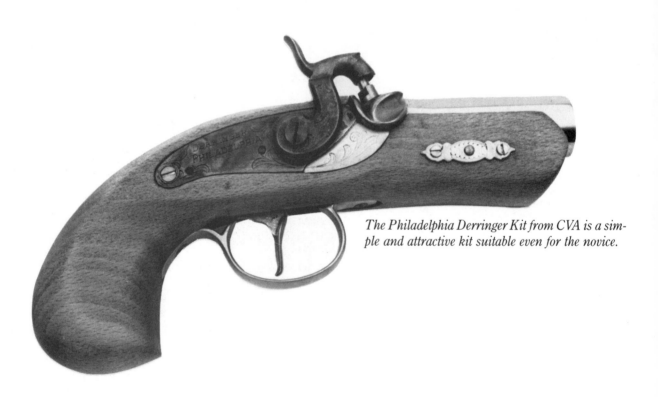

The Philadelphia Derringer Kit from CVA is a simple and attractive kit suitable even for the novice.

Introduction

Derringer is a generic term pertaining to a class of blackpowder percussion pistols manufactured and popularized by Henry Deringer (spelled with one r) of Philadelphia in the late 1830s. Although the gun was named after its inventor and the term originally spelled with one r, it was so often misspelled, (sometimes deliberately by imitators wishing to avoid litigation) that the double r spelling became the more commonly used (although not necessarily preferred) form. Some present-day aficionados of the derringer use the *deringer* spelling only to apply to the weapons manufactured by Henry Deringer.

Henry Deringer's guns were all percussion models; however, later model derringers were often manufactured as cartridge models. Although the term derringer conjures up an image of a tiny fist-sized weapon, the originals varied in barrel length from one and one-half to nine inches. Henry Deringer's guns quickly gained popularity and notoriety. (Indeed, one of Deringer's pistols was used to assassinate Abraham Lincoln.) In Philadelphia alone, Deringer-like imitations were being produced by no less than fourteen other gun companies; hence the term Philadelphia Derringer. The calibers and barrel lengths of these pistols varied widely, but .41 caliber was probably the most common caliber size, and three inches an average length.

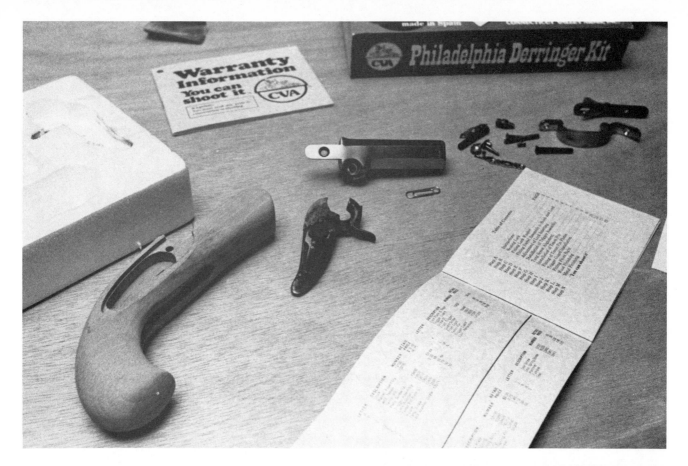

The kit comes complete with excellent assembly instructions and a detailed warranty booklet.

(Longer barrels — seven to nine inches — were found on the larger dueling size derringers.)

CVA's Philadelphia Derringer replica is a .45 caliber percussion model which differs from some of its 19th century predecessors in that it has a one-piece, rather than two-piece, barrel assembly. The barrel is three and one-fourth inches long.

Preparation

Being a rookie in the business and having built no other guns previously, I was a little reluctant to tackle this kit gun. The first thing I did was look at the instruction manual. The manufacturer's assembly instructions and procedures are written for the individual with a moderate understanding of gunsmithing. Since my knowledge of gun parts was very limited, I spent a lot of time going back and forth to the parts list and the exploded diagram in the assembly manual. Everybody knows what a barrel is but few non-gun enthusiasts can relate to a sear. It brings to my mind a large department store and tells my wife how to cook meat. It would have been helpful if a picture of the part being discussed in the assembly instructions had been included next to the text describing it, but life is not all roses. Perhaps CVA will eventually choose to modify its assembly instructions to better accommodate the novice gun builder.

The first actual step in assembling the Philadelphia Derringer was to make the lockwork (left hand) learn to love the stock (right hand).

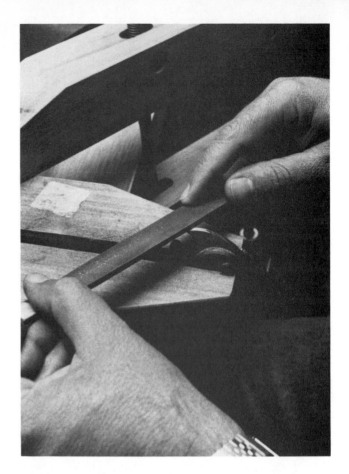

Right: Fitting the lockwork required a little judicious filing and (below left) some careful work with a sharp knife.

Below Right: The lockwork had to be drawn into the frame in order to check the progress of the fitting operation.

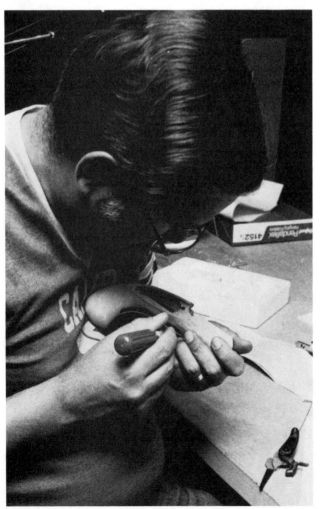

Much of the shaping of the stock, for which CVA specifies the use of a chisel or sharp knife, can be accomplished with a Dremel tool.

A disclaimer appears in the instructions stating that the warranty only applies to unworked parts. Because assembling the gun involves working with the parts, this presents a dilemma. Since this is a low-cost gun (list price $39.95), it's worth taking a chance; so go ahead and work the parts and forget the warranty. If you are serious about shooting this gun, please pay extra attention to the parts that operate under pressure; nobody wants to lose an arm or hand.

The Philadelphia Derringer gun parts are described at the beginning of the assembly manual. After checking all the parts against the manifesto (all parts were there), I was ready to begin the assembly.

CVA recommends the following tools:

a. Electric drill and ¹⁄₁₆″, ⅛″, ⁹⁄₆₄″, ¼″, ⁵⁄₁₆″ drill bits
b. Small flat file and round needle file
c. Small chisel or carving tool
d. Spotting compound
e. Sand paper (various grades) and steel wool
f. Wooden mallet
g. Screw drivers (various sizes)
h. Vise
i. CVA finishing kit

The instructions also mention using a metal punch, a propane torch, masking tape, and a good ruler calibrated to ¹⁄₃₂″. You will find that by using a Dremel tool with a cutting bit and a polishing/buffing wheel, the assembly is simplified considerably. Of the tools required, I was able to omit c, d and i listed above. I added a small candle for spotting purposes. If you have access to a drill press, then

you may omit the electric drill.

Assembly

The assembly of the gun is divided into thirteen individual steps, labelled A through M. Some are very long, others are extremely short.

Step A: The instructions describe the assembly process and include a short pep talk. The instructions are clear, brief, easy to understand and, in general, well written.

Step B: Seating Lock. This part is a little time consuming. The manufacturer tells you to use a chisel or a sharp knife (X-acto type) to remove excess wood from the stock. You soon realize that there are easier ways to achieve the same objectives. I used a Dremel tool to work on the stock. Since the stock is made of a fairly hard wood, the bit does not remove large amounts of material — thus ensuring that the novice woodworker does not make large gouges in the wood. This method is definitely much easier than working with a sharp knife. In order to complete step B, the sear in the percussion lock had to be filed down. In addition, the inside of the stock had to be enlarged to accommodate said sear. I successfully reduced the sear with a medium-coarse file.

Step C: Fitting of the Lock Washer. This is the first step that calls for the use of the drill. Remember, not only must the hole be drilled to the correct width, but also to the correct depth. I used a piece of masking tape wrapped around the drill bit to mark the proper hole depth. Once the drill bit had penetrated the wood to the edge of the tape, I knew the hole was the proper depth. This step

The best way to check the fit of a part, in this case the barrel, is to blacken it with a candle.

When the part is installed, the blackening will be transferred to the stock where the fit is close.

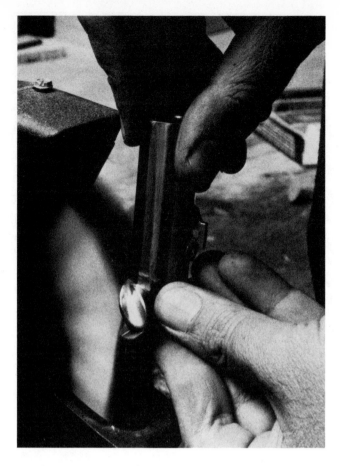

I wanted a mirror-like finish on the metal parts of my derringer. After using files to remove the obvious scratches and emery paper to remove the file marks; a buffing wheel and polishing compound were just the ticket.

was fairly easy to implement.

Step D: Fitting Barrel Assembly to Stock and Lock. This step was definitely a time-consuming activity. I found that the barrel did not fit on the stock. To determine which parts needed to be reduced in size by the Dremel tool, the barrel was spotted. This process is very simple. Either apply some spotting compound to the barrel, or light a candle and run the flame along the barrel surface. Darkening of the barrel will result. Then place the barrel into the stock briefly, remove it, and notice where the wood has been darkened. Remove a slight amount of the darkened wood and repeat the process until you achieve a perfect fit. This process may have to be repeated several times until the barrel is seated properly against the stock and lockwork.

Step E: Adjustment of the Lock Inletting. This is a relatively easy step. If you have completed the previous step correctly, step E is merely a fine tuning operation. However, in step E CVA includes a statement concerning the hammer fit which struck fear in the heart of this novice kit gun builder. It says, "If the hammer does not strike the nipple properly, recheck for correct inletting. It may be necessary to bend the hammer. Remove it from the stock and heat it to cherry red with a propane torch, then bend it to the desired angle. This should be done carefully to avoid breakage." Wow! Good-bye warranty. Fortunately, this wasn't necessary. (What a relief.) A suggestion to CVA: how about a little better quality control?

Step F: Installation of the Trigger Assembly. Dropping

the trigger assembly into the stock is relatively easy. If the fit is too snug, use the Dremel tool to remove excess material from around the edges of the hole in the stock. You may want to remove the lockwork to prevent marring its finish.

Step G: Tang Screw Adjustment. The tang screw, tang, and trigger assembly should be in alignment. If they aren't, the hole in the stock must be enlarged with a drill to accommodate them.

Step H: Installation of the Tenon Pin. This is the most critical part of the whole assembly. You must drill a hole perpendicular to the stock, hitting the tenon on the barrel and breaking through the stock on the other side in exactly the correct place to match the side where you began the hole. (This is not the time to learn how to use a drill. Young teens assembling one of these kits could probably benefit from some drilling help from Dad.) You can take a chance and drill the ⅛" hole as specified; however, I did not have that much confidence in my own measurements so I used a very small drill bit to drill an exploratory hole. If a correction is necessary, a very tiny hole is much easier to correct than a large hole. Fortunately, the first hole was perfect and was easily expanded to the required size. Using a drill press assures you that the hole is as straight as possible — meaning perpendicular to the tenon and the barrel. Take your time because the appearance of your gun will depend on how well you execute this step.

Step I: Fitting of Tenon-Pin Plates. This requires more drilling to set the tenon-plate screws, but isn't too difficult.

The Dremel tool was perfect for those areas where the buffing wheel would not fit. Here, the inside of the trigger guard is polished after being filed and sanded.

The screws used on the tenon-pin plates were steel. The tenon-pin plates were brass. Steel on brass didn't appeal to me, so I went down to the hardware store and bought four brass screws. In addition, I replaced one of the trigger guard screws with a brass screw since the trigger guard was also brass.

Step J: Trigger Guard Installation. This also is relatively easy, but requires drilling a hole for the rear trigger-guard screw.

Step K: Fitting Front Sight. First a philosophical digression. The derringer-style weapon was designed for defense (and in some cases, offense) at very close ranges; typically less than 20 feet and usually in very much in a hurry. Under these circumstances, the addition of a front sight is unnecessary. I decided to omit the sight provided in the kit for these reasons. I also rationalized that since I wanted a smoothly-finished barrel, the front sight would only interfere with that goal. A word of caution: if you decide to install the front sight and also plan to shoot the gun, be sure not to drill the necessary hole any deeper than $5/32''$, as specified in the assembly manual.

Step L: Wood Finishing. I finished my stock with Formby's Tung Oil, which is a blend of linseed oil and assorted herbs and spices (just kidding, Mr. Formby). After sanding the stock to the desired finish, I applied four coats of Tung oil to the stock with a clean, lint-free, cotton rag, and finished as directed between coats. The results were fantastic.

Step M: Metal Finishing. Finishing the barrel and other metal parts proved to be extremely time consuming. Since my barrel had some fairly deep scratches in it, I initially used a relatively coarse file to smooth it. From there I went to a finer file; then to progressively finer grades of emery paper and finally to steel wool. After using the steel wool, I used a buffing wheel and polishing compound to polish the barrel to a mirror-like finish. The same operation was applied to the brass parts with equally gratifying results. No browning or bluing was applied to the barrel, as I preferred the metal to achieve a natural patina with time. I polished the inside contours of the trigger guard with the Dremel tool and a felt bob; that operation alone justified the use of this tool.

Summary

CVA's Philadelphia Derringer is more difficult to assemble than, for example, the pepperbox described elsewhere in this publication; it requires some finishing touches on the inletting and some precision drilling at eight different points in the assembly process. The total assembly time was about 12 hours for this novice gunsmith. At least half of those hours were spent finishing the gun to my personal satisfaction.

Epilogue

The CVA Philadelphia Derringer now rests in my living room. Though I have no intention of shooting it for now, I know it will be ready when I am.

MILITARY WEAPONS KITS

Pistols, Rifles, and Machineguns

Sarco, Inc., has been supplying military surplus guns and parts to collectors, dealers, and the military for nearly 20 years. Listed on this page are kits for many of the weapons used by the U.S. Military for the last 70 years. All kits can be purchased by anyone and no special license is required. Each kit does require a receiver to make it into an operable firearm (the receiver is the part bearing the serial numbers—usually, the barrel screws into it). A Federal Firearms License is required to purchase a pistol or rifle receiver. Receivers are available from other suppliers in the trade. Machinegun receivers require special Federal "Form 1" registration before purchase or manufacture.

Thompson Sub-Machinegun Kits

The most famous sub-machinegun of all time! The "Tommy Gun" was the first successful sub-machinegun, and is now regarded as a classic firearm. Our kit contains all the parts with which to assemble a gun except the receiver and the trigger frame. All parts are either original U.S. Army W.W. II surplus, or brand new manufacture.

We have two basic variations of the Thompson:

Kit #1—M1928A1—This was the early style gun with detachable buttstock—caliber .45 ACP.
Kit Price **$238.96**
(plus $7.00 shipping)

Kit #2—M1A1—The last version of the Thompson developed for mass production in W.W. II—caliber .45 ACP.
Kit Price **$154.96**
(plus $7.00 shipping)

M1 Garand Rifle Kit

The M1 Garand, in caliber .30-06, was the main battle rifle of the U.S. Army throughout World War II and the Korean War. The quick-shooting semi-automatic Garand proved itself against the slower bolt-action Mauser rifles of Germany and Japan. Now you can assemble a fully operational M1 for yourself. Our M1 Garand Kit has almost all the parts needed to do the job. Those few parts which are not included are available separately from Sarco or other dealers.

Kit #1—All parts for the M1 except receiver, barrel and operating rod . . **$110.96**
(plus $7.00 shipping)
Kit #2—Same as Kit #1, but includes a very good condition barrel . . . **$175.96**
(plus $7.00 shipping)
Kit #3—Same as Kit #1, but includes a new unfired G.I. issue barrel . . **$220.96**
(plus $7.00 shipping)

M1 Carbine Kit

The .30 caliber M1 carbine is the all-time favorite military rifle for most collectors and shooters. Rapid semi-automatic fire and light recoil make the carbine a fun gun to shoot.

Our M1 Carbine Kit contains all M1 parts except the receiver. You will get a stock, sights, bolt, trigger, etc. etc. All parts are in good condition. The barrel has been cut off at the front end by a few inches, so we'll include an extra front barrel end. The operating slide has also been de-militarized (cut) in the back end. We include the piece so you can weld it back together.
M1 Carbine Kit **$79.96**
(plus $6.00 shipping)

.45 Automatic Pistol Kit

The Colt .45 M1911 pistol is such a classic firearm that little needs to be said about it here. Now, with our ".45 Builder's Kit" you can assemble your own custom .45. Thanks to a special purchase from a government contractor, we are able to offer a complete set of parts for the M1911A1 "Government" model .45 automatic pistol. Our kit contains ALL the parts in the gun except the receiver.

The .45 Builder's Kit contains all the parts necessary to assemble a gun, including barrel, slide, grips, magazine, hammer, trigger, sear, springs, etc. etc. (Receiver not included.)
.45 Builder's Kit **$165.96**
(plus $5.00 shipping)

Ordering Instructions
1. Include handling and shipping with your order.
2. Send money order or certified check.
3. C.O.D. order service available. All C.O.D.s add $5.75 for extra handling. All C.O.D.s will come CASH ONLY for delivery—NO CHECKS.
4. Visa or Mastercard also welcome—minimum order $25.00.
5. Put all inquiries on a separate sheet of paper and include a self-addressed envelope.
6. Average delivery time is 3 to 4 weeks.

Special Note Concerning Our Machinegun Kits

If you decide to build a .30 caliber Browning 1919 or M37 or a .50 caliber M2 yourself, you may do so legally if you file a "Form 1" with the BATF and comply with your state laws. To assist you, we supply free of charge a set of blueprints for the sideplates, but only ON RECEIPT of a copy of your approved "Form 1". The "Form 1" is not required to order our kit, only to get the receiver prints. We will send the prints later after your kit is ordered and the "Form 1" is approved by the BATF. Our reason for this requirement is that we do not wish to assist an illegal act. Prints supplied for the M37 will be 1919A4 prints, but these can be easily transposed to M37 by using the remaining pieces of sideplates as patterns for those dimensions that are different.

Many of our customers purchase kits to make non-firing display guns. This is especially popular with the Browning machinegun as it is fairly simple to construct a dummy receiver using plexiglass, wood, or other material and then using our kit parts to complete the model. These can then be mounted on a Jeep or other military vehicle, displayed in a gun room, store window, etc.

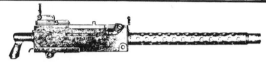

Browning M1919A4 and M1919A6 Machineguns

The .30 caliber M1919 Brownings were the standard-issue machineguns for the U.S. for nearly half a century. Many of these fine guns are still in use in armies around the globe. The M1919A4 is basically used as a tripod-mounted weapon, while the M1919A6 is fitted with a shoulder stock, flash hider, and bipod for use as a light machinegun.

These kits include all parts for a M1919A4 or M1919A6 Browning except the 2 receiver sideplates. The trunion block and top and bottom plates are included. The top plate supplied may have to be repaired, but we'll include overlapping pieces to make it easy to repair. All sights are included, barrel will have excellent bore and all parts will be in excellent, serviceable condition.
M1919A4 Kit **$895.96**
(+$15.00 shipping)
M1919A6 Kit **$995.96**
(+$15.00 shipping)

Browning M37 Machinegun

The M37 is a caliber .30-06 short-action version of the 1919-series machineguns. Designed for use in tanks and other vehicles where space is limited, the M37 has a shorter receiver and different style cocking assembly than the full-size guns. It is an alternate feed gun, similar to the .50 caliber. We also supply a standard cocking handle with the kit in case you decide not to use the retracting slide. This gun has never been on the market, and the few examples in private collections have been offered at $5,000 to $7,000 each. The general configuration is the same as the .30 caliber 1919A4 and most parts are the same, but there are some differences. These have had 2 inches removed from both sideplates according to Federal ATF regulations. These kits are in truly excellent condition and are virtually new.
M37 Kit **$995.96**
(+$15.00 shipping)

Browning .50 Caliber M2 Machinegun

Still the standard U.S. heavy machinegun, the "50" has been in service for over half a century, and it's still going strong! Our kit includes all parts to build a gun including barrel, sight, bolt, etc. The receiver has been "de-militarized" by the Army so it no longer functions as is. This process involves putting 1/8" wide cuts in the top cover, top plate, bottom plate and trunion. The receiver side plates were also cut in two and a piece was removed. To re-manufacture the receiver, you will have to fabricate sideplates and weld-up and machine the other cuts. Again, all parts for the gun are included except sideplates. The standard cocking handle, all sights, and internal parts are included. All parts are in serviceable condition and bore condition is very good or better.
.50 caliber M2 Kit **$1,456.96**
(shipped truck collect)

Guarantee

If you are not satisfied with any item ordered, you have 5 days to contact us for authorization to return it for a replacement or a refund. All returns must be accompanied by a letter with your invoice number and an explanation of the problem. All returns must be in the same condition in which you received them. Any alterations or work will void the guarantee.

Send all shipments pre-paid. C.O.D.s will be refused. Any items returned due to customer error are subject to a 10% re-stocking charge.

As we don't install the parts we sell, we cannot guarantee that they will function when installed by others.

How Self-Loading Firearms Work

by Gary E. Reisenwitz

A basic understanding of how self-loading firearms work is essential to any hobbyist who desires to work with, modify or construct a modern self-loading firearm. In order to obtain this basic understanding, a detailed description and analysis of the four most common principles of operation is offered here.

A self-loading firearm, by definition, uses a portion of the force or energy generated by the firing of the cartridge to mechanically extract the depleted casing, cock the firearm, chamber a new cartridge and otherwise prepare it for a subsequent firing. These firearms normally operate in a semi-automatic mode; i.e. a separate, distinct trigger pull is required for each shot. A fully automatic firearm, on the other hand, will continue firing shot after shot until the trigger is released or the ammunition supply has been expended.

Fully automatic weapons merely possess an additional mechanical capability, but this has no bearing on the principle of operation utilized to effect the cycling of the firearm. A firearm that is capable of firing several shots in succession by means of an external power source, such as a hand crank (Gatling gun) or electric motor (U.S. Army 20mm Vulcan), is not considered a self-loading firearm and will not be covered in this article.

A good self-loading design is one that successfully manages the forces of operation involved in the firing and cycling of the firearm. These forces are considerable, and their careful management is critical. Upon firing, the chamber of a modern firearm may experience pressures in excess of twenty tons per square inch. The soft brass shell casing can only act as a flimsy gasket when exposed to pressures of that magnitude.

The firearm, especially the bolt face and chamber, must safely contain this force for a short period of time, typically a few milliseconds. The minimum amount of time that these forces must be contained for safe operation is the time from primer ignition until the pressure of the expanding gas within the bore of the firearm drops to near atmospheric levels. Only then can the chamber be safely opened and the depleted shell casing extracted.

Techniques

There are two principle techniques to ensure that the chamber and bolt (or breech) support the cartridge for the required period of time. The first technique is to lock the bolt to the firearm's barrel or receiver, utilizing some form of mechanical construct, such as a locking lug. The second method is to ensure that the bolt's inertia is sufficient to delay the inevitable response to the cartridge combustion for the required time period. A method of effectively increasing bolt inertia without increasing bolt mass is to use the technique of preignition or mechanical disadvantage. Both of these techniques will be discussed at length when the blowback and delayed blowback principles of operation are described.

Nearly all current and successful self-loading firearms utilize one of four operating principles to perform the cyclic functioning of the firearm. These principles are: recoil operation, gas operation, blowback operation and delayed-blowback operation. There are other techniques but they have not been considered successful and no time need be spent on them.

Examples of all four operating principles can be found in current-production self-loading firearms around the world. These principles have resulted in designs which have stood and, in all likelihood will continue to stand the test of time. This does not mean that improvements and innovations cannot be made upon any of the current designs, or that new designs are not possible; but rather, it is more likely than not, that one of the four basic principles described herein will be utilized.

Recoil Operation

The first design principle to be discussed is that of recoil operation. Recoil-operated self-loading firearms were among the first successful designs. It was probably assumed that the most consistent and powerful force to be harnessed would be that of the ever-present recoil. Recoil-operated firearms are usually typified by having a barrel that moves a short distance forward and backward, relative to a fixed receiver or frame, during the course of firing. The purpose of this movement is to facilitate the operation of a mechanism to unlock the bolt from the barrel during recoil, while ensuring that the bolt is locked to the chamber at the instant of firing.

Prior to firing, the bolt is usually locked to the barrel, or a portion of the barrel extension, when a cartridge is chambered. Upon firing, the bolt and barrel, still locked, begin to move toward the rear of the weapon under recoil. After traveling a short distance together, a mechanism unlocks the bolt as the barrel ceases rearward motion. After the bolt is unlocked, its inertia carries it back further, extracting the fired casing, cocking the striker and compressing the recoil spring. Upon reaching the rearward limit of travel, the bolt moves forward — propelled by the compressed recoil spring, strips a fresh cartridge from the magazine or ammunition belt, chambers the car-

tridge and locks itself into the barrel as it returns to battery. A subsequent pull of the trigger releases the hammer or striker, ignition occurs and the cycle is repeated.

A fully automatic firearm, utilizing the recoil principle of operation, employs one additional mechanism — a disconnector. The purpose of a disconnector is to act as an automatic sear tripper or hammer release; allowing continuous cycling of the firearm as long as the trigger is held to the rear.

The design of the disconnector is critical in that the hammer or striker must not be released prior to the bolt reaching the locked position. If this occurred, a pre-locked ignition could result, causing possible damage to the weapon when the unsupported cartridge casing exploded.

A less-dangerous condition exists when the hammer or striker simply follows the bolt forward. When this occurs, ignition would be unlikely, or at best, sporadic. The bolt would probably slow the hammer or striker down to a velocity below that necessary to hit the primer with sufficient force to ensure ignition. Another problem that could occur with such a deficiency is that a protruding firing pin on the bolt face might interfere with the chambering of a cartridge by blocking the rise of the cartridge-case head, thus causing a jam. In any case, the nature of a disconnector is rather critical and great care should be taken when modifications on, or the manufacture of, a disconnector mechanism are anticipated.

Some examples of recoil-operated firearms are as follows: the Johnson Rifle, the Maxim and Browning machine guns, nearly all semi-automatic pistols greater than .380 ACP in caliber and Browning semi-automatic shotguns.

Recoil Operation

1: before firing

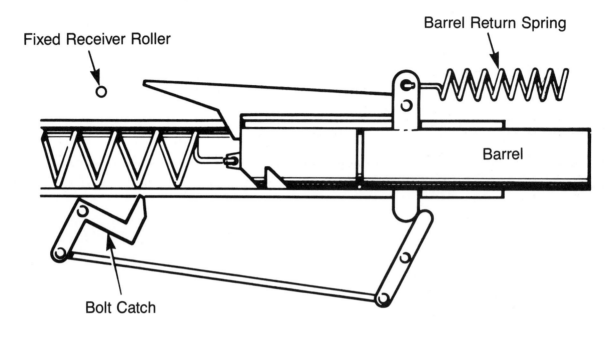

Fixed Receiver Roller

Barrel Return Spring

Barrel

Bolt Catch

2: at firing

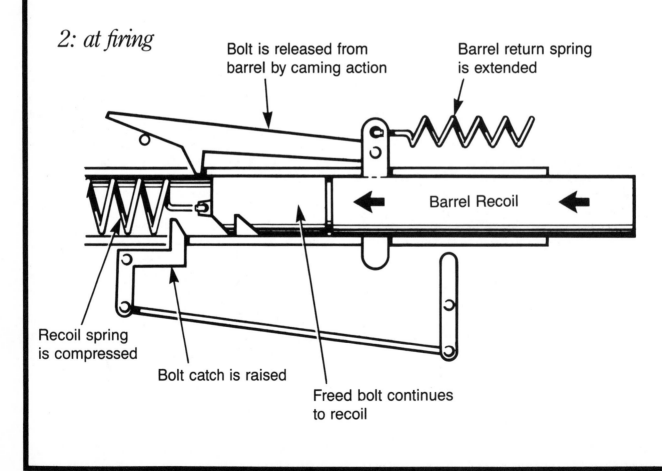

Bolt is released from
barrel by caming action

Barrel return spring
is extended

Barrel Recoil

Recoil spring
is compressed

Bolt catch is raised

Freed bolt continues
to recoil

3: extraction

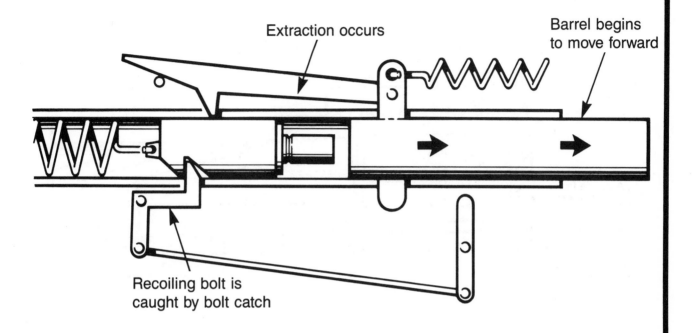

Extraction occurs

Barrel begins
to move forward

Recoiling bolt is
caught by bolt catch

4: bolt release

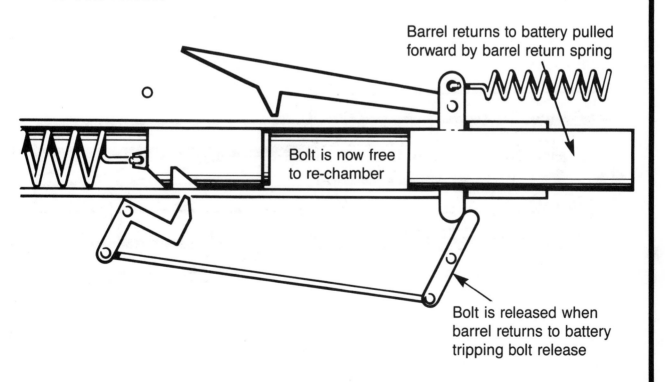

Barrel returns to battery pulled
forward by barrel return spring

Bolt is now free
to re-chamber

Bolt is released when
barrel returns to battery
tripping bolt release

Gas Operation

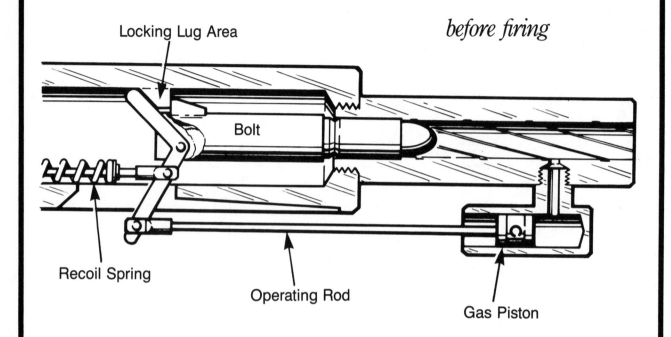

Locking Lug Area

before firing

Bolt

Recoil Spring

Operating Rod

Gas Piston

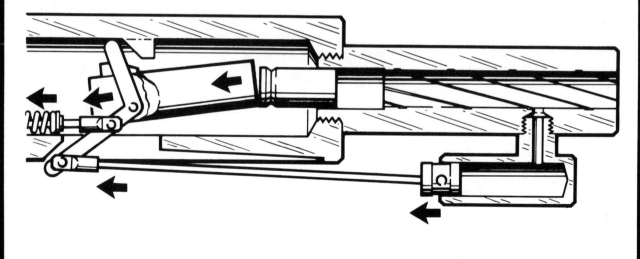

after firing

Gas Operation

The next design principle to be discussed is that of gas operation. Gas-operated firearms have been in production for approximately as long as recoil-operated firearms. Gas operation is currently enjoying tremendous popularity among designers of modern combat rifles and assault rifles.

The principle of gas operation usually involves bleeding high-pressure gas from within the barrel through one or more gas ports. The gas pressure is directed to act on a piston or ring, which is normally connected to an operating rod. The operating rod acts upon the bolt to unlock it from the barrel or receiver. The operating rod continues to force the bolt to the rear of the firearm, extracting the fired casing, cocking the hammer or striker, and compressing the recoil spring. The recoil spring then forces the bolt forward, stripping and chambering a fresh cartridge and re-locking the bolt into the barrel or receiver. The firearm is thus prepared for a subsequent pull of the trigger.

An advantage of gas operation is that it allows for a fixed barrel, and a weapon that is relatively light in weight. The delay, necessary for safe operation, is accommodated in this design principle by several factors including: how far from the chamber the gas port is located, the size of the gas port, the surface area of the gas piston or ring, and the combined mass of the entire reciprocating assembly.

In this design, care must be taken to ensure that not too much gas pressure is bled-off to operate the action. There will be no noticeable effect on the exterior ballistics if the mechanism is subjected to excessive force; however, breakage will almost certainly occur. It is important to remember that the high-pressure gas that is capable of driving the bullet out of the barrel with such tremendous force, is the same pressure utilized to cycle the action.

The chief drawback to gas operation is the problem created by powder fouling. Gas ports tend to clog; gas pistons may stick; and direct gas-action firearms (M-16, AR-l5) have their chamber areas and receivers repeatedly flooded with extremely hot combustion gases and powder residue.

There are many variations of the gas operation principle. Some firearms do not use separate pistons and operating rods, but instead combine them into devices commonly referred to as bolt carriers. Both the Kalishnikov and the AR-15 series firearms use bolt carriers to combine this function. The AR-15 is a direct gas-action type and the Kalishnikov is a more traditional closed-system design. These designs do differ considerably, yet still utilize the same basic principles of gas operation. The mechanical principles for allowing fully automatic fire are identical for both recoil and gas-operated firearms. The requirement for a disconnector remains the same.

Some examples of gas-operated firearms are: M1 Garand, M1 Carbine, M-14, FN-FAL, Ruger Mini-14, Colt AR-15, M-16, AR-18, AK-47, all Kalishnikov variants, U.S. M-60 machine gun and most commercial semi-automatic shotguns.

Blowback Operation

The third principle of operation to be discussed is blowback operation. Blowback operation is more recent than either recoil or gas operation in production firearms. It is also the simplest of the four principles of operation discussed here. Its simplicity, however, has limited its effective application to firearms using pistol ammunition.

The principle of blowback operation relies on the phase shifts produced by a massive bolt and an elastic combustion gas. In order to understand how such a phase shift can occur, imagine yourself riding in a stiffly sprung vehicle, such as a Jeep, along a bumpy road. When an especially large bump is encountered, you are thrown upward from the seat and may strike your head on the ceiling.

What has actually occurred, is that the motion of the vehicle and your body has become out of phase. While *you* are moving upward, the Jeep has already reached its maximum upward excursion and has either stopped its upward motion or is even moving downward toward your head. Your motion has been delayed by the elasticity of the seat cushions. This same phase delay applies to blowback operated weapons. The mass of the bolt is the primary determinant of the phase delay.

The requirement for a massive bolt renders the application of this principle to heavy calibers impractical due to the requirement for excessively massive components. For example, to safely use a blowback design to fire 7.62mm Nato ball ammunition would require a 10-pound bolt!

In a blowback-operated firearm, the bolt must possess sufficient inertia at firing to safely support the case head of the cartridge. If insufficient inertial resistance exists, combustion will force the bolt face away from the chamber and the unsupported casing will rupture. One method of insuring adequate inertia is to create the conditions for pre-ignition.

Pre-Ignition

In a pre-ignition design, the firearm is fired from an open bolt and possesses a fixed firing pin on the bolt face. When the trigger is pressed, the bolt — under pressure from a compressed recoil spring — is released and moves forward. The bolt then strips a cartridge from the magazine and forces it into the chamber. Upon chambering, the fixed firing pin on the bolt face begins to strike the cartridge primer before the bolt has come to rest. Complete ignition and peak chamber pressure are normally reached while the bolt is still several thousandths of an inch from rest. The forward momentum of the bolt effectively provides a much higher inertial resistance to the forces of combustion than if the bolt were totally at rest.

Simple-Blowback Operation

before firing

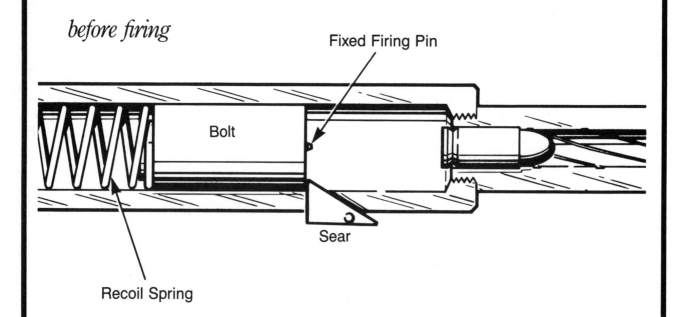

Fixed Firing Pin

Bolt

Sear

Recoil Spring

after firing

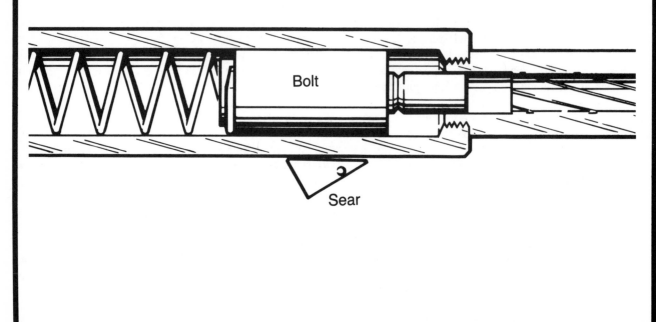

Bolt

Sear

The pre-ignition principle can be found in the designs of modern submachine guns such as the UZI, MAC 10, MAC 11, and STEN.

Closed-Bolt Blowback Systems

Blowback-operated firearms that do not fire from an open bolt typically do not possess a fixed firing pin but are constructed to more closely resemble recoil or gas operated firearms.

The most common examples of closed-bolt blowback firearms are found in .22-cal rimfire firearms. Most semi automatic pistols in calibers below .380 ACP are also blowback operated.

Fully Automatic Blowback Operation

Obtaining fully automatic fire from a blowback-operated firearm usually involves different mechanical principles than those used in recoil or gas-operated designs. The simplicity of design in an open-bolt blowback firearm lends itself to fully automatic fire. Such a firearm can have fewer moving parts than required for semi-automatic fire because it is only necessary to allow the bolt to move in and out of battery, unrestricted, when firing. Firing is terminated by releasing the trigger, causing the sear to engage and hold the bolt in the cocked position.

Design considerations for open-bolt blowback operation are somewhat different than those of other designs. The design must include a means of damping the bolt and spring assembly (if only inadvertently) to preclude resonant vibrations from interfering with operation. The bolt must have sufficient mass to support the chamber pressure, but not be so massive as to be incapable of full travel back to the cocked position. The spring rate of the recoil spring must be sufficient to ensure that the bolt has enough velocity at firing to provide sufficient inertial resistance for safe operation. However, it must not be so stiff as to impede bolt travel rearward to the cocked position. A final, major consideration must be made concerning the location of the bolt, when cocked, in relation to the chamber. If the sear locks the bolt too far to the rear, low-powered ammunition may not impart sufficient energy to the bolt for it to reach the locked position. The result could be a runaway gun, with no easy method of discontinuing the firing cycle as long as ammunition remains. Obviously, this can be quite dangerous.

If the sear positions the bolt too close to the chamber when cocked, and if the bolt can travel a significant distance to the rear, another danger may exist. A relatively massive bolt, under considerable spring tension, may strike the sear with considerable force when the trigger is released. This repeated action may eventually break the sear, or wear the bolt to the point of failure. Again, a runaway gun may result with its inherent dangers.

Some bolt over-travel, beyond the sear lock point, must be designed into the system to allow for ammunition differences. A buffer is sometimes used to physically limit bolt over-travel while cushioning the bolt during recoil. This system is used with the MAC 10- and MAC 11-series submachine guns. The advantage of the blowback principle is based primarily on its simplicity. Designs based on the blowback principle typically require fewer critical dimensions in their construction.

An additional advantage to using a blowback system is the ability to tailor a design to a specific cyclic rate-of-fire. This is because there are several, essentially independent, variables which affect the cyclic rate-of-fire. They are: the spring rate of the recoil spring, the bolt mass, the amount of reciprocating friction, and the momentum imparted by the cartridge.

Under most cases, the reciprocating friction — which is the friction between the bolt and the receiver during a firing cycle — is disregarded, and efforts are usually made to keep it to a minimum. In general, a stiffer spring when coupled with a lighter bolt results in an increased cyclic rate-of-fire. Artificially restricting bolt over-travel through the use of a buffer usually acts as a stiffer spring, and subsequently increases the rate-of-fire. A heavier bolt coupled with a lighter spring usually results in a lower cyclic rate. The momentum generated by the fired cartridge can usually be regarded as a constant, since the variances within factory ammunition of the same caliber are typically slight. With an understanding of these factors, it is apparent that it is possible to modify the operational characteristics of a blowback-operated firearm in a variety of ways.

If the blowback firearm utilizes a separate hammer or striker and fires from a closed bolt, the modifications necessary to permit fully automatic fire do not normally differ from the modifications necessary for the conversion of gas or recoil operated firearms. The exception to this rule is with the .22 caliber rimfire firearms. The soft brass casings of this type of ammunition require much less force to initiate ignition than normal center-fire primers. As a consequence, a modification allowing the hammer or striker to follow the bolt forward may allow the firing pin to strike the cartridge rim with sufficient force to produce ignition. However, this method is generally unreliable and should not seriously be considered as an option. The construction and emplacement of a disconnector is the only reliable method of ensuring fully automatic fire.

Delayed-Blowback Operation

before firing

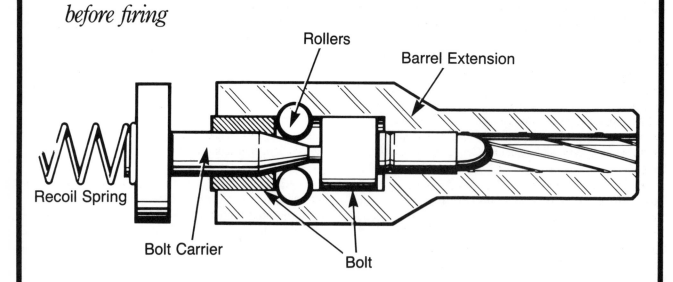

Rollers

Barrel Extension

Recoil Spring

Bolt Carrier

Bolt

after firing

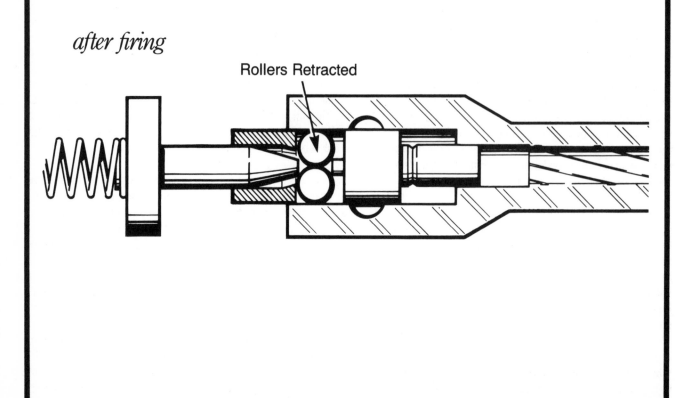

Rollers Retracted

Delayed-Blowback Operation

The final principle of operation that will be discussed is delayed-blowback operation. This is the most recently developed design and offers several advantages over designs incorporated in the three previous principles of operation. A delayed-blowback system uses the same energy source as the blowback system to perform the self-loading function. The difference is that the delayed-blowback firearm also uses either a gas system or a system of mechanical disadvantage to retard the bolt, thus preventing its premature movement out of battery.

With a mechanical system, the bolt is normally a multipiece assembly with rollers, levers or cams to provide a mechanical disadvantage toward rapidly moving the bolt to the rear. The mechanical disadvantage acts as a force multiplier, effectively increasing the inertial resistance to motion with a relatively low bolt mass. The mechanically increased inertial resistance ensures that the bolt remains forward for a long enough time to allow the bore pressure to decay to near atmospheric levels. After the mechanical disadvantage is overcome, the bolt is accelerated by the blowback forces to the rear, forcefully extracting the fired casing, cocking the hammer or striker, and compressing the recoil spring. The bolt is then driven forward by the recoil spring, stripping and chambering a fresh cartridge, and returned to battery. At battery, the bolt mechanism resumes its configuration in preparation for the next shot.

A second design incorporating the principle of delayed blowback involves using a friction device to slow the movement of the bolt within the receiver. A very well known example of this principle is the 1928 Thompson submachine gun. This design, as a means of slowing bolt travel, has not proven very effective and friction devices should be avoided due to their inefficiency.

A third design for delayed blowback uses gas operation. In this design, the high-pressure gas generated during firing is bled from a ported barrel and directed to act on a piston, or sleeve, to force the bolt closed. This is exactly the opposite of a gas operated firearm. It is, however, simpler than the gas operated firearm in that it allows for an unlocked bolt.

The advantages of delayed-blowback operation are several. First, the barrel remains stationary which allows for easier production and increased accuracy. Normally, there are no gas parts required, which reduces machining cost and complexity as well. The lack of gas pistons and their related mechanical parts reduces the cleaning requirement and tends to increase reliability. Second, the simplicity of blowback operation is obtained while allowing low bolt mass which permits the construction of a lighter firearm than for a blowback firearm of the same caliber. Third, the principle of operation is very versatile and can be used within the entire range of center-fire small arms ammunition with complete safety. Fourth, control of a de-layed-blowback firearm during fully automatic fire is improved over simple blowback design by the elimination of the large moving bolt mass. All of these factors contribute to the current commercial success of firearms using the delayed-blowback principle.

Fully automatic fire from a delayed-blowback firearm is possible with any of the designs utilizing this principle of operation. Almost all delayed-blowback firearms utilize separate hammers or strikers and do not utilize fixed firing pins. These firearms must incorporate a disconnector mechanism in order to achieve consistent and reliable fully automatic fire.

Some of the most popular firearms employing a delayed blowback principle of operation were designed to include the capability for fully automatic fire. These are the German MG-42, MG-3, and the entire line of Heckler and Koch assault rifles and machine guns.

A Final Note

A final note on fully automatic firearms is in order. Many hobbyists have found, sometimes accidently, that firearms can be modified to fire in the fully automatic mode. Hobbyists and collectors have also found that it is often much less expensive to convert a semi-automatic firearm into a machine gun than it is to purchase one outright.

It is legal for most people to own a fully automatic firearm. The legal requirements to be met are very similar whether the fully automatic firearm is converted or purchased. These legal requirements were established by the National Firearms Act of 1934 and are strictly enforced by the Bureau of Alcohol, Tobacco and Firearms. Failure to comply with the Federal laws pertaining to the possession or manufacture of a fully automatic firearm could result in severe legal penalties and felony convictions. The legal requirements must also be met before a purchase or conversion is made. Since it is generally not worth the risk, it would be very wise to comply with all Federal and local laws prior to undertaking any project involving fully automatic firearms.

The principles of operation described here should provide the reader with a basic understanding of how self-loading firearms work. It is hoped that this basic understanding may prove useful to the reader whether he or she wishes to attempt repair work, modification or construction of self-loading firearms. Whatever course of action is taken, never lose respect for, or underestimate, the power of the forces involved in firearm operation. The cartridge that can propel a bullet through plate steel is an extremely powerful albeit small package. The firearms designed to contain and harness these forces are constructed with close tolerances and of the finest steels and alloys available. Never attempt to modify or design a firearm without very careful planning and full consideration of all the factors that have been discussed here.

the Essex Arms Corp 45 ACP

by the KG&HG Staff

The Government Model 45 ACP is just about our favorite gun. It has earned a well-deserved reputation during two world wars and numerous smaller skirmishes as a reliable man-stopper. It is easy to service and find parts for, and it just shoots and shoots with rarely a fuss.

New 45s from Colt have risen in price to something over $450 just for the basic model. If you want something better or just different, the cost is extra. As a minimum, we like to replace the sights with modern high-visibility sights. The factory sights on the basic government model are nearly impossible to pick up in a hurry, especially in poor light conditions. We also like to put Pachmayr grips on any gun that we can. They seem to give any gun so-equipped a very reassuring feel in the hand. Add a few other niceties — such as a commander style hammer, beavertail grip safety, extended thumb safety, adjustable trigger — and

in short order one can replace over a hundred dollars worth of parts. This pushes the price for a *personalized* 45 to well over $550. This greatly exceeds our threshold of pain.

It seems to us that there must be a better way. Over the years, there have been lots of parts manufactured by lots of companies. Some of these parts, including slides and receivers, were made under government contract to satisfy the needs of the military. Some of these parts were also rejected by the government as not meeting the specifications of the military. Some of these parts were manufactured strictly for the commercial market. Unfortunately, it is sometimes difficult to tell which part belongs in which category — even for an experienced gun enthusiast. To add to the confusion, some commercial 45 parts will not fit into a standard 45 without modification. Also some aftermarket slides and receivers will not accept

standard parts without some modification.

What do you do? You can buy a part and just try it out, or you can buy only parts of a known *pedigree* based on your own (or someone else's) experience. We tried it both ways and aim to tell you about it.

Getting Started

Obviously, the foundation for our 45 project had to be the receiver and slide. These are the most expensive parts to acquire and in the case of the receiver, an FFL was required to purchase it. There must be a dozen different manufacturers of slides and receivers to choose from and initially we were a little bewildered. After checking around we decided to try a receiver and slide manufactured by Essex Arms Corp. Essex has been satisfying the needs of both professional and amateur gunsmiths for over 15 years.

Essex's catalog shows one basic receiver that can be used to build a 1911-A1 style gun in .38 super, 9mm and .45 calibers. Essex states in their catalog that the receivers are investment-cast in either 4140 chrome-moly steel or 416 stainless steel. Grip-screw bushings are installed at the factory and the plunger tube and ejector can be factory-installed as an option. We decided to order a 4140 receiver with the plunger tube and ejector installed.

Essex shows two styles of slides in their catalog: a regular 1911-A1 style slide and a ribbed slide. The ribbed

Above: Here are the parts necessary to build your own 45. The slide and receiver were obtained from Essex Arms Corp. The other parts were obtained elsewhere, mostly at gun shows.

Above: The slide was assembled to the receiver with no problems whatsoever. For small orders, Essex hand-selects a slide and receiver combo that fit together without hand fitting. If the customer prefers, they will select a tighter fitting slide and receiver that must be lapped together. Here, we were making sure that the barrel can be fully inserted into the slide/receiver assembly.

slide may be ordered with or without serrations and/or sight cuts. Both slides are investment-cast in either 4140 or 416 steel. We decided to order a 1911-A1 style slide in 4140 steel.

The slide and receiver arrived in about two weeks. Since the slide had been assembled to the receiver for shipment, it was obvious that we would not have to spend a great deal of time fitting the slide to the receiver. We suspected that Essex had specially selected a slide/receiver combo that fit, so we gave them a call to find out what was going on.

What we found out was that — yes indeed — they had selected a slide and receiver that slid right together, but that they do that as a standard practice unless the customer specifies otherwise (such as if the customer wanted to specially fit the slide to the frame) or unless the order is for a large quantity of parts. We inquired about the finish (which we weren't too impressed with) and commented that we probably were going to custom finish it ourselves anyway. They informed us that they would have been glad to supply the parts in the white if we had requested it, as it naturally saves them some work. Apparently many of their customers do request that the parts be shipped without any finish. They will also omit their logo on the slide if the customer so specifies. All you have to do is ask.

We went back and checked the slide and receiver more closely after our conversation with Essex. The fit between

the slide and receiver was plenty good for us. The only tweaking we had to do was to stone a little material off the side of the ejector where it was rubbing on the slide. After that, the slide had a barely perceptible play from side-to-side and from top-to-bottom.

Checking Out the Slide and Receiver

Once we were satisfied that the slide and receiver were going to work together properly, we disassembled the boss's 45 (while he was gone) and tried assembling the Essex parts with genuine Colt parts. Everything went together without a hitch and the action even appeared to work correctly without any fitting. Having satisfied ourselves that the Essex slide and receiver were not going to present us with any problems, we drove over to a gun show that was playing in town that weekend to find some parts to put the 45 together. We had some pretty specific ideas about what we wanted for sights and grips etc., but weren't too fussy about all the pins and springs and such that were necessary to make everything play together.

At the show we found a guy who had what appeared to be a corner on the surplus 45 parts business — complete with tons of cosmoline or some such gooey stuff to keep the parts from rusting over the last 70-odd years. We picked out the parts we needed and after several hours of otherwise amusing ourselves at the show we drove back to the shop.

Above: The fit of the barrel link and slide-stop pin must be checked. This was accomplished by assembling the barrel link and barrel-link pin to the barrel, then the barrel assembly to the receiver. While the barrel was held firmly down to the receiver, and as far to the rear as possible, the slide-stop pin was checked to be sure that it swung freely.

FIRST EDITION

Above: It's a good idea to polish the feed path from the magazine to the chamber. This was accomplished easily with some improvised tools.

Right: The trigger was installed through the rear of the receiver. It should slide freely, at least for the last one quarter inch or so.

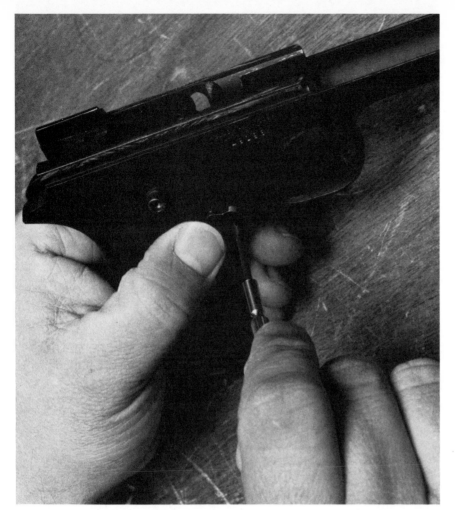

The magazine catch is installed to retain the trigger. We experienced a few problems installing the catch due to its dubious pedigree.

After washing the parts in solvent, we started to build up the 45. Some of the parts looked pretty crude. We had obviously picked up some non-GI parts. Despite appearances, which we could fix anyway, the parts all looked functional.

Fitting the Barrel

Since the Essex receiver was ordered with the grip-screw bushings, plunger tube, and ejector installed at the factory, the first step in the assembly process was to check the fit of the barrel to the receiver. With the slide assembled to the receiver and fully to the rear, we inserted the barrel through the front of the slide. The barrel was pushed back as far as possible to check for binding or obstruction.

In our case, the barrel mated perfectly to the receiver. If it had not, the problem would have to be corrected by judicious filing of the receiver or barrel. Usually the problem is that the barrel bed, i.e., the dished portion of the receiver which the barrel fits down into during feeding, has not been machined deeply enough into the receiver to accommodate the barrel.

Next the barrel link and barrel-link pin were assembled to the barrel and the fit of the barrel link was checked. This check is performed by installing the barrel in the receiver and inserting the slide-stop pin through the hole in the receiver engaging the barrel link. Hold the barrel down firmly and to the rear of the receiver. The slide-stop pin should move freely; ours did.

If your slide-stop pin does not move freely, then the link is not the proper length for your combination of barrel and receiver. At this point you don't know whether it is too long or too short. Disassemble the barrel and link and inspect the link. If it has been stamped S, 13, 17, or 21, it is likely that the link is too long (the numbers indicate the extra distance between the two holes in thousandths of an inch over a regular link). If your link is so stamped, then find a regular length (unstamped) link. If your link is not so stamped, it could either be too long or too short. Time to experiment.

To find out if your link needs to be longer, place a piece of masking tape on the rear of the link lugs. Be sure not to have any tape wrapping around the edge of the lugs. Now, reassemble the barrel link to the barrel and then the barrel assembly to the receiver. Does the binding of the slide-stop pin get better or worse? If the fit got worse,

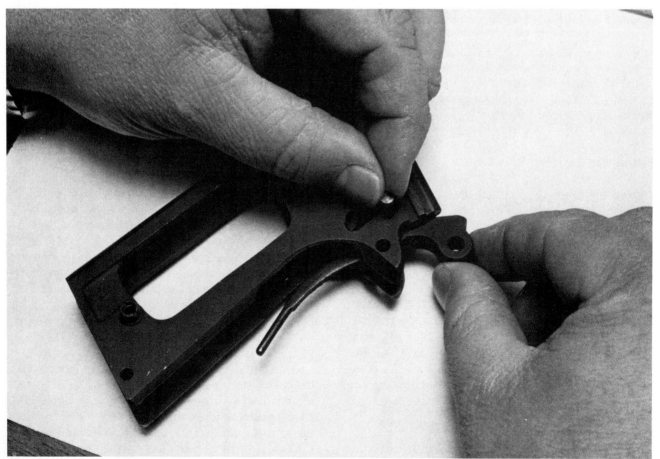

Right: This is the proper orientation of the hammer, hammer strut, sear, and disconnector. The sear fits over the disconnector with its arch facing toward the front of the receiver. Install the sear and disconnector into the receiver before installing the hammer assembly.

Below: The hammer is held in place by the hammer pin. The pin is flanged on one end and must be inserted into the frame from the left.

KIT GUNS & HOBBY GUNSMITHING

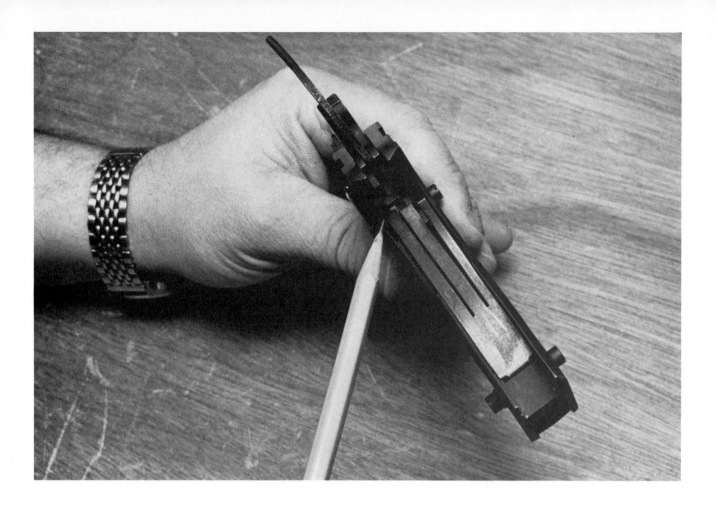

it is likely that your link is too long. If it got better, it is almost a certainty that your link is too short. In the latter case, a longer link is the answer.

If the fit got worse, you will have to do some further investigation. The problem is that you cannot be sure that you haven't gone past the optimum fit by placing the relatively thick masking tape on the rear of the lugs. Remove the masking tape and instead use a piece of Scotch tape or equivalent. If the slide-stop pin still does not swing freely, then the link is probably too long and metal will have to removed from the rear of the link lugs. Using a fine file, preferably with a safety edge toward the barrel, file a small amount of material away from the barrel. Try to keep your file cuts square and file the complete rear lug area. Check your progress often; it is always easier to remove metal than to add it. Stop when the slide-stop pin swings freely.

Polishing the Feed Ramp

Once the barrel has been fitted to the receiver it is a worthwhile precaution to polish the feed path from the magazine well up into the chamber. The M1911-A1 was designed to feed only FMC hard-ball ammo.

If you want to shoot anything else — ever — then assemble the barrel to the receiver, pushing it fully to the rear of its recess in the receiver. Next, wrap a stout rubber band around the barrel and receiver to hold it in place (or

Above: Installation of the sear spring is straightforward. Be sure that the three leaves of the spring appear as shown. The wide lip of the spring fits into a recess cut into the lower part of the receiver.

Above: The mainspring housing was slid part way over the sear spring, locking it in place.

Right: The safeties were installed next. We had to grind a little material off of the grip safety to accommodate the non-standard commander-style hammer.

KIT GUNS & HOBBY GUNSMITHING

carefully clamp the barrel and receiver together using a 3″ C clamp). Now make yourself a tool from a 12″ length of ½″ wooden dowel. Glue a 6″ x 1″ strip of 240 grit emery paper to the dowel, wound in a spiral. Now repeat the process with a strip of 320 grit emery paper at the other end of the dowel.

At last the fun begins. Insert the 240-grit end of the polishing tool up through the magazine well and place it against the barrel and receiver feed ramps. Apply pressure and rotate the dowel checking to see if you are removing material evenly from both the barrel and receiver. Adjust your angle to achieve even polishing. When the barrel and receiver feed ramps blend together, switch to the 320-grit end and clean up the finish. It should not be necessary to continue with finer grits but there is no harm if you wish to continue to achieve a better finish.

Trigger Installation

We removed the barrel assembly and set it aside. The trigger assembly that we had purchased was a special long match model with an adjustable stop for overtravel. We ran the overtravel-limit screw into the trigger assembly as far as it would go and then used a pair of pliers to bung up the threads a little. A dab of Locktite would have worked just as good but we didn't have any on hand. The limit screw was then screwed back into the trigger assembly and the assembly was inserted into the receiver.

Above: With the hammer fully de-cocked, the mainspring housing is inserted fully into the receiver. Be sure that the hammer strut fits properly into the mainspring cap. This usually requires some fiddling to get it right. Finally, the mainspring-housing pin can be inserted.

The assembled slide-stop plunger, safety-lock plunger, and plunger spring. Note the kink in the plunger spring. It is there to prevent the whole assembly from shooting across the shop when the thumb safety is removed.

At this point it was necessary to check for two things: first, the trigger must move freely within the receiver, at least for the last 1/4″ or so. Second, the trigger must not bind up when a magazine is inserted into the magazine well. We did not experience any trigger binding with the Essex receiver and our trigger. If the trigger does not move freely within your receiver, check that the trigger bow has not been bent. If the trigger bow has not been bent, then check the trigger bow-relief inside the receiver for any obvious burrs or obstructions. The trigger-bow relief will have to be opened up with a file until the trigger moves freely. Go slowly though, as you do not want to have a sloppy-fitting trigger. One technique that can be used to identify where metal must be removed, is to carbon black the trigger and check inside the receiver to see where the black has rubbed off. This will work best if the receiver has been left in the white.

Installing the Magazine Catch

Next, the magazine catch was assembled with the magazine-catch spring and magazine-catch lock. With our parts of dubious pedigree, we had to file the magazine catch slightly to permit the installation of the magazine-catch lock into the hole in the magazine catch. We also had to file the exterior of the magazine catch in order to be able to insert it into the receiver.

With the trigger installed in the frame and fully forward, the magazine-catch assembly was inserted into the receiver until the release button was flush with the left side of the receiver. The magazine-catch lock was then rotated one quarter turn clockwise, causing the magazine catch to spring into place. If your lock will not turn, push the catch carefully back and forth in the receiver until the lock aligns with the lock recess in the receiver. If the lock still will not turn, it is possible that there is an obstruction in the lock recess or that the lock recess was improperly machined. If this is the case, try to return the receiver as it is very difficult to machine this recess with ordinary hand or machine tools. We experienced no difficulties with the Essex receiver here.

Installation of the Lockwork

We next proceeded to the installation of the hammer, sear, springs and safeties. First, the mainspring was in-

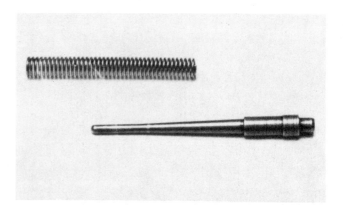

Not at all apparent in this photo is that the firing-pin spring is tapered down slightly at one end. This is supposed to prevent the spring from riding up over the firing pin. Our first spring was not tapered enough because the spring did ride up onto the firing pin, jamming the firing pin inside the slide. Lessons learned: Get a properly designed firing-pin spring or do not dry fire your gun!

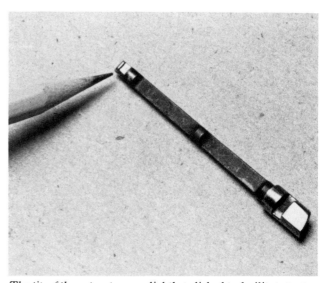

The tip of the extractor was lightly polished to facilitate proper feeding. Normally, the rim of the cartridge case slides up into the recess just behind the extractor hook as the case is stripped from the magazine. Burrs inside this recess can cause mysterious feed jams.

stalled in a Pachmayr style "B" mainspring housing. This was done to provide a neoprene-covered surface around the entire grip. Next, the mainspring housing was set aside and the hammer strut was assembled to the hammer. Be sure that the strut arches *forward* when installed on the hammer. Next, the sear and disconnector were assembled together and installed into the frame. Refer to the photos for the proper orientation of these critical parts. Finally, the hammer assembly was installed and secured with its pin.

With the receiver pointing towards the floor and the hammer fully uncocked, the hammer strut was flipped up out of the way and the sear spring was installed into the rear of the receiver. The wide lip at the bottom of the spring fits into a recess cut through the bottom rear of the magazine well. The small lip at the top of the leftmost spring leaf fits just to the left of the sear. The middle leaf was centered on the disconnector and the rightmost leaf arched backward. The spring dropped freely into the rear of the receiver. If it had not, then the receiver would have had to be inspected for obstructions and appropriate corrections made.

The mainspring housing was inserted into the receiver and slid part way up the sear spring, locking it into place. The hammer strut was flipped down and positioned over the mainspring cap. The main-spring housing was then slid up slightly more, securing the hammer strut.

Above: The slide-stop pin should be checked for squareness of fit before final assembly. With the slide-stop pin inserted into the receiver, a visual inspection will reveal any problems.

Right: With the barrel, recoil spring, and recoil spring guide installed in the slide, the slide assembly is installed on the receiver.

At this point we were ready to install the safeties: grip and thumb. Here we encountered our first major fitting operation. We had chosen to install a commander-style hammer with the longer 1911-style grip safety. This seemingly peculiar combination provides some of the flesh-saving advantage of the beavertail-grip safety at a surplus-parts price. We installed the grip safety in the receiver and inserted the thumb safety into the receiver to hold it in place. The hammer was partially cocked in order to determine where to remove material from the grip safety. Next the grip safety was removed and metal was ground away with a die grinder (a half-round file will do). Then the safeties were reinstalled in the receiver and the fit checked. This was repeated until the hammer could be fully cocked.

The grip safety was installed in the receiver and again secured with the partially installed thumb safety. With the hammer uncocked, the mainspring housing was inserted fully into the receiver and secured with the main spring housing pin. Next the slide-stop plunger, safety-lock plunger and plunger spring were assembled and inserted into the plunger tube. The hammer was cocked and the thumb safety positioned over its recess in the receiver. Depressing the safety-lock plunger with a small screwdriver, the thumb safety was slid into place.

Now the correct operation of the lockwork could be verified. With the thumb safety in the safe position, the trigger was squeezed. Mercifully, the hammer did not fall. Next the safety was switched down to the fire position

and with the grip safety not depressed, the trigger was squeezed again. Again the hammer did not fall. Finally, the receiver was gripped normally and the trigger squeezed again. This time the hammer fell!

The final operation to be performed in assembling the receiver was to adjust the trigger for correct over-travel. This was very straight-forward, consisting of adjusting the triggerstop screw inward until the hammer could not be made to fall and then backing the screw out until it would just fall when the trigger was squeezed.

Slide Assembly

The assembly of the slide is very simple compared to the receiver. It has only two main components associated with it: the extractor and the firing pin.

The firing pin presented us with an unusual problem. When the hammer was snapped on an empty chamber, the firing pin would leap forth from the breach with great vigor (we presumed) and become hopelessly jammed, pro-truding nearly ½″ from the breach face. Experimentation with various combinations of slides, firing pins and firing-pin springs isolated the problem to the firing-pin spring. One end of this spring should be a noticeably smaller di-ameter than the other end. This makes for a very tight fit over the firing pin and prevents it from slipping inside the spring and wedging the whole mess inside the frame. Replacement of the offending spring cured this problem and we proceeded on to the installation of the extractor.

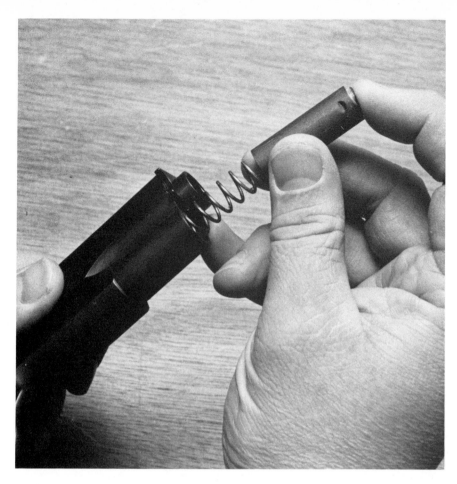

Left: Finally, the recoil-spring plug was installed over the recoil spring and pushed into the slide. The barrel bushing was rotated into place and we were done.

The extractor gave us no problems. We did, however, take the precaution of polishing the inside faces of the extractor to prevent possible feed jams. For those of you who are not familiar with the detailed operation of the 45 (as well as most other auto-loading pistols), the extractor does not normally ride up over the rim of the cartridge. This function of the extractor only occurs when the bolt or slide is closed on an already chambered round. During normal feeding operation, the rim of the cartridge slips up to and behind the extractor as the cartridge is stripped from the magazine and driven into the chamber. Many failures to feed properly can be solved by lightly polishing the inside surfaces of the extractor where the cartridge rim must slide.

Installation of the Sights

We chose to install the MMC white outline fixed rear sight with the MMC white bar cross front sight. This combination is very popular with the combat hand-gunner crowd.

Installation was uneventful, although we did end up buying a special front-sight staking tool (which we probably won't use again for at least a year). The rear sight fit right into the dovetail machined into the slide by Essex.

Final Assembly

Before we could finish the assembly of our custom 45 we had to check the slide-stop pin for squareness and fit

to the receiver. The slide-stop pin was installed into the receiver and the frame to slide-stop pin fit checked. The gap between the slide-stop pin and the frame was uniform and not excessive. We removed the slide-stop pin and proceeded on to final assembly.

The barrel was inserted into the slide and the bushing installed with the aid of a bushing wrench. The recoil spring and recoil-spring guide were inserted into the slide through the rear. Next the slide, barrel and recoil spring were installed onto the receiver and the slide-stop pin inserted through the receiver and barrel link. Finally, the recoil-spring plug was placed over the end of the recoil spring, pressed into the slide and secured with the barrel bushing.

Conclusion

The total cost of our home-brew 45 was $276.20. This was as follows:

Essex slide and receiver $121.50
Assorted surplus parts 96.80
Pachmayr grips and mainspring housing 28.00
MMC high visibility sights 29.90

Total $276.20

For a few hours labor we built a perfectly functional 45 for less than half the cost of a factory gun. What are *you* waiting for?

the XM–15 Shorty Kit

by Gary E. Reisenwitz

Illustrated, step-by-step assembly instructions for the XM–15 begin at the end of this article.

The Quality Parts Company's XM-15 Shorty kit is one of a number of similar kits being offered to the kit gun building enthusiast. I was attracted to Quality by the great variety of M-16/AR-15 configurations available. It is possible to get Shorty (CAR) kits with heavy barrels or regulation barrels, and standard AR-15 kits with heavy barrels (20" and 24" length) or regulation barrels (20" only).

A Shorty kit was ordered for our first project. I have a decided preference for short, handy guns, and this fit the bill nicely. The gun arrived, via UPS, in a plain brown cardboard box. Since it came disassembled, the box was only 17" across at its widest dimension.

The kit was organized into major subassemblies: barrel group, upper receiver, lower receiver and buttstock, each securely wrapped in heavy paper to protect against damage to the finish. Small parts came poly-bagged and were divided into functional groups such as the sight group; the

receiver pins and springs; the M-16 hammer, trigger, selector and disconnector group; the bolt assembly, etc. This undoubtedly helps Quality keep their inventory organized; it is also a great help for the kit builder unfamiliar with the M-16 and its variants.

Quality includes with each of its kits: a sling, a 30-round magazine (note: Ohio, and possibly your state, defines any semi-automatic firearm which is capable of firing more than 21 cartridges without reloading, with the specific exception of 22- caliber rimfire firearms, as an *automatic firearm),* and a manual to help in the assembly/disassembly of their kit. The manual is the standard GI issue Direct and General Support Maintenance Manual (TM9-1005-249-34). Of particular interest to kit builders is Chapter 3, Repair Instructions.

I unpacked the XM-15 kit and placed all the pieces on the workbench. I then turned to the manual for instruction. The manual actually describes the disassembly proc-

The instruction manual supplied with the kit actually shows you how to get to this point from a completely assembled gun. This article reverses the procedure to get you from this point to the firing range.

ess which, when reversed, constitutes the assembly process. Flipping to the back of Chapter 3 (pages 4 through 14), I prepared to begin assembly of the lower receiver.

Assembling the Lower Receiver

Locating the poly-bag with the miscellaneous lower receiver components and dumping them into a shallow box in front of me, I placed the lower receiver on its side with the magazine well to the right, as shown in figure 3-12 of the manual. I located the trigger guard and trigger guard spring (roll) pin and placed the pin in its hole in the lower receiver. Holding the trigger guard in place and carefully supporting the lower receiver, I tapped the trigger guard pin partly into place with a soft-faced hammer. The pin was then fully seated using an ⅛" punch.

I next located the magazine catch and catch button, but could not locate the catch spring. This is no problem, I thought, recalling the words of an old gunsmith I once knew who said, "A spring is a spring." I visited the local hardware store, and sure enough, there was my spring. It fit perfectly on the shaft of the catch and was long enough so that I could trim it to the proper length, if necessary. As it happened, the spring needed no further alterations, so I assembled the magazine catch to the receiver and proceeded on to the next step: assembly of the bolt catch.

Assembly of the bolt catch is fairly routine, although it would help to have three hands. If you have three hands (see photo), then proceed by assembling the bolt catch spring and plunger in the frame. Start the bolt catch pin in the frame, hold the bolt catch in alignment with the pin and hole in the frame, and seat the pin with a ³⁄₃₂" punch.

If you do not have three hands (or can't borrow one like I did), place the lower receiver in a padded vise and tap the bolt catch pin into its hole just far enough to hold the bolt catch, but not so far that you can't fit the bolt catch in at all. Due to the clearance required between the bolt catch and the lower receiver, this is not very difficult to accomplish.

The next step is assembly of the trigger and disconnector. I had a little difficulty deciphering the diagram in the manual to determine the proper orientation of the trigger spring. Once I finally determined the correct orientation (see photo), I could recognize the same assembly organization in the manual. The large end of the disconnector spring is inserted into its recess within the trigger. The disconnector is placed into its groove in the trigger, and then the assembly is lowered into the receiver. The trigger pin is then placed into the frame and pushed through using finger pressure to fully seat the pin in the frame. (The manual advises using a punch, but I did not find this

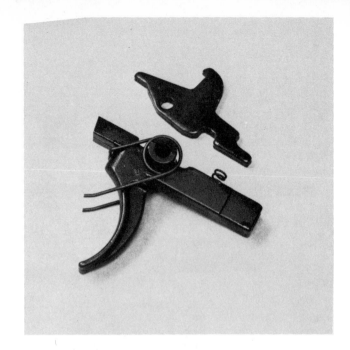

This is the proper relationship between the trigger and the disconnector. Note the location and orientation of the springs. This is not clear in the Army manuals. The trigger and disconnector are installed in Step 5.

necessary.) It will be necessary to manipulate the trigger and disconnector to align the various holes. Sighting through the hole on the other side of the receiver (opposite of the pin) helps. If necessary, the pin can be tapped into place using a punch or a soft-faced hammer.

One final note: Be sure that the trigger and disconnector move freely on the trigger pin. If they do not, first check the fit on the hammer pin. They look, and as far as I know, are supposed to be identical; however, I found that one pin was slightly larger than the other and would not allow the trigger and disconnector to function properly. If the trigger and disconnector still bind, it will be necessary to lightly polish the trigger pin using a drill and emery cloth. Go slowly and check the fit often; you want a free fit, not a loose one.

The selector lever and sear are shown to be assembled next. This stopped me for moment, as I could find neither a sear nor a hole for the sear pin. Then I realized that my AR-15 frame would not permit assembly of this critical M-16 part. If the gun had accepted this part, the receiver would have to be registered with the BATF and a $200 tax paid. I placed the selector lever into its hole, turned the receiver over, and placed the selector detent pin into its hole directly beneath the selector, on the side away from the lever. Placing the selector detent spring into its hole in the top of the grip, I mated the grip to the receiver and bolted the grip securely in place.

I placed the hammer spring on the hammer, making sure that the ends faced to the rear of the hammer. These ends fit into a notch cut into the trigger pin securing that pin within the frame. The hammer pin is secured by a small spring within the hammer. Placing the hammer into the frame and making sure that the spring ends rested upon the trigger pin, I inserted the hammer pin and drove it flush with a ⅛″ punch. The hammer could now be cocked

and proper operation of the hammer, trigger, disconnector and safety was verified.

The front and rear push pins were assembled next. The front push pin was a real adventure to assemble, as this retaining spring and plunger had to be compressed down into their holes in the frame while the pin was inserted into its hole, capturing the plunger. I stopped counting how many times I shot the plunger across my workshop. Finally, I was able to grip the plunger with needle-nose pliers to start it into its hole, then press it down flush with the end of the push pin and then slip the push pin into its hole in the frame. The rear push pin is much simpler because its retaining spring and plunger are inserted through the rear of the frame and held in place by the buttstock assembly.

After inserting the rear push pin into the frame, I screwed the buttstock assembly into the frame. The threads on the buttstock assembly that I received were very rough, and I managed to pick up a painful sliver in my finger. I suggest some caution here. I also suggest that you dress these threads with a fine triangular file to remove any burrs before assembling the buttstock to the lower receiver.

Before completely screwing the buttstock into place, the buffer retainer and buffer retainer spring are placed into their hole in the receiver. Depressing the buffer retainer, continue to screw in the buttstock, preventing it from popping out of the receiver, until it extends past the shoulder on the retainer. The rear push pin retainer and spring may now be installed through the rear of the frame and held in place by the buttstock index plate. The plate is held securely to the receiver by the retaining ring.

The plunger and plunger spring can be inserted into the buttstock by depressing the buffer retainer with a small

The various components of the bolt assembly are installed in Steps 9 through 12.

screwdriver and pushing the plunger down past it. Releasing the retainer secures the plunger and spring within the buttstock.

Assembling the Bolt and Bolt Carrier

Quality ships the bolt carrier and bolt partially assembled. The bolt carrier key has been assembled to the bolt carrier and the screws torqued to the proper specs and staked in place. The bolt comes with the ejector and extractor already attached. The bolt also has the gas rings installed, thus preventing an enthusiastic, but inexperienced, builder from distorting them. The position of the ring gaps should be checked to see that they are all equally spaced to prevent gas leakage.

The bolt is assembled into the bolt carrier with the extractor to the left, as viewed from the front. The bolt cam pin is placed into position and then rotated 90 degrees. The firing pin is inserted from the rear of the bolt carrier and secured with the firing pin retainer. The bolt carrier assembly thus completed, I proceeded on to the upper receiver.

Assembling the Upper Receiver

The forward assist plunger comes preassembled. It is inserted into the upper receiver along with its spring and secured with a roll pin. Be sure that the pawl faces the center of the receiver (toward the bolt carrier).

The rear sight is installed next. As delivered, my rear sight spring was slightly oversized (or its recess into the upper receiver undersized). To correct this, I bent the ends of the spring up further on each side to permit the spring to be compressed. I found that the hole in the windage drum had to be widened slightly so that the roll pin could fasten the windage drum to the windage screw. Further assembly of the rear sight proceeded with no difficulties.

The ejector port cover was assembled to the upper receiver along with its spring. Be sure to attach the small clip to the cover retaining pin before assembly. It is more difficult to attach after the pin has been assembled to the frame.

The upper receiver was set aside while I assembled the barrel group and handguard.

Assembling the Barrel Group

The barrel supplied by Quality Parts Company comes with the barrel nut and front sight already installed. This is made necessary by the flash hider extension which is brazed onto the front of the barrel (to provide the legal minimum barrel length of 16″). All that was necessary to complete the barrel group was assembly of the handguard slip ring, handguard slip ring spring and handguard slip ring retaining ring onto the barrel nut. A set of slip ring

The barrel, barrel nut, handguard slip ring, handguard slip-ring spring, and handguard slip-ring retaining ring are installed in Step 16.

pliers should be used to assemble the slip ring retaining ring onto the barrel.

The barrel was slipped into the upper receiver and the barrel nut was torqued into place. I think the barrel remover fixture, i.e., barrel vise jaw blocks, and combination wrench are absolute necessities for this task. I consulted some government armorers regarding the proper way to install the barrels on an M-16. The way that the final torque is reached is very important due to the dissimilar metals in contact. The proper procedure is to clamp the barrel in the proper fixture and assemble the upper receiver to the barrel. The barrel nut should be tightened at least three times to the proper torque value and then loosened. This serves to precondition the materials and to clear the threads of any foreign materials which might affect reading of the proper torque. Finally, the alignment of the barrel nut may be checked with the alignment gauge (an $^{11}/_{64}''$ drill will do in a pinch). The proper alignment of the barrel nut must be obtained by loosening and retightening the nut as many times as necessary to align the gas tube hole. The proper torque value should not be exceeded in an effort to align the gas tube passage.

The gas tube can be fitted to the upper receiver by first inserting the open end of the gas tube into the receiver and then sliding the tube forward toward the gas port in the front sight assembly. Push the tube into the gas port until the retainer hole is aligned with the hole in the front sight. Insert a roll pin into the hole and seat with a $^5/_{64}''$ punch.

Assembling the Handguard

When I attempted to assemble the handguard to the barrel, I discovered that the handguard was warped slightly, preventing both ends of the handguard to close completely. I cured this quickly enough by installing the handguard slip ring over one end of the handguard assembly and winding a large rubberband around the other. I then placed the entire assembly in a pot of boiling water. The water softened the plastic handguard just enough to remove the warpage and permit the two ends to close simultaneously.

The two halves of the handguard were assembled to the barrel by first inserting the front of each half into the cap at the front sight, and then snapping the rear into place, while retracting the handguard slip ring against its spring. The spring tension is quite high; I'm sure the handguard is not going to fall off.

Final Assembly

Before assembly I applied a generous coating of gun oil to the exterior of the bolt carrier assembly, a drop of oil into the bolt carrier key and several drops into the two holes in the right side of the bolt carrier (to lubricate the bolt's gas rings).

The charger handle, which was also preassembled, is placed partially into the upper receiver. The bolt carrier assembly is fully extended by snapping the bolt carrier

KIT GUNS & HOBBY GUNSMITHING

Step 1: Secure the trigger-guard spring pin with a 1/8" punch. Be sure to firmly support the underside of the frame where the pin fits. Failure to do this may result in a cracked frame.

sharply downward, then inserted with the carrier key fitting into the recess on the underside of the charging handle. The bolt carrier and charging handle can be pushed forward until the bolt carrier is flush with the rear of the upper receiver and the charging handle catches in place.

The upper receiver is mated to the lower receiver at the front pivot point and the front push pin pushed all of the way into the receiver, securing the upper receiver. Cocking the hammer and making sure the selector is in the safe position, the receivers may be closed together and the rear push pin inserted fully into the receiver.

Final Comments

Quality guarantees that their kits are shipped with the correct headspacing for the barrel and bolt. As with any

modern firearm, correct headspacing is essential for safe operation. If you contemplate using a different combination of barrel and bolt, it would be wise to purchase a headspacing gauge and learn how to use it.

I am very impressed by the fit and finish of the Quality Parts Co. XM-15 Shorty kit and I look forward to taking it to the range for test firing. Total assembly time was under two hours, including the side trip to the hardware store for a missing spring. I have no doubt that you can finish this kit in the same amount of time, even if you have never seen an M-16 before.

I am now planning some interesting modifications soon (such as a full auto conversion) which I will report to you in the next issue of KG&HG. Stay tuned.

FIRST EDITION

Step 2: Insert the magazine catch through the frame from the left side; slide the catch spring over the shaft and screw on the magazine-catch button.

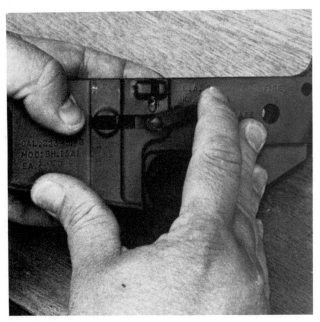

Step 3: Push the catch button in as far as possible and rotate the magazine catch until it contacts the receiver. Align the catch with its recess and allow it to retract into the receiver.

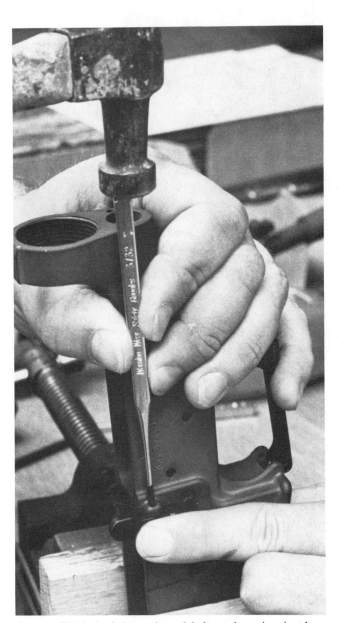

Step 4: Hold the bolt catch and bolt-catch spring in place while the bolt-catch pin is drifted into position with a 3/32" punch.

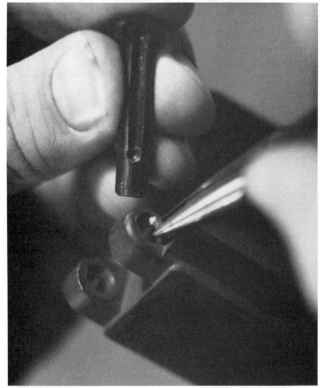

Step 5 (above left): The trigger pin can be driven home with a slight blow from a soft-faced hammer.

Step 6 (above right): Insert the hammer pin and drive it home with a ⅛" punch.

Step 7 (left): Assemble the front and rear push pins to the frame. Be careful not to shoot the plunger for the front push pin across the room. The rear push pin is much simpler as its plunger and spring are held in place by the buttstock assembly.

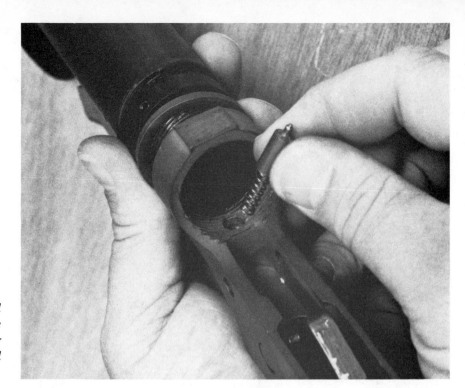

Step 8: Insert the buffer retainer and spring into the lower receiver. Hold the retainer down with a small screwdriver (not shown) as you load the plunger and plunger spring into the buttstock.

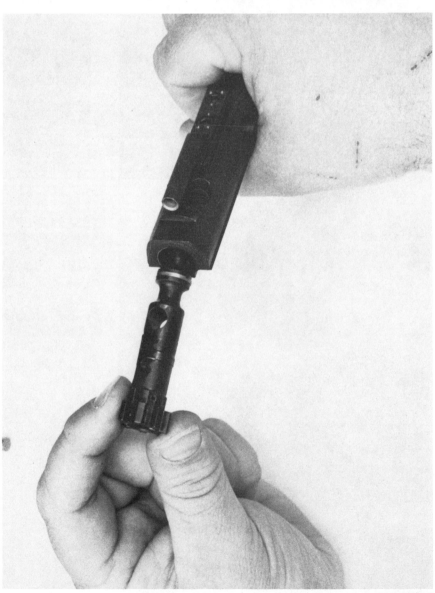

Step 9: Start the assembly of the bolt group by loading the bolt into the bolt carrier.

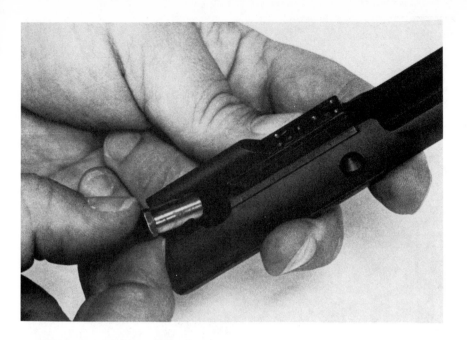

Step 10: Insert the bolt cam pin into the bolt carrier assembly. Note that you have to install it at right angles to the final operating position.

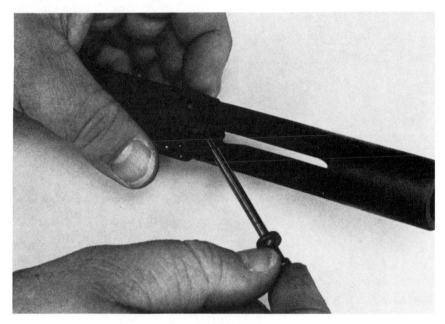

Step 11: Insert the firing pin into the rear of the bolt carrier assembly.

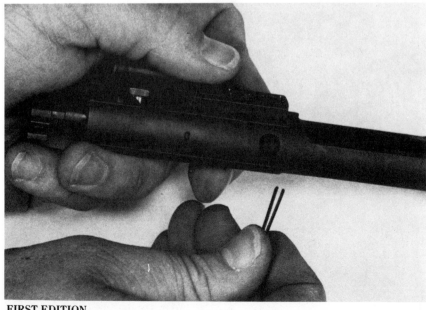

Step 12: Secure the firing pin with the firing-pin retainer.

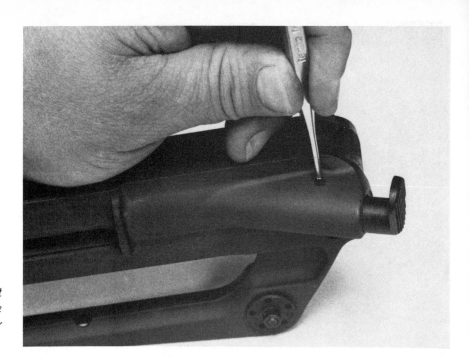

Step 13: Insert the forward assist plunger into the upper receiver with the pawl facing inward. Secure the plunger with a roll pin.

Step 14: Secure the windage drum to the rear sight with a roll pin.

Step 15: Install the ejector-port cover and the ejector port cover spring. Install the e clip onto the hinge pin before installing the pin into the receiver.

Step 16: Assemble the handguard slip ring, the slip-ring spring and the slip-ring retaining ring to the barrel nut.

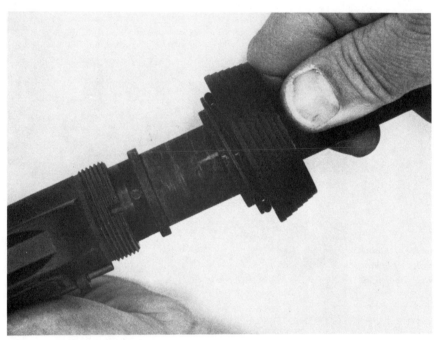

Step 17: Install the barrel on the upper receiver using the barrel nut. The barrel nut can be started using finger pressure.

Step 18: Secure the barrel in a vice and tighten the barrel nut to proper torque with a torque wrench and a special tool called an armorer's wrench (available from Quality Parts). Custom barrel vice jaw blocks are highly recommended, but wood blocks may be substituted in an emergency.

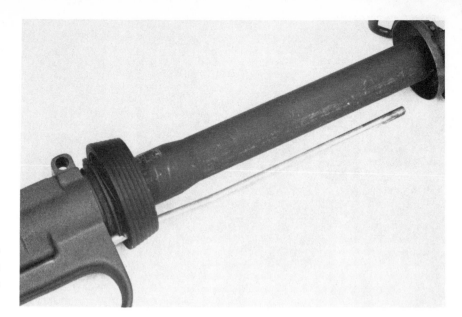

Step 19: The gas tube is installed by inserting it into the upper receiver. Note that it must fit through the the handguard retaining ring and the barrel nut.

Step 20: Install the two halves of the handguard by inserting the front of each half into the cap at the front sight and then snapping the rear portions underneath the handguard slip ring.

Step 21: Apply a generous coat of gun oil to the bolt carrier before installing it in the upper receiver.

104

Step 22 (left): Insert the charging handle part way into the upper receiver, then insert the bolt-carrier key into the recess in the charging handle. Permit the bolt carrier and charging handle to slide into the upper receiver until flush with the rear of the upper receiver.

Step 23 (below): Install the upper receiver onto the lower receiver and secure it with the front push pin. Cock the hammer and make sure that the selector is in the safe position. Close the receivers and secure them with the rear push pin. You're done!

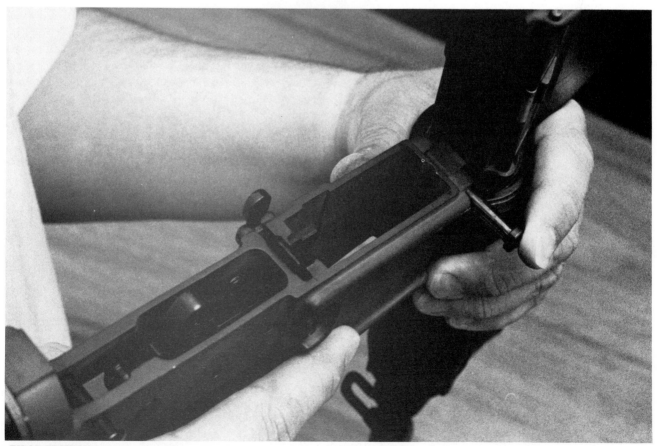

Rhino Evaluation

by Gary E. Reisenwitz

Editor's Note: Capt. Gary E. Reisenwitz is a graduate of West Point and a long-time student of both exotic and conventional weaponry. When we first contacted him about evaluating the Rhino M-16/AR-15 conversion kit, he had serious misgivings about the design philosophy. In spite of his misgivings, we gave Rhino International a call and arranged to obtain a converted upper receiver assembly. Now we consider ourselves converts to the Rhino system.

With the continuing popularity of the M-16 rifle and the many aftermarket variants (ER-15, XM-15 etc.), it is not surprising that there is such a large number of accessories available to either customize or improve the basic weapon. The Rhino system is a modification that is strictly functional. It was designed for those who are serious about improving the function and reliability of their weapon.

For all of its good points, the M-16/AR-15 has one significant flaw; it uses a direct gas-action mechanism. The M16 operates by bleeding high-pressure (and high-temperature) gas from the barrel and routing the gas through a metal tube into a chamber within the bolt-carrier assembly. There the gas acts on the bolt and bolt carrier; forcing them apart with equal and opposite gas pressure. This pressure imparts a momentum to the bolt carrier, causing it to move rearward. As the bolt carrier moves rearward, it cams the bolt open and separates it from the barrel as the bolt and bolt carrier continue rearward to full recoil. In the process, the end of the gas tube is exposed within the upper receiver and residual gas is vented into the upper receiver — fouling the bolt, bolt carrier and, inevitably, the inside of the upper receiver. Continued firing results in continued fouling and eventual stoppages. These stoppages are due both to powder fouling and the high temperature of the gases vaporizing the lubricant within the bolt carrier.

The Rhino System

The Rhino system eliminates both the heat transfer and the powder fouling associated with the conventional direct gas action system. Gas is bled from the barrel port, just as with the conventional M-16. In the Rhino system, however, the gas enters a variable-volume gas-piston chamber where it forces a piston and operating rod to the rear. The operating rod is of the same diameter as the conventional gas tube and enters the upper receiver through the same passageway.

The gas-piston assembly is retro-fitted to a standard front-sight base which requires minor handguard modifications for clearance. No modifications of any sort are required to either the upper receiver or barrel. The bolt carrier is fitted with a special bolt-carrier key which contains a series of steel and urethane discs to act as a shock cushion. This minimizes any shock loading of components which may occur during operation. The bolt-carrier key is self-contained and requires no servicing.

In operation, the Rhino gas system is intrinsically self-cleaning. The exhaust vents clear the piston chamber of deposits and pose no hazard to the shooter. The cyclic rate of fire can be adjusted by varying the volume of the gas-piston chamber. This is done by turning the spring-loaded adjustment screw located at the front of the gas piston assembly. Screwing in the adjustment screw decreases the available expansion chamber volume and increases the pressure exerted on the piston during firing. This serves to increase the cyclic rate of fire to a maximum of approximately 750 rpm with regulation-length barrels. *Short-barreled models utilizing the Rhino system are reported to be capable of cyclic rates of fire exceeding 900 rpm reliably!* Backing the screw out increases the effective volume, reducing pressure and the cyclic rate to a minimum functional rate of approximately 425 rpm. Backing-out the

Above: The Rhino-converted upper receiver mounted to a Jon Ciener-modified ER-15 lower receiver.

screw further will cause the weapon to fire in the single-shot mode, as the action will not cycle.

Some people might question the utility of a variable cyclic rate-of-fire. The value of this feature becomes immediately apparent upon use. First, it is difficult to describe the difference in controllability between firing at 750 rpm and firing at 425 rpm. The latter is not only more enjoyable, but can also result in a significant savings in ammunition. This is desirable from both an individual and an organizational standpoint. Second, even if full-auto firepower is not used, the gas-pressure regulator can be used to ensure reliable semi-automatic functioning of almost any conceivable handload which might not function reliably in a conventional direct gas-action weapon. This adds a degree of versatility and reliability to any usage.

A further advantage of the Rhino system may be of importance for specific applications; namely, firing from an enclosed position such as a vehicle. Normally the gas vented from the bolt carrier causes a considerable amount of gas and particulate emissions in the immediate vicinity of the shooter. Sustained firing of an unmodified M-16 from a poorly-ventilated enclosure can be very unpleasant.

Enough of this problem is known so that military vehicles using the M-16 as a firing-port weapon must use forced air ventilation to exhaust gases through the weapons port to the outside. For these applications, the M-16 has been modified to fire from an open bolt to aid in this evacuation. The Rhino system, if utilized in this application, should preclude the need for positive ventilation.

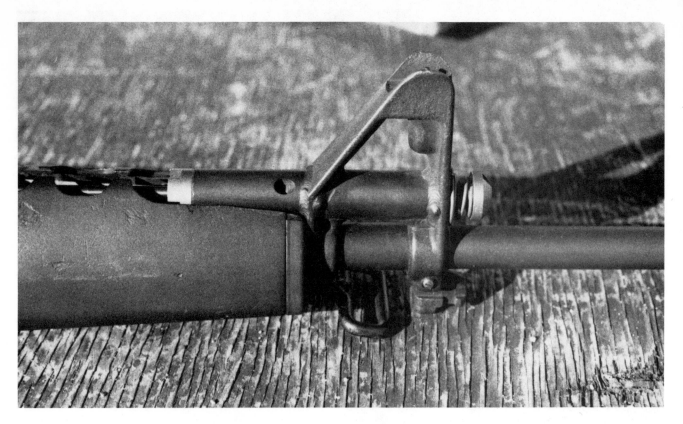

Above: The only changes that are apparent with the Rhino conversion unit are the front-sight assembly, with its newly added gas piston, and the cut-away portion of the handguard to provide clearance for the gas piston.

Evaluation of the Rhino System

The differences in the method of operation of the Rhino system caused me some initial concern. In the conventional M-16 there is an equal and opposite force imparted to the bolt and bolt carrier which causes the bolt carrier to be forced back. In effect, the bolt carrier pushes-off from the bolt thereby initiating recoil. With the Rhino system, this equal and opposite force is absent and the bolt is, in effect, dragged away from the barrel by the bolt carrier. My concern was that this mechanical difference might result in increased bolt and barrel-locking lug or cam-pin wear. Cam-pin wear is rather inconsequential, affecting function more than safety. Locking-lug wear can directly affect headspacing if the rear portions of the bolt locking lugs, or the front portion of the barrel-locking lugs, are being worn. Increases in headspacing create a dangerous firing condition and are expensive to repair. Wear on the bolt lugs requires bolt replacement, and wear on the barrel lugs requires barrel replacement.

Range Testing

In order to determine if accelerated bolt wear could be caused by the Rhino system, I set up a simple experiment using an unmodified M-16A1 type upper-receiver/barrel assembly equipped with a Colt chrome-plated bolt. The Rhino-equipped upper half also used a chrome bolt. I carefully degreased and cleaned each barrel and bolt. I then applied a commercial cold-bluing solution to the worn surfaces at the rear of the locking lugs on each bolt and re-lubricated them. After reassembling each upper half, I proceeded to the range.

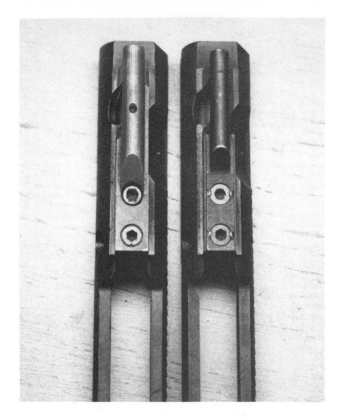

The Rhino-modified bolt carrier (far left) has a much beefier carrier-key assembly than the unmodified bolt carrier on the right.

At the range, I used commercial reloads approximating M193 military ball ammunition. An XM-15 semi-auto lower receiver was used for this portion of the test. First, I installed the conventional upper half on the XM-15 and fired twenty rounds down-range. After changing the upper receiver, a second string of twenty rounds was fired with the Rhino-equipped top half.

I gathered the expended casings and inspected them for signs of unusual operation — such as evidence of hard extraction or ballooning from premature extraction. Comparison of the casings from the Rhino receiver with those from the standard receiver showed no sign of excessive pressure or any other problem.

The bolt carriers and bolts were removed from the upper receivers, degreased and inspected for wear patterns on the locking lugs. There was no appreciable difference in the wear between either bolt. Wear on both was very light and not significant. No significant wear patterns were found on the parkerized Rhino cam pin, and I elected not to conduct a similar test on it. I reasoned that if there was no increase in bolt locking-lug wear, there should be no increase in cam-pin wear.

This was the only area in which I was skeptical regarding the Rhino conversion. I was happy to find that there was no additional component wear induced by the Rhino operation and began to note the many benefits of the system.

In order to fully evaluate the effectiveness of the Rhino system, I felt a full-auto test was in order. A Jon Ciener modified ER-15 lower receiver, with M-16 internal parts and a CAR-type buttstock and buffer assembly, was used

for this test. The full-length Rhino-equipped upper receiver/barrel assembly was installed and I continued to use the commercial reloads approximating U.S. military M-193 ball ammo.

I began my first 30-round string with the gas regulator screwed all the way in, to provide for the maximum cyclic rate of fire. Upon firing, I began to have misfires every three to four rounds. Examination of the misfired cartridges indicated that all of the observed misfires resulted from light strikes — as if the hammer were following the bolt. I believe the problem was due to the use of the full-pressure setting with the short spring and small buffer in the CAR buttstock. The adjustment screw was backed-out one revolution for the next 30 rounds, and I had no further problems whatsoever. I proceeded to fire 90 additional rounds as quickly as I could, to note any heating problems. The cyclic rate-of-fire remained at approximately 750 rpm and there were no malfunctions of any sort. Upon checking for heat buildup, I was pleasantly surprised to find the bolt carrier merely warm and easy to handle. The handguards were never uncomfortable, and even the front-sight base was not nearly as hot as a conventionally equipped top half under similar conditions.

Then I experimented with different settings of the gas regulator to test its effectiveness on lowering the cyclic rate of fire. Making periodic adjustments between bursts, I was able to lower the rate to approximately 425 rpm. The remainder of the 300 rounds were fired at this setting, and I found the weapon much more controllable and pleasant to shoot. Two and three round bursts were easily obtained and, for once, I found that a 30-round magazine could last a while.

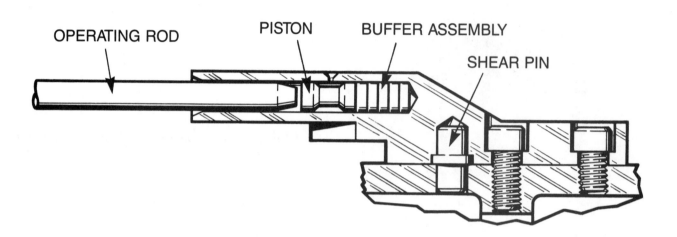

OPERATING ROD   PISTON   BUFFER ASSEMBLY

SHEAR PIN

Above: The Rhino bolt-carrier key assembly showing the operating rod, the buffer assembly, and the shear pin. The shear pin provides a precise mechanical link between the bolt carrier and the bolt-carrier key.

When the 300-round test was completed, I examined the weapon for heat buildup and found that it remained cooler than a standard M-16 at all times. I also inspected the bolt and bolt carrier and found them to be remarkably clean! Even after 300 rounds there was hardly any grime, powder fouling or anything that looked like it could contribute to a malfunction. If you've seen a conventional bolt and bolt carrier after 300 rounds you will surely be able to appreciate this.

Cleaning the Rhino-equipped top half was easy. The bolt and bolt carrier only needed to be wiped-off and re-oiled. The inside of the upper receiver was remarkably clean. The Rhino gas piston assembly is self-cleaning and required no maintenance whatsoever. Most of the gas piston components are stainless steel to ensure reliability.

Observations

The success of the Rhino system is due to a combination of factors, the first of which is design. It is an excellent design that ensures a minimum of parts with minimum modifications. There are no extraneous parts to clean, break or lose. The quality of machine work and workmanship is top-notch. The choice of materials also appears to be excellent. It seems that no effort has been spared to produce a system that performs. The Rhino system should provide the user with years of trouble free service and reliably consistent performance. I don't think anyone could ask for more.

Analysis of Malfunction During Full-Auto Testing

The malfunctions observed during full-auto testing, at the maximum cyclic rate-of-fire, appear to be due to excessive momentum imparted to the bolt-carrier and recoil-buffer assemblies by the operating rod. This causes the recoil buffer to bottom in the shortened CAR stock assembly, effectively altering the spring constant for the bolt-carrier system. This, in turn, causes the bolt carrier to rebound earlier than normal.

Under normal operating conditions, the bolt-carrier assembly, recoil buffer and recoil-buffer spring comprise a modified simple harmonic oscillator. As such, and ignoring friction, the classical differential equation of motion for a harmonic oscillator is given by:

$$d''x/dt'' - (K/M)x = 0 \qquad (1)$$

where x is the position of, in this case, the bolt carrier as a function of time, t; K is the effective spring constant; and M is the combined mass of the bolt-carrier assembly, recoil buffer and recoil-buffer spring. The solution of equation (1) is given by:

$$x = A \sin \omega t \qquad (2)$$

where A is the maximum amplitude of the bolt carrier's motion and ω is the natural undamped frequency of the bolt carrier system and is given by:

$$\omega = \sqrt{K/M} \qquad (3)$$

From equation (3) one can readily see that if the spring constant, K, is increased, the frequency of oscillation will increase. Likewise, if the combined mass, M, is decreased, the frequency of oscillation will also increase.

The time, T, for the bolt-carrier assembly to recoil fully and then return to battery is related directly to ω and is given by:

$$T = \pi/\omega$$

$$T = \pi \sqrt{M/K} \qquad (4)$$

Thus, one can see that if the effective spring constant is increased, the cycle time for the bolt-carrier assembly will decrease.

The sear is also a harmonic oscillator, with its own characteristic frequency and cycle time. Normally, the sear's cycle time will be less than that of the bolt-carrier assembly. However, if the bolt carrier cycles too rapidly due to bottoming of the recoil buffer, the sear may have insufficient time to return to its proper relationship with respect to the hammer-sear notch. The result is that occasionally, the sear fails to engage the hammer, and the hammer follows the bolt carrier into battery.

This can be corrected by reducing the sear's time constant with the use of a stiffer sear spring. However, I found the 750 rpm maximum cyclic rate-of-fire attainable with the standard issue sear spring to be more than adequate, so I chose instead to back-off slightly on the gas-pressure adjustment screw.

Conversations with Walter Langendorfer, the inventor of the Rhino conversion system, supported my analysis of the observed malfunctions. Rhino encourages the buyer of their conversion kit to send their weapon to the factory to be professionally modified. At the factory, the length of the gas regulator screw is tailored to the specific weapon, thus ensuring optimum performance throughout the entire range of settings of the gas regulator screw.   GER

ATF Form 1

Ticket to Full-Auto Conversion — Legally

by Jeffrey C. Marnell

There was a time when firearms were virtually uncontrolled. Prior to enactment of the National Firearms Act (NFA) in 1934, it was legal and relatively easy for a US citizen to own a machine gun, silencer, short-barrelled rifle or shotgun.

In 1934, however, congress made such unregulated frivolity illegal, and required that all such devices be registered and a tax paid. In 1968, stiff new federal regulations known as the 1968 Gun Control Act (GCA) were put into effect, severely limiting interstate and intrastate trade in firearms. The National Firearms Act was incorporated as Title II of the Gun Control Act, and additional regulations were imposed on weapons termed "destructive devices" which had been previously unregulated.

Restricted Weapons

As the law stands now, the following classes of firearms are restricted under Title II of the GCA: machine guns, silencers, short-barrelled rifles, short-barrelled shotguns and destructive devices.

Machine guns are defined to be "any weapon which shoots, is designed to shoot, or can be readily restored to shoot, automatically more than one shot, without manual reloading, by a single function of the trigger." The term machine gun also applies to "the frame or receiver of any such weapon, any combination of parts designed for use in converting a weapon into a machine gun, and any combination of parts from which a machine gun can be assembled if such parts are in the possession or under control of a person."

A silencer is defined as "any device for silencing or diminishing the report of any portable weapon, such as a rifle, carbine, pistol, revolver, machine gun, submachine gun, shotgun, fowling piece, or other device from which a shot, bullet, or other projectile may be discharged by an explosive."

A short-barrelled rifle "means a rifle having one or more barrels less than 16 inches in length and any weapon made from a rifle (whether by alteration, modification, or oth-

erwise) if such weapon, as modified, has an overall length of less than 26 inches." The definition of a short-barrelled shotgun is nearly identical to the short-barrelled rifle, except that the barrel (or barrels) may not exceed 18″ in length.

A destructive device is defined to be a potpourri of weapons such as a bomb, mine, hand grenade, explosive, poison gas or other unpleasantry of that general type. It also means devices capable of firing projectiles in excess of .50 caliber, with the specific exemption of antiques, signaling devices, and shotguns or other weapons which are intended solely for sporting purposes.

These devices are required to be registered with the Bureau of Alcohol Tobacco and Firearms (BATF), US Treasury Dept. Any restricted weapon in existence prior to enactment of the GCA, and not registered by October 31, 1968, is considered to be contraband and illegal for private ownership. A significant exception to this rule (which is especially applicable to imported weapons such as the Sten) is that if the weapon is reduced to parts and the receiver destroyed, the weapon can be remanufactured by an individual or a licensed Title II manufacturer. These restricted weapons, or other restricted weapons manufactured after enactment of the GCA, have to be registered with BATF and a $200 "making" tax paid.

Failure to register a machine gun or other Title II firearm with the BATF can result in stiff federal, and sometimes state, penalties. These penalties can include the following: Ten years in a Federal prison, a $10,000 fine, confiscation of any vehicle found transporting or containing the firearm, prohibition from owning firearms of any nature in the future, and all of the fringe *benefits* of the conviction such as a felony record, publicity, etc.

While the GCA does restrict trade in "unusual" firearms such as machine guns, cannons, silencers and short-barrelled firearms, it does not restrict them to the extent that most people believe. This has caused a great deal of concern by the average citizen when he or she sees a military-type weapon in the hands of a civilian.

It seems that with all the confusion over firearms laws and restrictions, few people are aware that in most states, with the necessary Federal licensing, private ownership of machine guns, silencers, and destructive devices is entirely legal. It is also legal in most states to convert a semi-automatic weapon to full-automatic capabilities with *prior* Federal licensing.

After thinking about the penalties involved in being caught with an unlicensed machine gun, the costs of licensing a full-auto modification are nearly trivial. But, before we go into the licensing procedure, let me explain a few other intricacies of the GCA.

Once a gun is manufactured by someone as a machine gun, it is always a machine gun under the law; regardless of whether or not it is capable of full-automatic fire at any particular moment. Also remember that under normal circumstances, any machine gun manufactured before 1968 must have been registered as a machine gun on or before October 31, 1968 or it is illegal to own. By law it is considered contraband!

However, if a person legally modifies a semi-automatic weapon, formerly classified as an ordinary rifle, shotgun, or pistol, to full-automatic fire, it may (under some circumstances) be converted back to semi-auto fire only and sold as an ordinary firearm.

It is possible, if the firearm was converted to full automatic by the use of a conversion kit with no modifications to the receiver, and if no other modifications had been made such as shortening the barrel or altering the overall weapon's length, that the kit could be licensed as the registerable item. In this case, the kit itself is considered to be a machine gun and is therefore subject to all of the registration and transfer procedures. Removal of the kit from the weapon would leave it an ordinary non-registerable weapon, which could be sold (or otherwise transferred) without further ATF involvement. It should be noted with some emphasis, that the mere possession of all, or in some cases, just one of the parts necessary to make a full-auto conversion constitutes possession of a machine gun, even if the gun itself is not in one's possession.

Licensing Procedure

Since it is more popular for individuals to buy a semi automatic firearm and modify it to full-auto fire, than to buy a factory-made machine gun, silencer, or destructive device, I will deal only with the licensing of a semi- to full-auto modification in this article.

Before any modification can be attempted, and even before all of the full-auto parts are purchased, the person modifying the firearm (called the "maker") must receive a license granting him (or her) permission to modify and possess a full auto firearm or machine gun. This license is prescribed to be in the form of an approval stamp affixed to the original of your ATF Form 1 application. Refer to the sample ATF Form 1 included at the end of this article as specific topics are discussed. Recall that failure to obtain the necessary license can result in stiff federal, and sometimes state, penalties. I have found that law enforcement authorities take these regulations quite seriously; a violator is not apt to talk his (or her) way out of arrest when caught violating any provisions of the National Firearms Act.

Once an individual decides to convert a semi-automatic weapon to a full-automatic weapon, determination should be made as to whether it is allowed by law in their state and municipality. At present, according to the NFA Branch of the BATF, the following states generally prohibit possession of machine guns by private individuals: California, Delaware, District Of Columbia, Hawaii, Illinois, Iowa, Kansas, Louisiana, Michigan, Minnesota, New York, Pennsylvania, Rhode Island, South Carolina, and Washington. For the states of New Jersey, North Carolina and Wisconsin, a permit from the state would be necessary before the BATF could approve an application to purchase or make a machine gun.

The BATF cannot approve an application to make or possess a machine gun in a state where it would violate state law. Pennsylvania and Missouri only allow the possession of machine guns if they are certified as curios or relics. It would be unlikely that a person could modify a weapon in those two states. Since state and local laws change from time to time, I suggest that current information be obtained from the NFA Branch of the Bureau of Alcohol, Tobacco and Firearms, Washington, D.C. 20226. This may be done at the same time you request a copy of ATF Form 1 and the two FBI fingerprint cards which you will need to make your application.

If you are lucky enough to be in one of the 37 states not mentioned above, you should know that there is a cost of $200 per weapon modified in the form of a *making tax* (an additional $200 *transfer tax* is payable when buying or changing ownership of a machine gun). You must also have your fingerprints taken and submit two recent photos, in addition to properly filling out the application form (ATF Form 1) and having the chief law enforcement officer of the maker's place of residence sign the form.

The law enforcement officer only has to sign a statement saying "I have no information indicating that the maker will use the firearm or device described on this application for other than lawful purposes. I have no information that possession of the firearm described in item 4 on the front of this form would place the maker in violation of state or local law." Getting the law enforcement signature can often be the most difficult part of the application process as many police departments are either not familiar with laws governing this matter, or are otherwise hesitant to give their signature.

The application form itself is provided in duplicate, with 1-1/2 pages of instructions which must be very closely followed. Failure to follow the instructions can result in your application being rejected, or at least delayed. If the application is rejected, the $200 fee is returned to the applicant. The form is designed to give clear identification of both the person making the application, and the firearm or destructive device which will be made upon receipt of the approved application . Note that although the application asks for federal firearms dealer identification numbers in sections 5 thru 7, the applicant does not have to be a dealer in order to have his application approved.

In addition to making a full-automatic conversion, Form 1 can be used for licensing the manufacture of a shotgun having a barrel less than 18 inches long, a rifle with a barrel less than 16 inches long, a weapon made from a rifle or shotgun with an overall length of less than 26 inches, a muffler or silencer, or a destructive device. It can also be used for the manufacture of a group of weapons classified under the National Firearms Act as "any other weapon". These include smooth-bore pistols designed to fire shotgun shells, etc.

When filling out the duplicate Form 1, the BATF suggests that a carbon paper be used, thereby making an exact duplicate. However, all signatures must be in ink, and original; no carbon copy signatures will be accepted. After the forms are filled out completely, with the personal photographs attached in the proper places, it should be sent along with two completed fingerprint cards and a cashier's check, or money order, for $200, to the address

listed on the form. Processing usually takes from one to three months, with final approval of the application giving the applicant permission to modify the firearm as requested, and registering it in his (or her) possession.

After the firearm is registered as a machine gun, any sale of the weapon must be done through a licensed machine gun dealer and a $200 transfer tax paid. The maker of the firearm must at all times maintain control of the weapon, and must maintain the license forms with the firearm at all times, available for law enforcement inspection. He cannot lend it to anyone, and it is licensed only for his possession. Before the machine gun can be transported across state lines, request for approval must be obtained from BATF on Form ATF 7560.8. BATF cannot issue such approval if the state the machine gun is to enter has a law which prohibits its possession.

Generally, any law-abiding citizen of the United States, residing in a state permitting ownership of machine guns, can get an application approved for ownership. The exceptions are similar to those prohibiting any ownership of firearms; i.e., a person who (1) has been convicted in a federal, state or municipal court of a felony or (2) has been discharged from the Armed Forces under dishonorable conditions, or (3) has been judged mentally incompetent by a court of law, or (4) has renounced his U.S. citizenship, or (5) is an illegal alien.

True, this process does seem to be rather involved and costly at first glance. But just sit back and think of the fun you will have taking your machine gun to the range and shooting it in front of everybody! And while $200 is a lot of money to pay for a license, remember that it is good for as long as you own the weapon, and is nothing compared to the cost of supplying ammo for a "hungry" machine gun. Besides, if you get caught with a full-auto weapon that is not licensed what will it cost you?

Semi- to Full-Auto Conversion

The actual physical modification of the firearm is sometimes quite simple; many books have been written on the subject, covering weapons ranging from the M-1 rifle to semiautomatic Remington shotguns. Ads for these books can be found in many firearms and military magazines. Some of these modifications require that a person only file down a certain part of the trigger mechanism for full-auto fire; however, others are quite complex.

So if you are bound and determined to own a machine gun, or just always wanted one (like a lot of us), here is the way to fulfill that long-awaited dream. All it takes is the stamina to get through some red tape, a $200 tax fee, some mechanical ability, and a lot of ammo, assuming you live in one of the right states.

KIT GUNS & HOBBY GUNSMITHING

APPLICATION TO MAKE AND REGISTER A FIREARM
(Submit in duplicate. See Instructions attached.)

TO: National Firearms Act Branch, Bureau of Alcohol, Tobacco and Firearms, Washington, DC 20226

The undersigned hereby makes application, as required by Sections 5821 and 5822 of the National Firearms Act, Title 26 U.S.C., Chapter 53, to make and register the firearm described below.

1. TYPE OF APPLICATION *(Check one)*

☐ a. **TAX PAID.** Submit with your application a check or money order for $200 made payable to the Department of the Treasury. Upon approval of the application, this office will acquire, affix, and cancel the required "National Firearms Act" stamp for you.

☐ b. **TAX EXEMPT** because firearm is being made on behalf of the United States, or any department, independent establishment, or agency thereof.

☐ c. **TAX EXEMPT** because firearm is being made by or on behalf of any State or possession of the United States, or any political subdivision thereof, or any official police organization of such a government entity engaged in criminal investigations.

2. APPLICATION IS MADE BY:
☐ INDIVIDUAL
☐ BUSINESS FIRM   ☐ GOVERNMENT ENTITY

TRADE NAME *(If any)*

3a. APPLICANT'S NAME AND MAILING ADDRESS *(Type or print below and between the dots)*

●   ●

b. IF P.O. BOX IS SHOWN ABOVE, STREET ADDRESS MUST BE GIVEN HERE

c. COUNTY

IMPORTANT: COMPLETE THE REVERSE SIDE. INDIVIDUALS (INCLUDING LICENSED COLLECTORS) MUST ALSO SUBMIT, IN DUPLICATE, FBI FORM FD-258, FINGERPRINT CARD.

d. TELEPHONE AREA CODE AND NUMBER

4. DESCRIPTION OF FIREARM (Complete items a through i)

d. MODEL

a. NAME AND LOCATION OF ORIGINAL MANUFACTURE OF FIREARM (RECEIVER) *(If prototype, furnish plans and specifications) (See Instruction 2f.)*	b. TYPE OF FIREARM TO BE MADE *(Shortbarreled rifle, machine gun, destructive device, etc.)*	c. CALIBER, GAUGE OR SIZE *(Specify)*	
			LENGTH e. OF BARREL: *(inches)* f. OVERALL:
			g. SERIAL NUMBER *(See Instruction 2g.)*

h. ADDITIONAL DESCRIPTION *(Include all numbers and other identifying data which will appear on the firearm)*	i. STATE WHY YOU INTEND TO MAKE FIREARM *(Use additional sheet if necessary)*

5. APPLICANT'S FEDERAL FIREARMS LICENSE *(If any)*
(Give complete 15-digit number)

First 6 digits	2 digits	2 digits	5 digits

6. SPECIAL (OCCUPATIONAL) TAX STATUS

a. ATF IDENTIFICATION NO.	b. CLASS

7. EMPLOYER'S IDENTIFICATION NUMBER *(If applicable)*

IMPORTANT: GIVE FULL DETAILS ON SEPARATE SHEET FOR ALL "YES" ANSWERS IN ITEMS 8 AND 9

8. IS APPLICENT	YES	NO	9. HAS APPLICANT	YES	NO
a. Charged by information or under indictment in any court for a crime punishable by imprisonment for a term exceeding one year?			a. Been convicted in any court of a crime punishable by imprisonment for a term exceeding one year?		
b. A fugitive from justice?			b. Been discharged from the armed forces under dishonorable conditions?		
c. An alien who is illegally or unlawfully in the United States?			c. Been adjudicated as a mental defective or been committed to any mental institution?		
d. Under 21 years of age?			d. Renounced his or her citizenship, having been a citizen of the United States?		
e. An unlawful user of or addicted to marihuana or any depressant, stimulant or narcotic drug?					
10. A citizen of the United States					

UNDER PENALTIES OF PERJURY, I DECLARE that I have examined this application, including accompanying documents, and to the best of my knowledge and belief it is true, accurate and complete and the making and possession of the firearm described above would not constitute a violation of Chapter 44, Title 18, U.S.C., Chapter 53, Title 26, U.S.C., Title VII of the Omnibus Crime Control and Safe Streets Act, as amended, or any provisions of State or local law.

11. SIGNATURE OF APPLICANT	12. NAME AND TITLE OF AUTHORIZED OFFICIAL OF FIRM OR CORPORATION *(If applicable)*	13. DATE

THE SPACE BELOW IS FOR THE USE OF THE BUREAU OF ALCOHOL, TOBACCO AND FIREARMS

By authority of the Director, Bureau of Alcohol, Tobacco and Firearms, this application has been examined and the applicant's making and registration of the firearm described above is:

STAMP NUMBER

☐ APPROVED *(With the following conditions, if any)*   ☐ DISAPPROVED *(For the following reasons)*

EXAMINER	DATE	AUTHORIZED ATF OFFICIAL	DATE

ATF FORM 1 (7560.1) (12–82)

ADDITIONAL REQUIREMENTS

1. PHOTOGRAPH

The Chief of Police, Sheriff, or other official acceptable to the Director must complete the "Law Enforcement Certification" below. If the applicant is an individual (including a licensed collector) a recent photograph must be attached in the space provided and FBI Form FD-258, Fingerprint Card, completed in duplicate, must be submitted.

**AFFIX
RECENT PHOTOGRAPH HERE**
(Approximately 2" x 2")

2. LAW ENFORCEMENT CERTIFICATION (See IMPORTANT note below)

I certify that I am the chief law enforcement officer of the organization named below having jurisdiction in the area of residence of

_____

(Name of Maker)

I have no information indicating that the maker will use the firearm or device described on this application for other than lawful purposes. I have no information that POSSESSION OF THE FIREARM DESCRIBED IN ITEM 4 ON THE FRONT OF THIS FORM WOULD PLACE THE MAKER IN VIOLATION OF STATE OR LOCAL LAW.

_____

(Signature and Title of Chief Law Enforcement Officer—see IMPORTANT note below)

BY (See IMPORTANT NOTE BELOW)_____

(Signature and Title of Delegated Person)

_____

(Organization)

_____

(Street Address)

_____

(City, State, and ZIP Code)   (Date)

IMPORTANT: The chief law enforcement officer is considered to be the Chief of Police for the maker's city or town of residence, the Sheriff for the maker's county of residence; the Head of the State Police for the maker's State of residence; a State or local district attorney or prosecutor having jurisdiction in the maker's area of residence; or another person whose certification is acceptable to the Director, Bureau of Alcohol, Tobacco and Firearms.   If someone has specific delegated authority to sign on behalf of the Chief of Police, Sheriff, etc., this fact must be noted by printing the Chief's, Sheriff's, or other authorized official's name and title, followed by the word "by" and the full signature and title of the delegated person.

ATF FORM 1 (7560.1) (12–82)

APPLICATION TO MAKE AND REGISTER A FIREARM

DETACH THIS SHEET BEFORE COMPLETING FORM

INSTRUCTIONS

1. DEFINITIONS.

a. FIREARM. The term "firearm" means: (1) a shotgun having a barrel or barrels of less than 18 inches in length; (2) a weapon made from a shotgun if such weapon as modified has an overall length of less than 26 inches or a barrel or barrels of less than 18 inches in length; (3) a rifle having a barrel or barrels of less than 16 inches in length; (4) a weapon made from a rifle if such weapon as modified has an overall length of less than 26 inches or a barrel or barrels of less than 16 inches in length; (5) any other weapon, as defined in b. below; (6) a machine gun; (7) a muffler or a silencer for any firearm whether or not such firearm is included within this definition; and (8) a destructive device. The term "firearm" shall not include an antique firearm or any device (other than a machine gun or destructure device) which, although designed as a weapon, the Director, Bureau of Alochol, Tobacco and Firearms, or authorized delegate finds by reason of the date of its manufacture, value, design, and other characteristics is primarily a collector's item and is not likely to be used as a weapon.

b. ANY OTHER WEAPON. The term "any other weapon" means any weapon or device capable of being concealed on the person from which a shot can be discharged through the energy of an explosive, a pistol or revolver having a barrel with a smooth bore designed or redesigned to fire a fixed shotgun shell, weapons with combination shotgun and rifle barrels 12 inches or more, less than 18 inches in length, from which only a single discharge can be made from either barrel without manual reloading, and shall include any such weapon which may be readily restored to fire. Such term shall not include a pistol or a revolver having a rifled bore, or rifled bores, or weapons designed, made, or intended to be fired from the shoulder and not capable of firing fixed ammunition.

c. PERSON. The term "person" means any individual, company, corporation, association, firm, partnership, joint stock company, trust or society.

2. PREPARATION OF APPLICATION TO MAKE AND REGISTER A FIREARM, AND PAYMENT OF TAX, WHERE REQUIRED.

a. As provided in §5822 of the National Firearms Act, every person [other than a licensed manufacturer who has also paid the required special (occupational) tax to manufacture NFA weapons] seeking to make a firearm must complete, in duplicate, a separate application on this form for each firearm. The applicant maker must furnish all the information called for on this application form.

b. The applicant must present this form to the law enforcement agency having jurisdiction in his area of residence (Chief of Police, Sheriff, etc.) for completion of the Law Enforcement Certification on the back of the form. If the applicant is other than an individual, the trade name should be entered as "name of maker."

c. If the applicant is an individual (including a licensed collector), an unmounted photograph (2" x 2" taken within the past year) must be affixed in the indicated space on both copies of the form, and completed FBI Form FD-258, Fingerprint Card, must be submitted in duplicate. The prints should be taken by someone qualified to do so and must be clear, unsmudged and classifiable. In addition, the person taking the fingerprints must enter the identification data regarding the individual maker and must complete the Fingerprint Cards by signing as the person taking the fingerprints.

d. All required signatures must be entered in ink. It is preferred that the form be prepared by use of a typewriter, using carbon paper to make an exact duplicate. Pen and ink may be used, but under no circumstances will a form filled in by use of a lead pencil be accepted. The signature on both copies *must* be an original. Photocopies, other facsimiles, or carbon copy signatures are not acceptable. All changes made on the form must be initialed and dated by the applicant.

e. Unless the making of the firearm is tax exempt (see instruction 4 below), a $200 making tax must be paid (Title 26 U.S.C., Chapter 53, §5821(a)).

f. Item 4a. of the form should clearly indicate if the parts of a receiver which has been destroyed in accordance with Department of Defense (DOD) demilitarization standards will be used to "make" the receiver of the firearm. The name of the manufacturer of the original receiver should be shown, as well as any serial number appearing on such receiver. Please note that a machinegun receiver which has not been destroyed according to current DOD demilitarization standards may be classified as a National Firearms Act (NFA) weapon in and of itself. It is unlawful to possess an NFA firearm which is not registered to the possessor and the weapon is subject to the seizure and forfeiture provisions of the law.

g. It is suggested that the Serial Number (item 4g on the face of the form) contain at least four digits, preceded by the maker's initials.

h. If any questions arise concerning the preparation of the form, contact the NFA Branch, Bureau of Alcohol, Tobacco and Firearms, Washington, DC 20226 or the nearest ATF office.

3. DISPOSITION OF APPLICATION TO MAKE AND REGISTER A FIREARM.

The applicant will forward both copies of the form to the NFA Branch, Bureau of Alcohol, Tobacco and Firearms, Washington, DC 20226, with a $200 check or money order (where required) made payable to the Department of the Treasury. If approved, the original of the approved form will be returned to the applicant and ATF will retain the duplicate. Approval by ATF will effect registration of the firearm to the applicant. The applicant shall not, under any circumstances, make the firearm until the approved form, with the "National Firearms Act" stamp attached, is received. The form must be retained by the applicant and be available at all times for inspection by Government officers until such time as the firearm may later be transferred after approval by this office. If the application is disapproved, the original and any accompanying check or money order will be returned to the applicant with the reason for disapproval.

4. EXEMPTIONS FROM PAYMENT OF TAX.

a. Under the provisions of §§5852 and 5853, National Firearms Act, firearms, as defined in 1a. and 1b., may be made by any person without payment of the making tax when made by, or on behalf of: (1) the United States, or any department, independent establishment, or agency thereof; or (2) any State or possession of the United States, or any political subdivision thereof, or any official police organization of such a government entity engaged in criminal investigations. The maker must apply on this form and obtain the approval of the Director before making the firearm. Documentation that the firearm is being made for a government entity must accompany the application. A U.S. Government Contract number or a State or local government purchase order would be acceptable documentation. Upon receipt of the approved ATF Form 1, and after the firearm has been made, the maker must apply on ATF Form 5 for the tax exempt transfer of the firearm to the government entity for whom it was made.

b. A manufacturer who has paid special (occupational) tax to manufacture firearms may make the kind of firearm that he is qualified to manufacture without payment of the making tax and he is not required to file this application form. However, the qualified manufacturer must report and register each firearm made by filing ATF Form 2, Notice of Firearms Manufactured or Imported, with the Director, immediately after manufacturing the firearm.

(Continued on reverse)

5. PERSONS PROHIBITED FROM MAKING A FIREARM.

Section 5822 of the National Firearms Act requires that the application to make a firearm be denied if the making or possession of the firearm would place the person making the firearm in violation of law. The term "law" in this statute includes Federal laws as well as State statutes and local ordinances applicable to the locality where the transferee resides. Under Title VII of Public Law 90-351, as amended, (18 U.S.C., Appendix, 1201-1203), the possession "in commerce or affecting commerce" of a firearm, including an unserviceable firearm which has a frame or receiver is unlawful when possessed by any person who:

(1) has been convicted by a court of the United States or of a State or any political subdivision thereof of a felony, or

(2) has been discharged from the Armed Forces under dishonorable conditions, or

(3) has been adjudged by a court of the United States or of a State or any political subdivision thereof of being mentally incompetent, or

(4) having been a citizen of the United States, has renounced his citizenship, or

(5) being an alien is illegally or unlawfully in the United States.

6. PENALTIES.

Any person who violates or fails to comply with any of the requirements of the National Firearms Act shall, upon conviction, be fined not more than $10,000 or be imprisoned for not more than 10 years, or both, in the discretion of the court. Moreover, any firearm involved in any violation of the provisions of the National Firearms Act or any regulations issued thereunder shall be subject to seizure and forfeiture. It is unlawful for any person to make or cause the making of a false entry on any application or record required by the National Firearms Act, knowing such entry to be false.

7. LATER TRANSFER OF THE FIREARM.

If the firearm is to be transferred later by the applicant, an application form covering the proposed transfer must be filed with the Director, Bureau of Alcohol, Tobacco and Firearms.

PRIVACY ACT INFORMATION

1. AUTHORITY. Solicitation of this information is made pursuant to the National Firearms Act (26 U.S.C. §5821 and 5822). Disclosure of this information by the applicant is mandatory for any person (other than a manufacturer qualified under the National Firearms Act) making a firearm as defined in the National Firearms Act.

2. PURPOSE. To verify payment of the tax imposed by 26 U.S.C. §5821; to determine that the making would not be in violation of law; and to effect registration of the firearm.

3. ROUTINE USES. The information will be used by ATF to make the determinations set forth in paragraph 2. In addition, to effect registration of the firearm, information as to the identification of the firearm, date of registration, and the identification and address of person entitled to possess the firearm will be entered into the National Firearms Registration and Transfer Record. No information obtained from an application, registration, or records required to be submitted by a natural person in order to comply with any provision of the National Firearms Act or regulations issued thereunder, shall, except in connection with prosecution or other action for furnishing false information, be used, directly or indirectly, as evidence against that person in any criminal proceeding with respect to a violation of law occurring prior to or concurrently with the filing of the application. The information from this application may only be disclosed to Federal authorities for purpose of prosecution for violation of the National Firearms Act.

4. EFFECTS OF NOT SUPPLYING INFORMATION REQUESTED. Failure to supply complete information will delay processing and may cause denial of the application.

PAPERWORK REDUCTION ACT NOTICE

This form is in accordance with the clearance requirements of Section 3507, PL 96-511, 12/11/80. The information you provide is used to establish that a transferee's receipt and possession of the firearm would be in conformance with Federal, State, and local law. The data is used as proof of lawful registration of a firearm to the manufacturer. The furnishing of this information is mandatory (26 USC 5822).

Considerations for Fully Automatic Fire Modifications

The easiest type of weapon to convert for fire in full-automatic mode, both safely and reliably, is a weapon that fires from an open bolt, has a fixed firing pin, and utilizes a large capacity magazine.

All that is necessary to modify such a weapon is to allow the bolt to fly in and out of battery freely until the trigger is released, or until the magazine is emptied. Modification of a weapon without adequate magazine capacity is, of course, rather pointless. Most semi-automatic weapons of this design were initially designed specifically for full-automatic fire which is why conversion is often relatively easy.

Modifying a bolt to provide it with a fixed firing pin usually will not work unless the bolt face is recessed to at least the same distance as that which the firing pin protrudes from the bolt face. Lack of proper recess will cause the cartridge-case head to catch on the firing pin as the cartridge is chambered, thus causing a recurring jam.

A semi-auto weapon that fires from a closed bolt and that incorporates a separate hammer or striker must employ a *disconnector* in order to achieve safe and reliable full-auto fire. The purpose of the disconnector is to time the release of the hammer or striker in such a way as to insure that the bolt is completely closed prior to ignition.

If the sear has been filed, or some other modification made so that the hammer merely follows the bolt into battery, reliable ignition is not likely to occur. The bolt will normally slow down the hammer to the point that it will not be able to impart sufficient inertia to the firing pin to ensure reliable ignition. This method does work occasionally with .22-caliber rim-fire weapons due to the soft brass casings, and hence relatively light impact required for ignition.

Another difficulty that might be encountered if the hammer is permitted to follow the bolt into battery, is that if the firing pin protrudes from the bolt face, feed jams may occur as discussed previously. There is also the possibility of a prechambered ignition if the hammer is merely permitted to follow the bolt into battery, or if the disconnector is poorly designed or constructed.

In conclusion, I would encourage the potential builder of a full-auto weapon not to underestimate the various factors which have been designed and built into today's modern weaponry. At the same time, I do not want to needlessly discourage a potentially talented, but inexperienced, weapons designer from experimenting with his designs. Just be careful and consider the potential harm that an out-of-control firearm may cause both to yourself and to others.

GER

the YAC STEN MK II Kits

KG&HG looks at a trio of STEN guns from the York Arms Company

After Dunkirk, the British army was in desperate need of weapons with which to rearm and a new submachine gun was high on the list of priorities. Two weapons designers, Shepherd and Turpin, at the Royal Small Arms factory in Enfield, submitted a design that was accepted for production under the name STEN (Shepherd Turpin ENfield). This design was based on knowledge gained from captured German MP40s.

The STEN was designed to be easily and cheaply mass produced. The barrel of the STEN, for example, was simply a drawn steel tube with only two rifling grooves (these were later increased to six). A total of 3,750,000 STENs were produced by U.K. factories. More STEN MK IIs were produced than any other version — over 2,000,000 in all. They were issued to all branches of the service and also air-dropped into occupied Europe to equip resistance and partisan forces. Under the widely diverse conditions of battle experienced by the STEN, it proved to be an excellent weapon.

Three Kits from YAC

The York Arms Company offers three kit versions of the venerable STEN MK II submachine gun. The first, and the one which we chose to build, is a faithful reconstruction of the STEN — fully capable of automatic fire. The second is a semi-auto replica of the STEN and the third is a single-shot replica.

We're not sure about the utility of a single-shot STEN, but we see no harm if that's what someone wants to build. The semi-auto STEN makes a lot of sense, however. With the semi-auto STEN kit, anyone could own a replica of the STEN gun that at least looks like the original but without having to obtain the federal (and possibly state) permits, or having to worry about a real honest-to-God submachine gun in the house.

Unfortunately, while the YAC semi-auto STEN is designed to only fire in semi-auto mode, the folks at ATF

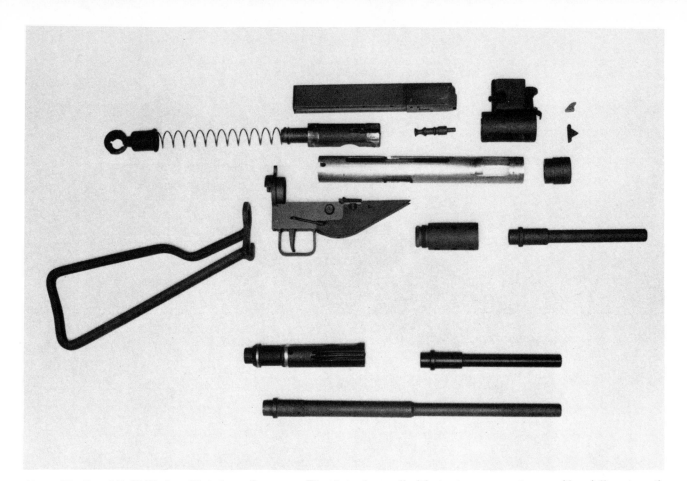

Above: The Sten Mk II Kit from York Arms Company. The photo shows all of the parts necessary to assemble a fully automatic Sten gun. Also shown (at the bottom of the photo) is the semi-auto bolt, dummy barrel and 16" barrel.

Below: A detailed view of the trigger housing assembly.

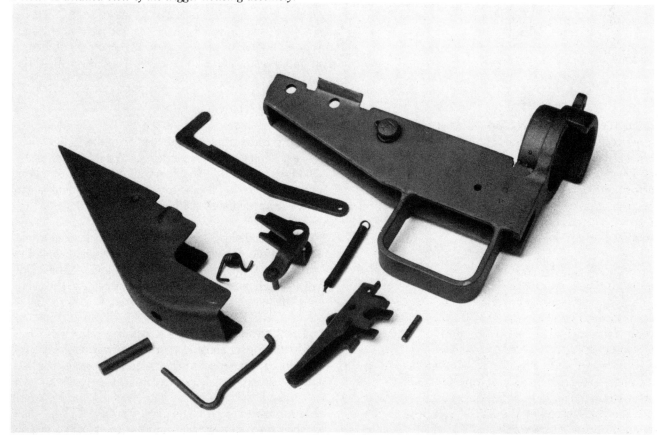

Close-up view of the semi-auto bolt. The weld line, just to the rear of the cocking handle, indicates where the bolt extension has been attached.

have decided to classify it as a fully automatic weapon. While we are not privy to the reasons for their decision, we can surmise that they felt that the semi-auto STEN could be too easily converted back to full-auto form by simply reversing the modifications made by YAC. This is always a problem when attempting to derive a semi-auto weapon from a full-auto weapon, especially when the operating principle is a straight blowback, such as in the STEN.

Semi-Auto STEN Kit

YAC created the semi-auto version of the STEN MK II by performing several modifications to the full-auto parts. The first, and most obvious, modification was to weld an extension onto the full-auto barrel to bring its overall length to the legal minimum of 16″.

The second modification by YAC was to weld an extension onto the bolt so that it is positioned just behind the magazine. At the same time, the full-auto disconnector relief was eliminated, forcing the disconnector to trip every time the bolt moves forward.

The third modification by YAC was to weld a safety block inside the trigger housing, thereby converting the normal SEMI/FULL function of the selector to a SAFE/FIRE function. Next, a short extension (YAC says it's a 1/4″ x 1/4″ roller bearing) is brazed onto the disconnector to further ensure that the trigger will disconnect every time the bolt travels forward. After all of the modifications to

The YAC-modified trigger housing assembly. Note the extension welded onto the disconnector. Note also, the block placed just in front of the disconnector.

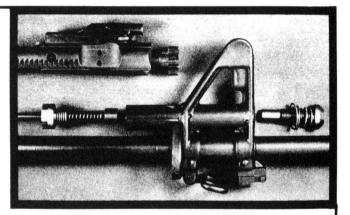

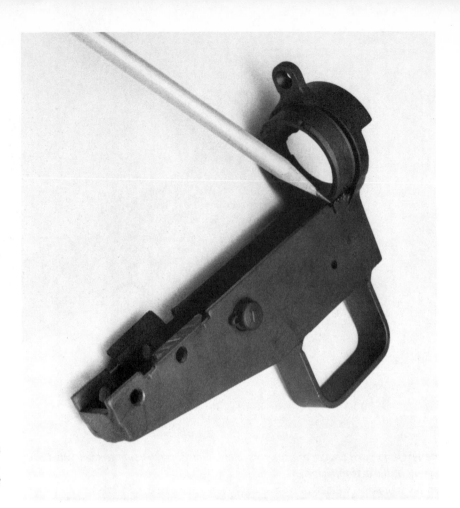

The original receiver was sawn through just forward of the rear head casing. Notice that somebody went just a little too far in this operation.

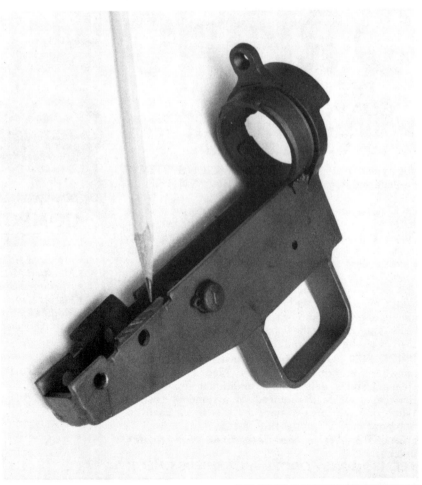

Two more cuts were made on either side of the receiver, as shown.

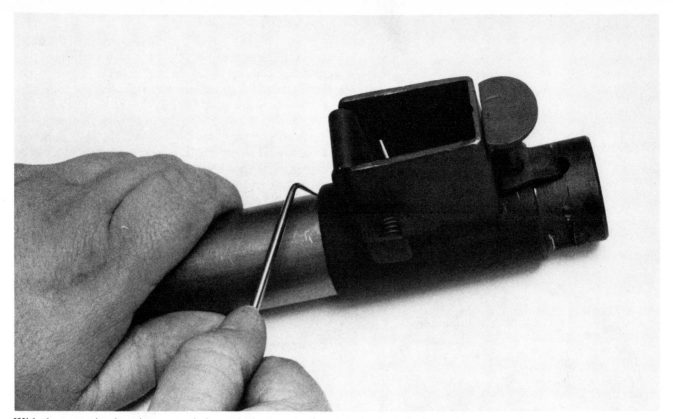

With the magazine housing correctly located, the new receiver tube is marked with a sharp tool.

the trigger housing have been performed, the trigger and sear pivot pins are welded into place to prevent tampering.

The fourth, and final, modification performed by YAC was to turn their new semi-auto bolt down to 1.310″ OD and to supply the kit with a thicker wall tubing (1.334″ ID) to prevent the installation of a full-auto bolt (1.375″ OD) into the semi-auto STEN.

As we said above, ATF is apparently not satisfied with the modifications performed by YAC to obtain a semi-auto STEN; they have ruled that it must be licensed as though a fully automatic weapon. We trust that YAC has appealed this ruling. So, if you would like to purchase a semi-auto STEN and want to know its current legal status, call the NFA branch of ATF at (202) 566-7371.

Single-Shot STEN Kit

This kit takes the semi-auto STEN kit one step further and in the process has apparently escaped the ATF Stamp of Disapproval. What YAC has done is to eliminate the magazine entirely; therefore, it matters little whether the gun is fully automatic or not. Since there is only one cartridge, which must be manually inserted into the chamber, the single-shot STEN can only fire once for each pull of the trigger. In this case, the only perceived difference between a *semi-auto* single-shot STEN and a *full-auto* single-shot STEN is that the bolt will close on an empty chamber for a full-auto version while it will stay back for a semi-auto version. The YAC single-shot STENs are designed to hold the bolt back after firing, thereby facilitating the loading of the next round.

We have misgivings about the concept of a single-shot STEN; however, considering the legal limbo of YAC's semi-auto STEN it may be the easiest path to owning something resembling a STEN. Even that has to be highly qualified, since the lack of a magazine seriously impacts the resemblance of the single-shot STEN to its full-auto brother. We would like to see YAC supply, as part of this kit, a dummy magazine welded into a normal magazine housing which could be slipped into place on the single-shot STEN receiver. Until YAC supplies this component, however, single-shot STEN kit builders may wish to perform this modification themselves.

Full-Auto STEN

Finally, the genuine article—the gun with which Great Britain fought WW II. First though, in order to understand the assembly process, it helps to understand a little about how and why these kits came into being.

Title II of the Gun Control Act (GCA) of 1968 prohibits the importation of certain types of weapons, such as short-barreled pistols (the famed Walther PPK was a victim) and machineguns. It does not prohibit the importation of gun parts (except the receiver) and the subsequent manufacture of said gun in the United States. Behold the STEN kit.

In Europe, the STENs are completely disassembled and the receiver is carefully cut away from the trigger housing. This is accomplished by making a vertical cut through the receiver tube just in front of the rear-head casing, and two small cuts on either side of the trigger housing just above the sear pin. The barrel sleeve is removed from the front of the receiver tube by cutting the tube just behind the magazine housing, sliding the magazine housing off to the rear, and then removing the excess tubing by turning the barrel sleeve in a lathe.

With the trigger housing and barrel sleeve removed from the receiver tube, the receiver remnants are discarded and the non-restricted parts imported into the U.S. and sold as replacement parts or as complete kits, such as the STENs described here.

To remanufacture a STEN gun using one of these kits, it is necessary to *obtain permission using ATF Form 1* and then merely weld a new receiver tube onto the old trigger housing. Weld the barrel sleeve back into place and, *presto*, you're back in action! Next, we will describe the actual steps that we took to remanufacturer our STEN kit.

Preparing the Receiver Tube

The receiver tube supplied by YAC comes cut to the proper length and has the cocking-lever slot completely milled out. Also, the beginnings of two "J" slots in the rear of the receiver tube were cut by YAC — presumably for orientation purposes (at least, that is how we used them). All that remained to complete the receiver tube was to cut the ejection and magazine ports, cut the sear slot, finish the "J" slots, and weld the ejector into place.

YAC supplies sketches of the receiver tube showing dimensions and other information necessary to complete the STEN kit. The sketches were — well — sketches and not as pretty as that of, at least, one competitor's drawings. On the other hand, YAC's sketches were 100% accurate and complete which we found to be lacking in the drawings of Brand X. Rather than attempt to transfer the dimensions of YAC's drawings to our receiver tube, we chose to use the various pieces (provided as part of the kit) as templates to show us where to cut.

Installing the Magazine and Ejector Ports

In order to locate the magazine and ejector ports, we first had to correctly locate the magazine housing on the receiver tube. Our first task was to position the magazine housing the correct distance, front to rear, to allow the barrel-nut catch to properly engage the teeth on the barrel nut.

This was accomplished by assembling the barrel, barrel nut and barrel sleeve; slipping the magazine housing onto the receiver tube; installing the barrel assembly onto the front of the receiver; and then adjusting the position of the magazine housing until the teeth of the barrel-nut catch were centered on the teeth of the barrel nut. Once the proper longitudinal position was established, the receiver was marked with a scribe so that the magazine housing could be readily restored to the proper location.

Above: This is how the front of the receiver should look with the bolt installed. A line can be drawn from the center of the extractor, through the firing pin and ejector relief, to the center of the magazine housing.

KIT GUNS & HOBBY GUNSMITHING

Above: After the outline of the ports had been scribed onto the new receiver housing, all that was necessary was to follow the outline with an end mill.

Even using a milling machine, we felt compelled to perform some fine adjustments with a file.

Next, the magazine housing had to be properly oriented in relation to the bolt assembly. The bolt assembly was inserted into the receiver tube and positioned so that the cocking handle could be installed. The bolt was then slid fully forward and the location of the extractor and ejector recess noted. A line drawn through the center-line of the extractor and the ejector recess should exactly bisect the ejector and magazine ports. With the magazine positioned to satisfy this requirement, the outline of the magazine and ejector ports were scribed onto the receiver tube with a sharp tool.

Once the proper locations for the magazine and ejector ports had been scribed on the receiver tube, all that was required was to cut out the ports by whatever means that we found handy. We took the easy way out by using a milling machine for most of the cutting; but, a drill, hacksaw and file would have also worked, albeit somewhat slower. As it happened, we found that it was necessary to use our files to make the ports cut into the receiver tube match the ports in the magazine housing. In part, this was cosmetic. It didn't seem right for the ejection port to have a multi-stepped contour. But, in the case of the magazine port, it was necessary to further enlarge the port in the receiver tube to permit complete insertion of the magazine.

Installing the Ejector

With the magazine and ejector ports cut in the receiver tube, a 1/8″ wide by 1/2″ long slot, centered to the rear of the magazine port, had to be created to allow the ejector to be welded to the receiver. YAC supplies an ejector which has been stamped to the exact shape required. We found this ejector too hard to hold in place to be welded, so we fabricated a new one from some scrap steel that we had lying around the shop. We left the new ejector about 1″ too long. This permitted it to be clamped in place in the receiver tube, firmly against the bolt, while at the same time permitting plenty of clearance to weld it to the receiver. After the ejector was firmly welded in place, the excess material was sawn off and the stubble dressed smooth with a file.

Installing the Sear Slot

The next operation, which sent us back to the milling machine, was to cut the sear slot. Again, although YAC supplied adequate drawings to machine the slot, we chose instead to use the trigger housing as a template to mark the sear slot outline.

First, we had to remove the surplus bit of material left behind in the rear head casing when the old receiver tube was cut away from the trigger housing. This was accomplished with a flat punch and hammer. To our relief, the receiver remnant popped out easily. Next we disassembled the trigger-housing assembly, paying special attention to the location of the sear and the disconnector.

A small slot had to be added to the rear of the magazine port to permit the ejector to be welded into place.

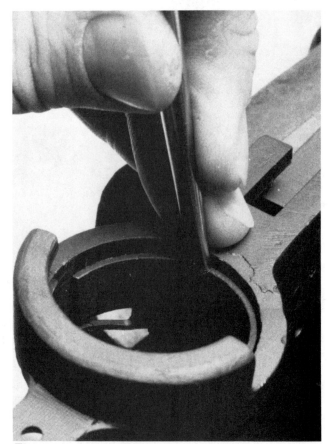

The remnants of the old receiver tube had to be removed from the rear head casing. Fortunately, a flat punch accomplished this task easily.

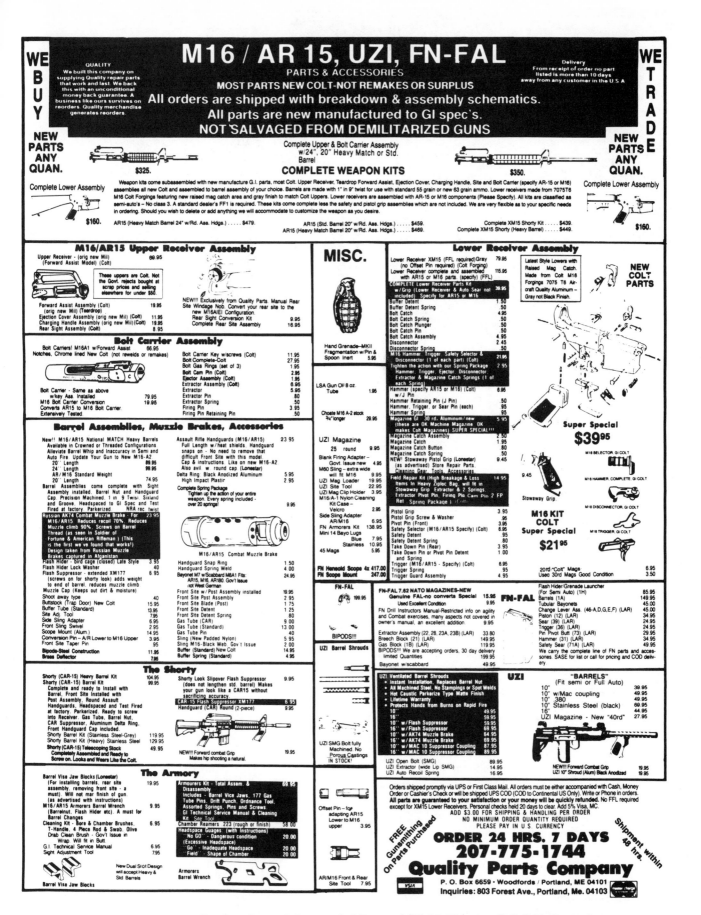

We Also Carry a Complete Line of 45 and M14 Parts SASE Catalog.

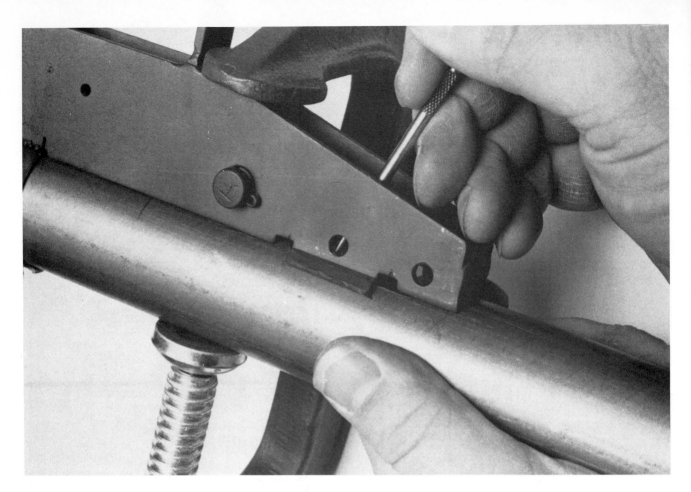

A small notch was cut into the top rear of the receiver tube to allow the tube to engage an alignment pin in the rear head casing. Next, the receiver tube was inserted into the rear head casing and — after checking that the trigger housing was perpendicular to the magazine — clamped securely with a C-clamp. The outline of the left and right inside edges of the trigger housing were scribed in the usual manner on the receiver tube and the approximate locations of the front and rear of the sear and disconnector were indicated with a felt-tip pen.

Then, the receiver tube was removed from the trigger housing; the dimensions marked with the felt-tip pen were checked against the drawings supplied by YAC. Since there appeared to be no discrepancies between our empirical determination of the correct location for the sear slot and that indicated in the drawings, we proceeded with abandon. In a short time, we had produced yet another hole in the receiver tube. Loosely assembling the trigger housing to the receiver tube, we found that some file work was necessary to make everything work correctly; however, we wanted to postpone that until we had welded the receiver tube onto the trigger housing.

Before we welded the trigger housing in place, we made some preparations to weld the barrel sleeve into place. Three 5/16″ holes were drilled through the receiver tube, approximately 1/4″ from the front edge, and spaced equally about the circumference with one hole centered on the ejector port. Next, the magazine housing was installed; using the magazine housing plunger hole as a guide, a 1/

Above: With the receiver tube firmly clamped to the trigger housing, the outline of the sear slot was traced with a sharp scribe.

4″ hole was drilled through the receiver tube.

Welding the New Receiver

Now we were ready to finish the required welding operations. The barrel sleeve was installed into the front of the new receiver tube and positioned so that a 1/4″ pin could be inserted through the magazine housing plunger hole. Next, the three 5/16″ holes were filled with weldment, securing the barrel sleeve permanently to the new receiver tube. This method of attaching the barrel sleeve provides the cleanest possible installation and, with a little file work, no visible evidence remains of any welding.

Finally, we were ready to weld the trigger housing onto the receiver tube. Again the receiver tube was inserted into the rear head casing, checked for alignment and clamped into place. Next, a bead was drawn on either side of the trigger housing just above the sear pin (where the old weldment was cut) securing the tube to the trigger housing. Then, just as a precaution, a bead was run around the entire outer circumference of the rear head casing where the old receiver tube had been sawed through. The rear head casing is a substantial piece of steel, which ab-

Opposite Page: Finally, the receiver could be welded together.

Not wishing to risk a run-away gun, the Sten was first loaded with one round.

solutely prevents the rear of the receiver tube from separating from the trigger housing, *provided* that the welds on either side of the trigger housing do not break. If these welds should ever break, there would be no way to stop the STEN gun from firing in full-auto mode until the magazine was empty. An extra weld around the rear head casing seemed like cheap insurance.

With the trigger housing welded into place, the receiver was essentially complete. We did have to go back and dress up the sear slot to allow the sear and disconnector to work without binding. We also performed some cosmetic filing and sanding to dress up the appearance of the STEN so we could show our mothers what a nice job we did before we sent it off to be re-parkerized. With all that completed, we assembled the STEN and headed off to the local range for testing.

Range Testing

When testing any new weapon, especially one that is capable of fully automatic fire, extreme caution must be exercised at all times to prevent accidents.

For our range testing of the STEN, a party of three persons, at least two of whom were familiar with basic first aid (stop the bleeding — call the doctor) techniques, departed to a local commercially owned range. For a nominal fee, we conducted our test in a completely controlled and cooperative environment.

Our confidence in the assembly process and the metallurgy of the surplus STEN parts was sufficient that we dispatched with the usual lanyard phase of range testing. As our first step, we loaded the magazine with just a single cartridge. Firing from the hip, and pointing generally down range, the trigger was pulled.

To our relief, almost everything worked perfectly. The barrel didn't blow up, the cartridge casing didn't rupture, the welds didn't crack — but, the bolt slammed forward on an empty chamber after the first shot. Thinking that perhaps we didn't understand the symbology on the selector switch, we chose the only other setting. Same result.

Ignoring that problem for the moment, we proceeded to load two rounds into the magazine. Sure enough, pull the trigger and two rounds fired. Hot damn! Full auto! No major problems either. We skipped three and four rounds in the magazine and leapt directly to five. We found that two-round bursts were easily performed with the STEN.

Next, we attempted to measure the cyclic rate of fire for the STEN. Loading ten cartridges into the magazine, we pointed the STEN down range and pulled the trigger until the magazine was exhausted. The burst lasted 1.2 seconds indicating a cyclic rate of 500 rpm.

We didn't do any accuracy tests while we were at the range because: (1) who cares, (2) it was 5 above zero, (3) we hadn't installed the front sight yet, and (4) we couldn't

KIT GUNS & HOBBY GUNSMITHING

Finally, the STEN operating under full-auto fire.

have seen the target through all the smoke.

We did, however, note with much pleasure that the STEN gun was very controllable. There was no evidence of the legendary muzzle climb of the Thompson submachine gun or even the M-16. We have no idea why this is, but we are also not the first to observe it.

Final Observations

The three STEN kits by YAC represent an attempt to provide three different types of kit builders with the opportunity to own a replica of the famous STEN gun. Unfortunately, for both YAC and anyone who wishes to own a semi-auto STEN, ATF requires the same licensing procedure for both the full-auto and semi-auto versions of the STEN.

We were pleased to see how easy it was to fabricate a new receiver tube. If we were to do it a second time (which we probably will) we estimate it will take about two hours to complete the receiver. This assumes the use of machine tools. With hand tools, we would guess the time would be more like six hours.

The assembly drawings and instructions were sketchy and not well organized but we had no problem building our gun using them and we found them to be accurate and complete. The STEN design is very forgiving about most of the dimensions, thus making it a good first gun for a would-be machinegun kit builder.

In conclusion, we feel that all three YAC STEN gun kits represent excellent values and can be easily constructed — even by a novice kit gun builder.

Add a Dummy Magazine to your Single-Shot STEN

Take a surplus STEN magazine and insert it into a STEN magazine housing. Be sure that the magazine is fully inserted into the housing. With a sharp tool, scribe the magazine where it extends beyond the inside diameter of the magazine housing. Just scribe the front and rear, you can mark the top and bottom after you have withdrawn the magazine from the housing.

Next, disassemble the magazine and set everything but the outer shell aside. With a hacksaw, cut off the top of the magazine and then file it down to the scribe marks. Re-insert the magazine into the magazine housing to check your progress; continue to file until the magazine no longer protrudes into the magazine housing.

Assemble the floor plate to the magazine and tack-weld it into place. Then insert the magazine into the magazine housing and weld (or braze) it securely into place. This prevents losing your specially modified magazine or letting someone discover that your magazine is a fake. It also insures that your single-shot STEN is still, in spirit as well as in fact, a single-shot STEN.

With the modified magazine housing completed, all that is necessary is to install it on your STEN. If the front sight has been welded into place, then the welds will have to be broken in order to remove the front sight. With the front sight removed, the magazine housing should slip right over the barrel, the barrel nut and the front part of the receiver. Position the magazine housing so that the barrel-nut catch properly engages the teeth on the barrel nut. Check that the magazine is perpendicular to the trigger housing and mark the magazine housing and receiver so that you can easily return the magazine housing to the proper position.

Next, remove the magazine-housing plunger and associated springs and pins from the magazine housing and scribe the outline of its hole onto the receiver tube. Push the magazine housing out of the way and drill through the receiver tube and barrel nut with a 1/4″ drill. Now you should be able to reassemble the magazine housing and snap it into position on your single-shot STEN.

Below: The outline of the magazine housing is scribed onto the magazine with a sharp tool.

Right: With the magazine disassembled, the portion of the magazine which protrudes into the receiver is removed with a hacksaw.

Below: The floorplate is assembled onto the magazine and tack welded into place.

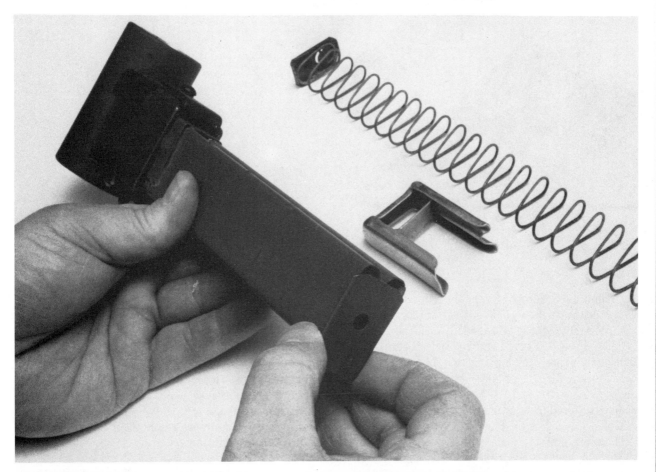

the Muffler Shop

by W. Kenneth Johnson

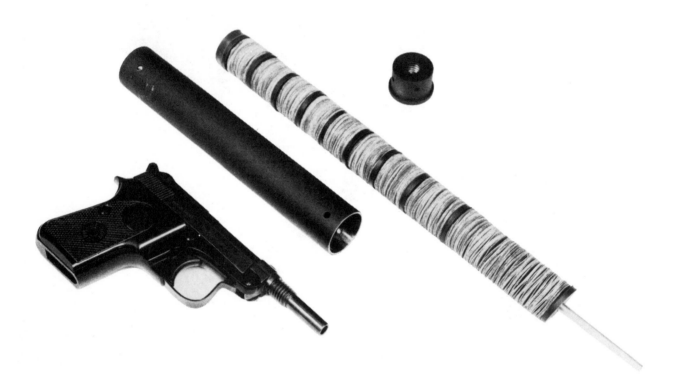

I am the first to admit that I have no practical need for a silencer. It doesn't make my bullets fly farther, or flatter, or more accurately. All that it does do is make them fly more quietly. Even that is not really practical; after all, half the fun of plinking is the big bang that the gun makes when you squeeze the trigger. Or is it?

I will leave it to you to determine your own reasons for owning a silencer, such as the Sionac .22-caliber unit that I built. There are probably some very good reasons why someone would want to own a silenced .22-caliber Beretta. *Because* seemed like an adequate reason to me.

Some words about silencers and things of that sort before I proceed. The government (Federal that is) does not outlaw silencers, per se. Instead they discourage wholesale traffic in them, as well as machine guns and other *class 3* weapons. This is accomplished by imposing a tax and licensing requirement on the manufacture and sale (transfer is the official language) of such weaponry. While silencers are not illegal (except where prohibited by state or local law), the mere *possession* of an unregistered silencer or machine gun is very much illegal.

I contacted the local office of the ATF regarding building

KIT GUNS & HOBBY GUNSMITHING

The Sionac silencer kit comes with a nice discussion of silencer theory. The internal parts come assembled on a .22-caliber wooden dowel to keep everything in order.

a silencer using the Sionac kit and found the agent that I talked to very friendly and informative. A few days after I called, a packet of forms and instructions arrived in the mail.

ATF Form 1

As described in another article in this publication, ATF Form 1 is the fundamental mechanism by which the ordinary citizen can build their own silencer or any other restricted weapon. The form isn't difficult to fill out nor is it long. There is one major gotcha, however. You have to get the signature of the *chief law enforcement officer* of your area of residence. I live in a fairly small community and I had some misgivings as to how to approach the Chief of Police to ask him to let me build a silenced pistol. I could just imagine having a patrol car parked outside the house for the rest of my life!

I called the police department and gave them a story about how I was some big-shot gun-writer doing an article about silencers, etc. and therefore had a legitimate reason to build the unspeakable. The girl that answered was yawningly polite: "Yup, we get people building silencers all the time." She said to drop on by and talk to Sgt. Soandso. I took a shower and shaved again, put on a tie, drove over to the police department and asked for the sergeant. He came out, shook my hand and invited me back to his office.

We joked awhile about why I wanted to do strange things like build a silencer. (I imagine they really enjoy these brief interludes in their lives of catching vermin and speeders.) We talked about my certifiable love of God and country, etc. We took a few fingerprints (mostly mine) in order to lend credence to my story and affixed said prints to my application form.

I got the distinct impression that the police were not particularly comfortable with the idea of me building a silencer or any other kind of out-of-the-ordinary weapon, but that they were acutely aware that I was legally entitled to do so unless specifically prohibited by law. In due course, I received the official blessing that I required and I sent my check for $200, and the ATF Form 1, off to Washington.

A few months passed (plan ahead, dear reader) by the time I received my original ATF Form 1 back, with all kinds of stamps and stuff all across it. Finally! I was able to legally do what any nit with a hacksaw could do in minutes.

Sionac provides plans for an outer tube assembly that requires only that the builder cut off a piece of aluminum tubing with a 1" inside diameter and drill a few holes to secure the end caps, which are supplied with kit. This allows the person without access to machine tools to assemble their kit in just an hour or so.

Right: For those of you who do not have access to machine tools such as a lathe, Sionac provides a set of plans to enable the "shade tree" gunsmith the means to assemble a working silencer. With Sionac's plans, the only tools that you will need are a hacksaw and a drill.

Below: Having spent $200 to have this silencer licensed and having access to a lathe over at the local high school, I wanted something that was at least as attractive as my newly bought Beretta. Shown in the photo is a new outer tube being fashioned out of some 1" I.D. thin-wall tubing that I could have blued to match the Beretta. I also turned up some new end caps out of some pieces of steel that were lying about the shop.

Above: The lathe was the logical place to polish the outer silencer tube.

Left: The new end cap which I had fabricated on the lathe was tapped to accept the SWD barrel.

Above: The barrel had to be worked on a little in order to get it to fit properly with my Beretta Minx.

Since SWD sells a replacement barrel for the Beretta Minx and Jetfire that is already threaded to accept a silencer, I decided to buy a Beretta Minx and the SWD barrel. Unfortunately, the threads on the SWD barrel do not match the threads on the Sionac end-caps. Since I had access to a lathe, I was not overly concerned.

I sketched a silencer-tube design of my own (see the drawings at the end of the article) which incorporated the changes required by the SWD barrel plus some fancy touches, such as knurled end-caps, etc. I turned up some new end caps from a couple pieces of steel that I had lying around the shop, and an outer tube from some thin wall 1" ID steel tubing that I picked up from a surplus metal yard. I stamped my personal serial number on the outer tube as proscribed by law and temporarily set it aside.

The SWD barrel had to be fitted to the Beretta. There was some extra material up near the barrel-pivot pin which prevented the barrel from closing properly. This was easily removed with a Dremel tool and a 1/4" sanding drum.

Assembly of the silencer was very simple. Some care was necessary, however, to avoid spilling what must have

been several hundred brass-screening washers all over my workbench. First, I screwed the front end-cap in to the outer tube. Then I removed the pin from the wooden dowel which had been inserted by Sionac through all of the internal silencer parts and inserted the silencer parts, dowel and all, into the silencer tube. Finally I screwed the rear end-cap into place, securing the whole mess.

Now I had an honest-to-God silencer. I was in the big league. Move over James Bond! Off to the range.

Test firing the silencer was a kick. Phutt! Phutt! Just like in the movies. Unfortunately, I can't say anything about the accuracy, since the silencer obscured the sights; but I hadn't planned to go to the NRA Nationals with this gun anyway. I do plan to make some additional tests on sound reduction and so forth, so I'll probably solder some sights on to the silencer and see how much it affects the accuracy of the little Beretta.

As I said starting out, there's nothing practical about silencers but they sure are fun to shoot and not really any more expensive to own than a good quality gun.

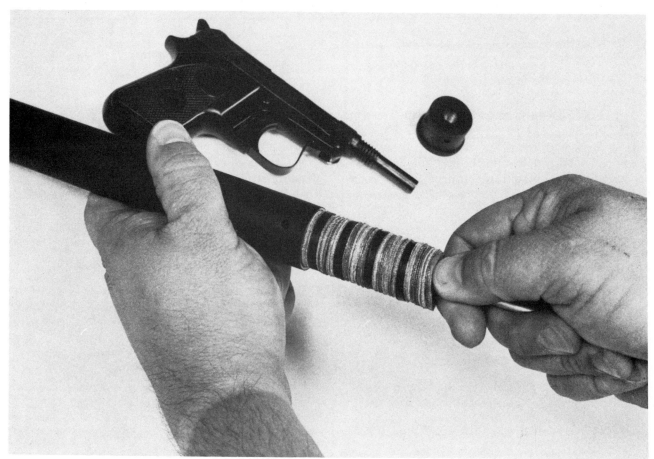

Above: The climax! The Sionac silencer was assembled by removing the pin from one end of the wooden dowel, and inserting the whole kit, dowel and all, into the silencer tube.

Below: I designed a slightly more refined silencer tube to accept the Sionac parts. I decided to use threaded and knurled end caps instead of the ones supplied by Sionac.

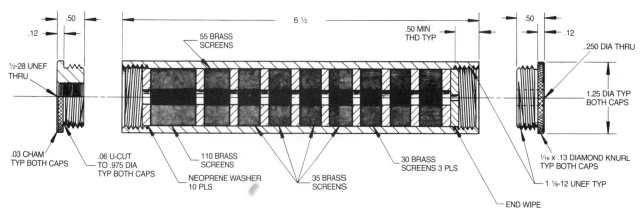

Electroless Nickel Plating

by the KG&HG Staff

Surface finishing the metal parts of a gun often remains a major stumbling block for the amateur gunsmith. A gun can't be considered "completed" as long as the surface is not properly "finished" by either bluing, browning or plating. Most finishes available to the amateur gunsmith, however, cannot measure up to those available to the professional.

When we noticed an advertisement for an electroless nickel-plating solution that the amateur gunsmith could use on his (or her) kitchen stove, we contacted the manufacturer, Electroless Specialties. We explained our interest, and they kindly shipped us a sample quantity of their plating solution.

Required Equipment

The instructions, provided with the plating solution, recommended (as a minimum) that the user have the following equipment.

Tank: 1 gallon minimum, glass or stainless steel.
Thermometer: 212°F, ±5°F.
Tongs: 8 inches or longer.

Surface Preparation

The first step required when plating a gun is to clean the parts to be plated in a standard cleaning solution. Electroless Specialties recommends gasoline, perchlorethylene or mineral spirits to perform this task. We prefer not to use gasoline for any task except fueling our automobiles.

Next, we were instructed to remove any rust or scale by blasting the surfaces to be plated with glass beads. We noted that the manufacturer recommended glass-bead blasting rather than sand blasting. We inquired about this, and they informed us that sand blasting tends to produce a somewhat greyish finish. The surfaces should be glass beaded until a uniformly dull, chrome-like finish is obtained and no dark spots remain.

After you have glass beaded the parts to be plated, do not handle them with your bare hands; this will prevent oil deposits and avoid a spotty finish. Return the parts to the cleaning bath after the glass-beading operation before attempting to plate them. The parts should be plated within 2 to 3 hours after glass beading. Further delay will allow surface oxidation (rust) to form, resulting in a poor finish.

Plating Procedure

The plating solution provided by Electroless Specialties must be diluted by 3 parts of water to 1 part of solution. Then bring the diluted mixture to a temperature of 190°F, ±10°F. When the solution is at the correct temperature, the parts should be placed in the solution with tongs. Be careful not to touch the parts with your bare hands. Large parts should be pre-heated in a water bath to prevent cooling of the plating solution.

Leave the parts in the plating solution for 30 to 40 minutes. Turn the parts periodically to assure even plating. After the treatment has been completed, the parts must be rinsed in cold, running water for 2 minutes. Finally, dry the parts with a clean cloth and set them aside.

If a hard, wear-resistant finish is desired, Electroless Specialties recommends that the nickel-treated parts be heat-treated by placing them in an oven (the kitchen oven is fine) set at 400°F for 4 to 5 hours.

Testing

We went out and bought a special pot (i.e., one that will never be used for cooking) for the nickel-plating solution. The plating solution contains nickel sulphate and the container carries a warning not to take the contents internally, or permit the solution to remain on the skin or splash in the eyes. We diluted the solution as the instructions directed, and heated it to the recommended temperature. Using a pair of tongs, we placed our prepared steel sample into the solution. (We used a piece of scrap steel for our test, rather than one of the boss's guns, out of concern for our hides.) After 30 minutes we removed the sample and inspected the finish.

We weren't sure what we were looking for, but we couldn't see any obvious defects like flaking, etc. The finish looked very much the same as it did when it went into the solution. All the gouges, pits and scratches were still there, however, the color had that characteristic electroless-nickel look. The wear characteristics of this plating technique are reported to be very good; obviously, we could not verify this with our limited test. Very shortly, however, we plan to plate one of our test guns using this product and to report on its performance. Since the solution is very inexpensive, we see no reason for the ambitious amateur gunsmith not to give it a try.

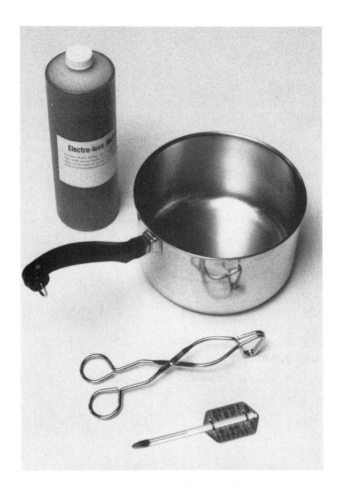

Left: Illustrated is the equipment required to nickel plate your favorite gun. Don't use utensils that you also use for preparing food.

Below: A pair of tongs is used to handle the parts to be nickel plated. The kitchen stove can be used to heat the plating solution, but extreme care must be exercised.

the Directory

Your Source for Information on Blackpowder, Modern and Exotic Weapons Kits

The information contained in this section is supplied by the manufacturers and is believed to be accurate at the time of publication. KG&HG, however, assumes no responsibility for errors, omissions or the claims of the manufacturers or suppliers.

Since prices and specifications are always subject to change without notice, we urge you to contact the manufacturers for the most current information. To assist you in this, we have included a convenient Business Reply Card at the end of this volume.

Blackpowder Kits

Allen Fire Arms   Pistols

Kit: 1847 Walker Revolver
Caliber: .44
Barrel Length: 9"
Price: $ 115.00
Color case-hardened frame and brass trigger guard. Overall length - 15 3/4", weight - 4.410 lbs.

Kit: 1848 Baby Dragoon Revolver
Caliber: .31
Barrel Length: 3,4 and 5"
Price: $ 110.00
5 shot cylinder, color case-hardened frame, brass backstrap and trigger guard. Overall length (4" barrel) - 9 1/2", weight - 1.430 lbs.

Kit: 1849 Pocket Revolver
Caliber: .31
Barrel Length: 3,4 and 5"
Price: $ 114.00
Octagonal barrel, color case-hardened frame, brass backstrap and trigger guard, 5 shot engraved cylinder. Overall length (4" barrel) - 9 1/2", weight - 1.480 lbs.

Kit: 1851 Navy Griswold Confederate Revolver
Caliber: .36
Barrel Length: 7 1/2"
Price: $ 99.00
The Navy Griswold is nearly the same as the 1851 Augusta except that the barrel is round forward of the lug and the cylinder is not engraved.

Kit: 1851 Navy Sheriff's Revolver
Caliber: .36
Barrel Length: 5"
Price: $ 110.00
Snub nose version of 1851 Navy Revolver. Overall length - 10 1/2", weight - 2.530 lbs.

Kit: 1849 Wells Fargo Revolver
Caliber: .31
Barrel Length: 3,4 and 5"
Price: $ 110.00
The Wells Fargo revolver is like the 1849 Pocket Revolver except that it has no loading lever.

Kit: 1860 Army Revolver
Caliber: .44
Barrel Length: 8"
Price: $ 115.00
Round tapered barrel, color case-hardened frame, 6 shot engraved cylinder, brass trigger guard. Overall length - 13 3/4", weight - 2.650 lbs.

Kit: 1851 Navy Revolver
Caliber: .36
Barrel Length: 7 1/2"
Price: $ 110.00
Octagonal barrel, color case-hardened frame, brass backstrap and trigger guard, 6 shot cylinder. Overall length - 13", weight - 2.750 lbs.

Kit: 1851 Navy Augusta Confederate Revolver
Caliber: .36
Barrel Length: 7 1/2"
Price: $ 99.00
The Navy Augusta is nearly the same as the Navy 1851 except a brass frame replaces the steel frame.

Kit: 1858 Remington New Army Revolver
Caliber: .44
Barrel Length: 7 1/2"
Price: $ 115.00
Tapered octagonal barrel, brass trigger guard. Overall length - 13 3/4", weight - 2.650 lbs.

Kit: 3rd Model 1851 Navy
Caliber: .36
Barrel Length: 7 1/2"
Price: $ 110.00
The 3rd Model Navy is nearly the same as the 1851 Navy except that the backstrap and trigger guard are steel instead of brass.

Kit: Texas Dragoon Revolver
Caliber: .44
Barrel Length: 7 1/2"
Price: $ 125.00
Color case-hardened frame, brass backstrap and square-back trigger guard. Overall length - 13 1/2", weight - 3.970 lbs.

Kit: 1862 Pocket Navy Caliber Revolver
Caliber: .36
Barrel Length: see below
Price: $ 104.00
Tapered octagonal barrel, 5-shot cylinder, color case-hardened frame, brass backstrap and trigger guard. Overall length - 10 1/2", weight - 1.680 lbs. Available in 4 1/2", 5 1/2" or 6 1/2" barrel lengths.

Kit: 1862 Police Revolver
Caliber: .36
Barrel Length: see below
Price: $ 104.00
Color case-hardened frame, 5-shot cylinder, brass backstrap and trigger guard. Overall length - 10 1/2", weight - 1.590 lbs. Barrel length available in 4 1/2", 5 1/2", and 6 1/2".

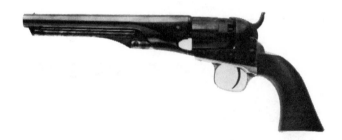

Kit: 1st Model Dragoon Revolver
Caliber: .44
Barrel Length: 7 1/2"
Price: $ 125.00
Color case hardened frame, brass backstrap and trigger guard. Overall length - 13 1/2", weight - 3.970 lbs.

Kit: 2nd Model Dragoon Revolver
Caliber: .44
Barrel Length: 7 1/2"
Price: $ 125.00
The 2nd Model is like 1st Model Dragoon except that it has a square cylinder bolt slot, instead of oval.

Kit: 3rd Model Dragoon Revolver
Caliber: .44
Barrel Length: 7 1/2"
Price: $ 125.00
Same as 2nd Model Dragoon except: 1) the loading lever taper is inverted, 2) the loading lever latch hook has been changed in shape, 3) a loading lever latch was added, 4) the backstrap is steel and 5) the frame has been cut for a shoulder stock.

Allen Fire Arms Cont.

Kit: 1861 Navy Revolver
Caliber: .36
Barrel Length: 7 1/2"
Price: $ 114.00
Color case-hardened frame. 6 shot cylinder. Overall length - 13", weight - 2.750 lbs.

Armsport   Pistols

Kit: 1851 Colt Navy Revolver
Caliber: .36, .44
Barrel Length: 7 1/2"
Price: $ 72.00
Comes with either brass or steel frame.

Kit: 1860 Colt Army
Caliber: .44
Barrel Length: 8"
Price: $ 78.00
Parts are prefitted and preassembled.

Kit: Corsair Two Barrel Pistol
Caliber: .44
Barrel Length: 8"
Price: $ 85.00
Parts are prefitted and preassembled. Twin percussion locks.

Kit: Dueling Pistol
Caliber: .45
Barrel Length: 10"
Price: $ 95.00
Parts are prefitted and preassembled

Kit: Kentucky Pistol
Caliber: .45, .50
Barrel Length: 10"
Price: $ 70.00
Prefitted and preassembled.

Kit: New Remington Army Steel Revolver
Caliber: .44
Barrel Length: 8″
Price: $ 110.00
Parts are pre-fitted and pre-assembled.

Classic Arms Ltd.   Pistols

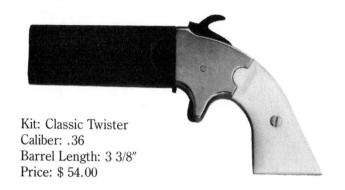

Kit: Classic Twister
Caliber: .36
Barrel Length: 3 3/8″
Price: $ 54.00

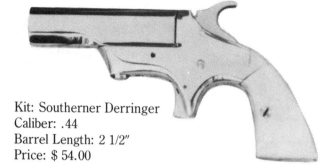

Kit: Southerner Derringer
Caliber: .44
Barrel Length: 2 1/2″
Price: $ 54.00

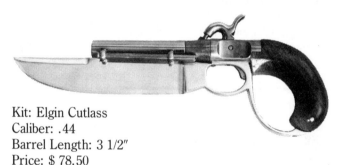

Kit: Elgin Cutlass
Caliber: .44
Barrel Length: 3 1/2″
Price: $ 78.50

Kit: Ethan Allen Pepperbox
Caliber: .36
Barrel Length: 3 1/8″
Price: $ 59.25

Kit: Duckfoot
Caliber: .36
Barrel Length: 2 7/8″
Price: $ 48.95

Kit: Snake Eyes
Caliber: .36
Barrel Length: 2 5/8″
Price: $ 54.00
This kit features a brass frame and barrel. All holes have been drilled and tapped, as required.

Kit: New Orleans Ace
Caliber: .44
Barrel Length: 3 1/2″
Price: $ 45.75
Only 1 to 3 hours average assembly time is advertised. Easy to assemble - only cosmetic finishing required.

Connecticut Valley Arms   Pistols

Kit: Mountain Pistol
Caliber: .45, .50
Barrel Length: 9″
Price: $ 115.95
Octagonal Barrel with 15/16″ flats and hooked breech for easy cleaning. Parts are ready to assemble and the stock is fully inletted. This gun uses the same lock and patented breech system as the Mountain rifle. The lockwork features an engraved design.

Kit: Colonial Pistol
Caliber: .45
Barrel Length: 6 3/4"
Price: $ 49.95
The Colonial Pistol features an engraved lockwork with a screw adjustable sear engagement. According to CVA's catalog this is one of their best sellers.

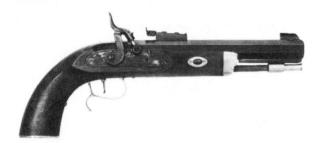

Kit: Hawken Pistol
Caliber: .50
Barrel Length: 9 3/4"
Price: $ 73.95
1" Flats on octagonal barrel. Hooked breech for easy take down.

Kit: Kentucky Pistol
Caliber: .45
Barrel Length: 10 1/4
Price: $ 62.95
Comes with engraved lock and brass front sight. Stocks are fully inletted. The metal parts require only final fitting and finishing.

Kit: Philadelphia Derringer
Caliber: .45
Barrel Length: 3 1/4"
Price: $ 41.95
Comes with color case-hardened and engraved lockwork with brass inlay and octagonal barrel.

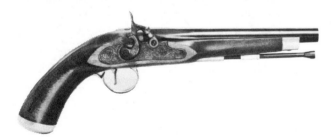

Kit: Tower Pistol
Caliber: .45
Barrel Length: 9"
Price: $ 73.95
Comes with engraved lock. Barrel is octagonal at breech, tapering to round at muzzle.

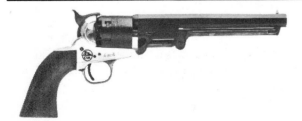

Kit: 1851 Colt Navy Revolver
Caliber: .36
Barrel Length: 7 1/2"
Price: $ 78.95
Comes with solid brass frame and octagonal barrel. The loading lever and hammer are color case-hardened.

Kit: 1858 Remington Army Revolver
Caliber: .44
Barrel Length: 8"
Price: $ 123.95
This kit features a color case-hardened hammer.

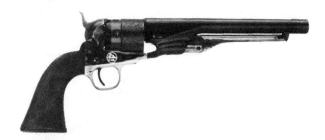

Kit: 1860 Colt Army Revolver
Caliber: .44
Barrel Length: 8"
Price: $ 121.95
Comes with brass trigger guard and color case-hardened
loading lever, hammer and frame.

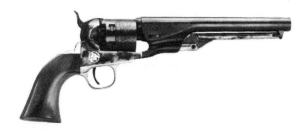

Kit: 1861 Colt Navy Revolver
Caliber: .36
Barrel Length: 7 1/2"
Price: $ 114.95
Available with either a brass or steel frame. The loading
lever and hammer are color case-hardened. The frame is
color case-hardened on the steel framed model only. Price
shown (KA621) is for the steel framed version.

Dixie Gun Works   Pistols

Kit: .44 Remington Revolver
Caliber: .44
Barrel Length: 6 1/2"
Price: $ 69.96

Kit: Brass Frame Derringer
Caliber: .41
Barrel Length: 2 1/2"
Price: $ 37.50

Kit: Dueling Pistol
Caliber: .40
Barrel Length: 9"
Price: $ 49.95

Kit: Jail Key Pistol
Caliber: up to .40
Barrel Length: 6 1/2"
Price: $ 12.95

Kit: Lincoln Derringer
Caliber: .41
Barrel Length: 2"
Price: $ 59.95

Kit: Model 1849 Baby Dragoon
Caliber: .31
Barrel Length: 5 1/2"
Price: $ 79.95

Kit: Model 1853 Colt Revolver
Caliber: .36
Barrel Length: 6"
Price: $ 79.95

Kit: Pennsylvania Pistol
Caliber: .44
Barrel Length: 10"
Price: $ 72.50

Kit: Spiller & Burr Revolver
Caliber: .36
Barrel Length: 6"
Price: $ 65.00

Kit: Steel Frame Derringer
Caliber: .40
Barrel Length: 3"
Price: $ 45.00

Kit: Tower Flintlock Pistol
Caliber: .65
Barrel Length: 9"
Price: $ 54.95

Kit: .36 Caliber Navy Revolver
Caliber: .36
Barrel Length: 6 3/4"
Price: $ 91.50

Kit: Model 1851 Navy Brass Frame Pistol
Caliber: .36
Barrel Length: 7 1/2"
Price: $ 72.50

FIRST EDITION

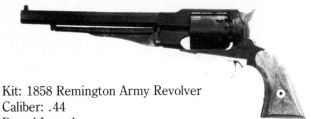

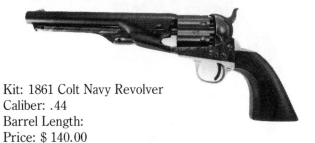

Kit: 1858 Remington Army Revolver
Caliber: .44
Barrel Length:
Price: $ 140.00

Kit: 1861 Colt Navy Revolver
Caliber: .44
Barrel Length:
Price: $ 140.00

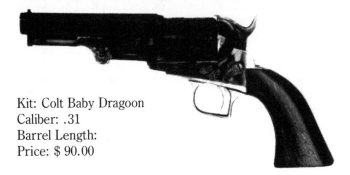

Kit: Colt 1851 Square Back Revolver
Caliber: .36
Barrel Length:
Price: $ 132.00

Kit: Colt Model 1862 Police
Caliber: .36
Barrel Length:
Price: $ 140.00

Kit: Colt Sheriff Revolver
Caliber: .36, .44
Barrel Length:
Price: $ 90.00

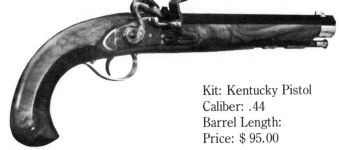

Kit: Colt Baby Dragoon
Caliber: .31
Barrel Length:
Price: $ 90.00

Kit: Colt Single Action Army
Caliber: .45
Barrel Length:
Price: $ 119.00

Kit: Harper's Ferry Pistol
Caliber: .48
Barrel Length:
Price: $ 150.00

Kit: Kentucky Pistol
Caliber: .44
Barrel Length:
Price: $ 95.00

Kit: Model 1851 Colt Navy Revolver
Caliber: .36, .44
Barrel Length:
Price: $ 90.00

Kit: Model 1860 Colt Army Revolver
Caliber: .44
Barrel Length:
Price: $ 140.00

Kit: Philadelphia Derringer
Caliber: .45
Barrel Length:
Price: $ 57.50

Kit: Walker Model 1847 Revolver
Caliber: .44
Barrel Length:
Price: $ 160.00

Kit: Rogers & Spencer Army Revolver
Caliber: .44
Barrel Length: 7 1/2"
Price: $ 125.00
Solid frame design with precision rifled barrel. Extra large nipple cut-out on rear of cylinder for ease of capping. Loading lever assembly and cylinder are easily removed for cleaning by half turn of retaining screw.

Kit: Army 1860 Revolver
Caliber: .44
Barrel Length: 8"
Price: $ 108.00
Traditional Colt 1860 Army Military design. 2-Screw model with frame cut for shoulder stock. Backstrap and trigger guard of polished yellow brass.

Kit: Navy 1851 Revolver
Caliber: .36
Barrel Length: 7 1/2"
Price: $ 70.00
Available in steel or brass & steel. Traditional Southern design with precision rifled barrel.

Kit: Remington New Model 1858 Revolver
Caliber: .44
Barrel Length: 8"
Price: $ 120.00
Solid frame design with precision rifled barrel

H.N. Company   **Pistols**

Kit: 1851 Colt Navy Revolver
Caliber: .36, .44
Barrel Length: 7 1/2"
Price: $ 39.95
Brass backstrap & trigger guard. Overall length - 13 1/4", weight - 44 oz.

Kit: 1851 Colt Navy Sheriff's Model
Caliber: .36
Barrel Length: 5"
Price: $ 34.95
Features a brass frame. This is a short-barreled version of the Colt 1851 Navy revolver. Overall length - 10 3/4", weight - 40 oz.

Kit: 1860 Colt Army
Caliber: .44
Barrel Length: 8"
Price: $ 49.95
Army 1860 Brass frame revolver with brass backstrap & trigger guard. Overall length - 13 3/4", weight 44 oz.

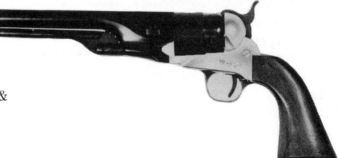

Kit: 1858 New Remington Army
Caliber: .44
Barrel Length: 8"
Price: $ 61.95
Remington New Army Revolver 1858 Steel frame, features a solid frame for increased accuraccy and reliability. Predecessor to the single action revolver. Brass backstrap & trigger guard. Overall length - 13 1/2", weight - 44 oz.

Kit: Kentucky Pistol
Caliber: .45
Barrel Length: 9 1/2"
Price: $ 43.95
Single shot pistol designed to match the Kentucky Rifle. Rifled octagonal barrel. Overall length - 15 1/2", weight - 40 oz.

Kit: Kentucky Pistol
Caliber: .45
Barrel Length: 10 1/2"
Price: $ 53.10
6 hours average assembly time. Conversion kit No. 706 ($39.95) contains flintlock, 3/8 x 16 stainless steel touch hole, flint & wrap and instructions for converting to flint lock operation.

Kit: Target Underhammer Boot Pistol
Caliber: .45
Barrel Length: 6 1/2"
Price: $ 55.20
4 hours average assembly time.

Lyman Products

Pistols

Kit: 1851 "Squareback" Navy .36
Caliber: .36
Barrel Length: 13"
Price: $ 119.95
This .36 caliber replica features a color casehardened steel frame, hammer and loading lever and steel cylinder engraved with the same Navy battle scene as found on the originals.

Kit: New Model Army .44
Caliber: .44
Barrel Length: 13 1/2"
Price: $ 134.95
Patterned after the popular 1858 New Model Army .44, this rugged replica features a steel frame, barrel, cylinder and loading lever. The trigger and hammer are color case hardened and the trigger guard is polished brass.

Kit: 1860 Army .44
Caliber: .44
Barrel Length: 13"
Price: $ 134.95
Features one-piece walnut grips, color casehardened frame, hammer and loading lever. The backstrap and trigger guard are nickel-plated brass.

Kit: The Plains Pistol Kit
Caliber: .50 and .54
Barrel Length: 15"
Price: $ 119.95
Companion to the "Great Plains Rifle". Produced in the original Hawken style, this pistol offers features found in custom-built costing hundreds of dollars more.

Navy Arms Company

Pistols

Kit: British Flint Dragoon Pistol
Caliber: .614
Barrel Length: N/A
Price: $ 295.00
100% Inletted stock. Only final fitting, polishing & finishing required.

Kit: Griswold & Gunnison Revolver
Caliber: .36, .44
Barrel Length: 7 1/2"
Price: $ 76.75
20 minutes average assembly time. All metal parts are completely milled and require only light buffing and polishing. Barrel, frame and cylinder are preassembled. Kit comes with brass frame.

Kit: Model 1851 Colt Navy Revolver
Caliber: .36, .44
Barrel Length: 7 1/2″
Price: $ 93.00
All internal parts are preassembled and timed. Only major components need to be assembled and cosmetic finishing done.

Kit: Model 1860 Colt Army Revolver
Caliber: .44
Barrel Length: 8″
Price: $ 93.00
All internal parts are preassembled and timed. Only major components need to be assembled and cosmetic finishing done.

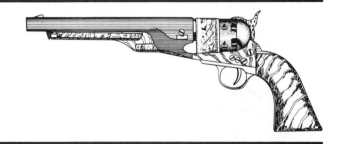

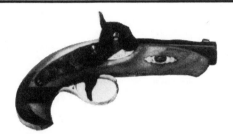

Kit: Philadelphia Derringer
Caliber: .45
Barrel Length: 3″
Price: $ 98.50
2 to 5 hour average assembly time. Stock is inletted but requires final fitting and cosmetic finishing.

Kit: Remington Style Revolver
Caliber: .36, .44
Barrel Length: 6″
Price: $ 106.00
All metal parts are completely milled and require only light buffing and polishing. The barrel is rifled and ready for finishing. Barrel, frame and cylinder come preassembled. All screws are furnished and all screw holes have been drilled and tapped.

Springs Import   Pistols

Kit: Corsair Pistol
Caliber: .44
Barrel Length: 8″
Price: $ 57.00
Pre-fitted and assembled.

Kit: Kentucky Pistol
Caliber: .45, .50
Barrel Length: 10″
Price: $ 45.00
Pre-fitted and assembled.

Springs Import Cont.

Kit: Model 1851 Colt Navy
Caliber: .36, .44
Barrel Length: 7 1/2″
Price: $ 39.00
Pre-fitted and assembled.

Kit: Model 1858 New Remington Army
Caliber: .44
Barrel Length: 8″
Price: $ 67.00
Pre-fitted and assembled.

Kit: Model 1860 Colt Army
Caliber: .44
Barrel Length: 8″
Price: $ 62.00
Pre-fitted and assembled. Available in steel or brass.

Kit: Spanish Patriot Pistol
Caliber: .45
Barrel Length: 10″
Price: $ 62.00
Pre-fitted and assembled.

Thompson/Center Arms   Pistols

Kit: Patriot Pistol
Caliber: .36, .45
Barrel Length: 9″
Price: $ 145.00

Kit: Santa Fe Hawken Rifle
Caliber: .54
Barrel Length: 32″
Price: $ 229.00
Double set trigger. Overall length - 50″, weight - 9.480 lbs.

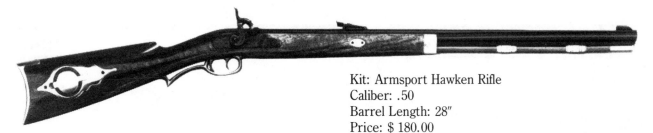

Kit: Armsport Hawken Rifle
Caliber: .50
Barrel Length: 28″
Price: $ 180.00
Chrome lined barrel. Parts are pre-fitted and pre-assembled.

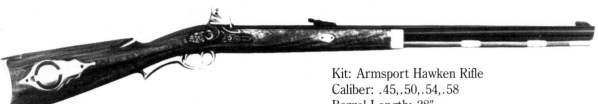

Kit: Armsport Hawken Rifle
Caliber: .45,.50,.54,.58
Barrel Length: 28″
Price: $ 170.00
Chrome lined barrel. Parts are pre-fitted and pre-assembled.

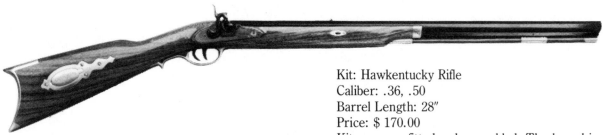

Kit: Hawkentucky Rifle
Caliber: .36, .50
Barrel Length: 28″
Price: $ 170.00
Kits are pre-fitted and assembled. The barrel is chrome lined.

Kit: Kentucky Rifle
Caliber: .45, .50
Barrel Length: 32″
Price: $ 165.00
Chrome lined barrel. All parts pre-fitted and pre-assembled.

Kit: Tryon Trailblazer Rifle
Caliber: .50, .54
Barrel Length: 28, 32"
Price: $ 275.00
Armsport advertises that this is the only mass-produced muzzle loading back-action lock hunting and target rifle. As usual, it comes with a chrome lined barrel and comes pre-fitted and pre-assembled.

Connecticut Valley Arms   Rifles

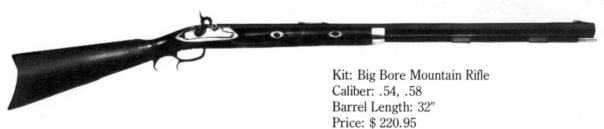

Kit: Big Bore Mountain Rifle
Caliber: .54, .58
Barrel Length: 32"
Price: $ 220.95
The stock is advertised as 95% inletted. The lockwork is engraved and features a screw adjustable sear engagement and an authentic v-type mainspring.

Kit: Frontier Rifle
Caliber: .45, .50
Barrel Length: 28"
Price: $ 157.95
The barrel is octagonal with 15/16" flats, hooked breech, 1 turn in 66" rifling and eight lands. The Frontier Rifle is compact and easy to shoulder comfortably.

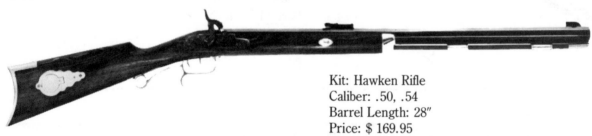

Kit: Hawken Rifle
Caliber: .50, .54
Barrel Length: 28"
Price: $ 169.95
Octagonal barrel has 1" flats, hooked breech for easy disassembly, 1 turn in 66" rifling and eight lands. This rifle can be assembled with a minimum of effort and with common workshop tools.

Kit: Kentucky Rifle
Caliber: .45
Barrel Length: 33 1/2″
Price: $ 117.95
Octagonal barrel, rifled 1 turn in 66″.

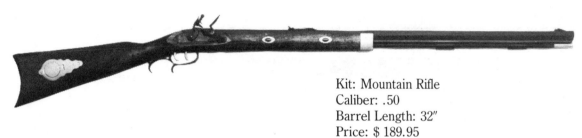

Kit: Mountain Rifle
Caliber: .50
Barrel Length: 32″
Price: $ 189.95
The Mountain Rifle features an engraved lock, double set triggers and german silver furniture. The stock is 95% inletted and ready for final fitting and finishing. The barrel is octagonal with 15/16″ flats and is rifled 1 turn in 66″.

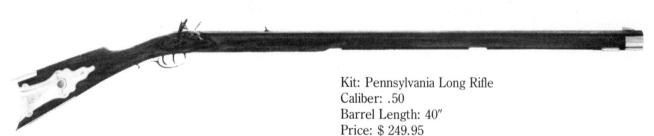

Kit: Pennsylvania Long Rifle
Caliber: .50
Barrel Length: 40″
Price: $ 249.95
The Pennsylvania Long Rifle features an engraved color case-hardened lock with screw adjustable sear engagement. The octagonal barrel is 7/8″ across the flats. The buttplate, toeplate and patchbox have already been inletted to assist the kit builder.

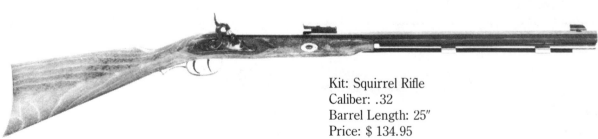

Kit: Squirrel Rifle
Caliber: .32
Barrel Length: 25″
Price: $ 134.95
The Squirrel Rifle features an octagonal barrel with 11/16″ flats and hooked breech. Rifled to one turn in 48″. A good starter gun.

Dixie Gun Works

Kit: 2nd Model Brown Bess Musket
Caliber: .75
Barrel Length: 41 3/4″
Price: $ 245.00

Kit: Hawken Rifle
Caliber: .45, .50, .54
Barrel Length: 29″
Price: $ 175.00

Kit: Pennsylvania Lancaster County Rifle
Caliber: .45
Barrel Length: 36″
Price: $ 139.95

Kit: Springfield Rifle
Caliber: .58
Barrel Length: 50″
Price: $ 225.00

EMF Company

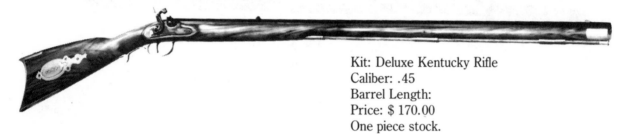

Kit: Deluxe Kentucky Rifle
Caliber: .45
Barrel Length:
Price: $ 170.00
One piece stock.

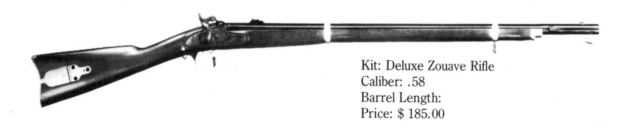

Kit: Deluxe Zouave Rifle
Caliber: .58
Barrel Length:
Price: $ 185.00

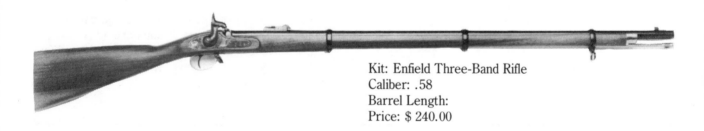

Kit: Enfield Three-Band Rifle
Caliber: .58
Barrel Length:
Price: $ 240.00

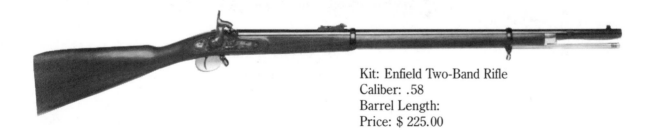

Kit: Enfield Two-Band Rifle
Caliber: .58
Barrel Length:
Price: $ 225.00

Kit: Enfield Musketoon
Caliber: .58
Barrel Length:
Price: $ 200.00

Kit: Deluxe Pennsylvania Rifle
Caliber: .45, .50
Barrel Length:
Price: $ 185.00

Kit: Minuteman Kentucky Rifle
Caliber: .45
Barrel Length:
Price: $ 120.00

Kit: Hawken Rifle
Caliber: .50
Barrel Length:
Price: $ 200.00

Euroarms of America   Rifles

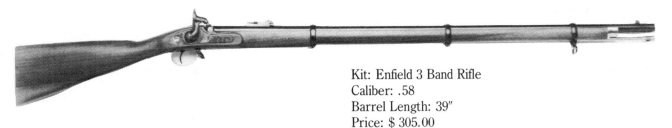

Kit: Enfield 3 Band Rifle
Caliber: .58
Barrel Length: 39″
Price: $ 305.00
Polished bright brass buttplate, trigger guard and nose-cap. Folding ladder rear sight can be adjusted to a maximum elevation of 900 yards to exploit the maximum potential of the Enfield's excellent long range accuracy.

Kit: Enfield 2 Band Rifle
Caliber: .58
Barrel Length: 33″
Price: $ 295.00
Buttplate and trigger guard are of solid cast and polished brass. Folding ladder rear sight that can be adjusted to a maximum elevation of 700 yards.

Kit: Enfield Musketoon
Caliber: .58
Barrel Length: 24″
Price: $ 255.00
Features removable breech plug. Buttplate and trigger guard are constructed of solid cast and polished brass. Folding ladder rear sight that can be adjusted to a maximum elevation of 700 yards.

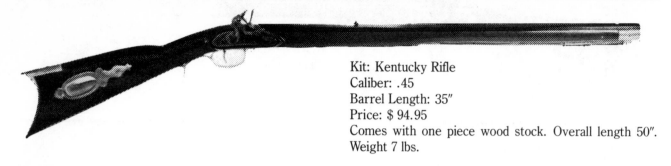

Kit: Kentucky Rifle
Caliber: .45
Barrel Length: 35″
Price: $ 94.95
Comes with one piece wood stock. Overall length 50″.
Weight 7 lbs.

Kit: Hawken Rifle
Caliber: .45, .50
Barrel Length: 29″
Price: $ 104.95
This rifle features adjustable rear sight, double set adjustable triggers, and a hooked breech. The one piece stock features a cheek piece and brass patch box. Overall length - 46″, weight - 9 lbs.

Hopkins & Allen

Rifles

Kit: Brush Rifle
Caliber: .36, .45
Barrel Length: 25″
Price: $ 99.50
8 hours average assembly time. Conversion kit No. 706 ($39.95) available to convert to flintlock operation.

Kit: Buggy Underhammer Rifle
Caliber: .36, .45
Barrel Length: 20, or 25″
Price: $ 131.80
6 hours average assembly time.

Kit: Deer Stalker Underhammer Rifle
Caliber: .58
Barrel Length: 28″
Price: $ 154.80
6 hours average assembly time.

Kit: Heritage Underhammer Rifle
Caliber: .36, .45, .50
Barrel Length: 32"
Price: $ 147.31
6 hours average assembly time.

Kit: Pennsylvania Hawken Rifle
Caliber: .50
Barrel Length: 29"
Price: $ 125.50
8 hours average assembly time. A conversion kit, # 706 ($39.95) is available to convert to flintlock operation.

Lyman Products   Rifles

Kit: The Great Plains Rifle Kit
Caliber: .50 and .54
Barrel Length: 50"
Price: $ 249.95
Replica of Great Plains rifles made by such builders as Hawken, Gemmer, and Demick to the specifications of experienced backwoodsmen. Companion to Great Plains pistol.

Kit: The Trade Rifle Kit
Caliber: .50 and .54
Barrel Length: 45"
Price: $ 199.95
Patterned after the sturdy rifles developed for the Indian and fur trade. Much sought after by trappers, Indians and other back woodsmen, these rifles provided basic hunting tools without expensive frills.

Mowrey Gun Works   Rifles

Kit: Mowrey Squirrel Rifle
Caliber: .32
Barrel Length: 28"
Price: $ 237.00
Rifled barrel with 1:60 twist.

Kit: Rocky Mountain Hunter
Caliber: .50, .54
Barrel Length: 28"
Price: $ 237.00
Rifled barrel with 1:60 twist.

Navy Arms Company   Rifles

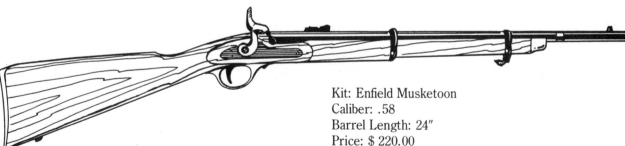

Kit: Enfield Musketoon
Caliber: .58
Barrel Length: 24"
Price: $ 220.00
Stock is 100% inletted. The barrel requires polishing and bluing.

Kit: Mark I Hawken Rifle
Caliber: .50, .54
Barrel Length: 26″
Price: $ 175.95
Manufactured in the U.S. Features cheek rest and double set triggers. Stock is inletted for lock and barrel. Requires only minimum of fitting and relieving to complete. Comes complete with assembly booklet.

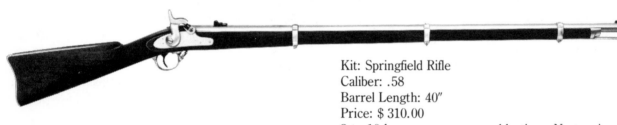

Kit: Morse Rifle
Caliber: .50,
Barrel Length: 26″
Price: $ 105.00
All parts are machined and ready for final assembly and finishing. Manufactured in the U.S.

Kit: Springfield Rifle
Caliber: .58
Barrel Length: 40″
Price: $ 310.00
3 to 10 hour average assembly time. No tapping is required. Stock is 90% inletted.

Kit: Brown Bess Musket
Caliber: .75
Barrel Length: 42″
Price: $ 342.00
3 to 10 hours average assembly time. This kit is assembled and the stock is 100% inletted. The stock requires sanding and staining.

Kit: Charleville Musket
Caliber: .69
Barrel Length: 44 5/8″
Price: $ 310.00
3 to 10 hours average assembly time. This kit requires some inletting or the stock and the metal parts require polishing.

Kit: Ithaca / Navy Hawken Rifle
Caliber: .50, .54
Barrel Length: 32″
Price: $ 320.00
Stock is inletted for lock and barrel. Requires minimum of fitting and relieving to complete. Manufactured entirely in the U.S.

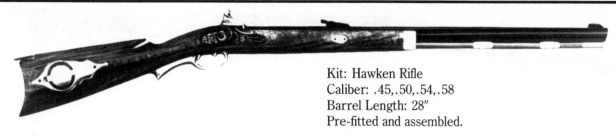

Kit: Hawken Rifle
Caliber: .45, .50, .54, .58
Barrel Length: 28″
Pre-fitted and assembled.

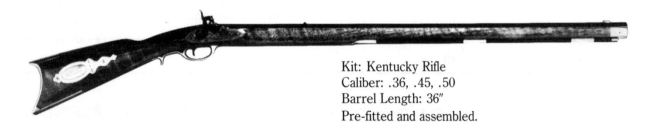

Kit: Kentucky Rifle
Caliber: .36, .45, .50
Barrel Length: 36″
Pre-fitted and assembled.

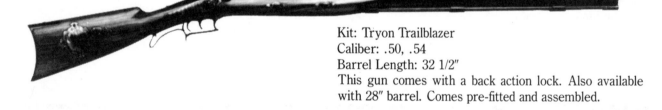

Kit: Special Kentucky Rifle
Caliber: .45
Barrel Length: 32″
Pre-fitted and assembled.

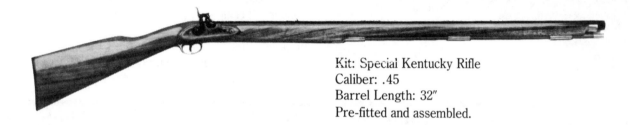

Kit: Tryon Trailblazer
Caliber: .50, .54
Barrel Length: 32 1/2″
This gun comes with a back action lock. Also available
with 28″ barrel. Comes pre-fitted and assembled.

Thompson/Center Arms   Rifles

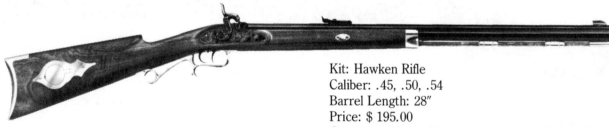

Kit: Hawken Rifle
Caliber: .45, .50, .54
Barrel Length: 28″
Price: $ 195.00
Comes complete with an excellent assembly booklet. Stock
is advertised as 100% inletted. Features a color case hard-
ened coil spring type lockwork and fully adjustable hunting
style sights.

Thompson/Center Arms Cont.

Kit: Renegade Rifle
Caliber: .50, .54, .56
Barrel Length: 26″
Price: $ 175.00
Available as a smoothbore musket for hunters in No Rifle states. Superb accuracy - beat all comers, including the T/C Hawken, in a target match. 100% American made using the finest materials available.

Connecticut Valley Arms   Shotguns

Kit: Double Barrel Shotgun
Caliber: 12 Gauge
Barrel Length: 28″
Price: $ 219.95
Comes with polished and engraved lock, trigger guard and tang. The stocks are 95% inletted but not checkered.

Dixie Gun Works   Shotguns

Kit: Double Barrel Shotgun
Caliber: 10 ga., 12 ga.
Barrel Length: see below
Price: $ 275.00
Comes in different barrel lengths: 12 ga.- 28″, 12 ga. mag.- 29″, 10 ga. & 10 ga. mag.- 30″. All barrels are modified or cylinder bore.

EMF Company   Shotguns

Kit: Deluxe Double Barrel Shotgun
Caliber: 12 gauge
Barrel Length:
Price: $ 265.00

Navy Arms Company   Shotguns

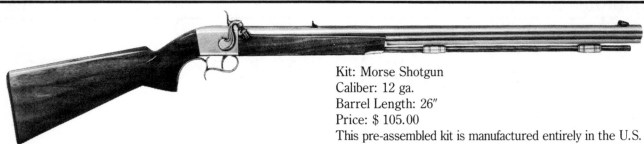

Kit: Morse Shotgun
Caliber: 12 ga.
Barrel Length: 26″
Price: $ 105.00
This pre-assembled kit is manufactured entirely in the U.S. Barrel requires draw filing and polishing. Stock requires sanding and staining. Stock is 90% inletted.

Kit: Classic Side by Side Shotgun
Caliber: 10 ga., 12 ga.
Barrel Length: 28″
Price: $ 265.00

2 to 10 hour average assembly time. This kit is 100% inletted. Wood requires sanding and staining. Barrel requires browning or bluing.

Modern and Exotic Kits

AR-15/M-16 — Full-Auto Conversion Kits

Kit: AR-15 Auto-Sear Base
Manufacturer: The Postal Armorer
Price: $29.88
Obvious attempt to avoid ATF restriction of auto-sears. You build it, you register it.

Kit: AR-15 Auto-Sear Trip
Manufacturer: Sgt. Sandy's Parts & Surplus
Price: $19.00
See The Postal Armorer for the other piece of this kit.

Kit: AR-15 To M-16 Kit
Manufacturer: Catawba Enterprises
Price: $35.00
Kit includes hammer, trigger, disconnector and safety-selector.

Kit: M-16 Auto-Sear
Manufacturer: Sparkey's Gun Tune
Price: $ 14.95
M-16 type auto-sear. Will fit into M-16 and properly modified AR-15 receivers.

Kit: AR-15 Lower Receiver Conversion
Manufacturer: J. Miniard
Price: $30.00
M-16 type auto-sear plus installation instructions.

Kit: M-16 Bolt Carrier Conversion
Manufacturer: Quality Parts Company
Price: $27.95
Converts AR-15 bolt carrier to M-16 carrier.

HK-91/HK-93 — Full-Auto Conversion Kits

Kit: HK-91/93 Auto-Conversion Kit
Manufacturer: AG Supply
Price: $100.00
All parts are ready to install.

Kit: HK-91/HK-93 Conversion Kit
Manufacturer: Lynn & Betty Fletcher
Price: $125.00

MAC 10 — Full-Auto Conversion Kits

Kit: Select-A-Sear
Manufacturer: C&C TUBING
Price: $25.00
Needs no modification to frame or upper receiver of gun.

Ruger Mini-14   Ruger 10/22 — Full-Auto Conversion Kits

Kit: Ruger 10/22 Selective Fire Conversion
Manufacturer: FKF
Price: $48.00
1000 Rounds per minute conversion.

Kit: Full Auto Conversion
Manufacturer: RGS
Price: $149.00
Requires substantial modifications to gun. Also requires some welding.

UZI — Full-Auto Conversion Kits

Kit: UZI Auto-Conversion
Manufacturer: 3-Way
Price: $29.95
No machining - easily installed.

Kit: The Kicker
Manufacturer: ARM-TEC
Price: $31.95

Kit: .22 Caliber Conversion
Manufacturer: Bro-Caliber International
Price: $127.00
Atchisson System

Kit: AK-74 type Muzzle Brake
Manufacturer: Alpha Armament Ltd.
Price: $36.95

Kit: Illuminated Front Sight
Manufacturer: Light Enterprises
Price: $ 17.95

Kit: 11 1/2" Barrel with Long Flash Hider
Manufacturer: Sparkey's Gun Tune
Price: $74.95
Legal to install on all AR-15/M-16s

Kit: 11 1/4" Barrel with Birdcage Flash Hider
Manufacturer: Sparkey's Gun Tune
Price: $ 74.95
Require's prior ATF approval

Kit: 16 1/4" Barrel with Birdcage Flash Hider
Manufacturer: Sparkey's Gun Tune
Price: $74.95
Legal to install on all AR-15/M-16s

Kit: AR-15/M-16 Heavy Match Barrel
Manufacturer: Texas Armament Company
Price: $82.50
20" Length and 1 in 9 twist.

Kit: AR-15/M-16 Heavy Match Barrel
Manufacturer: Texas Armament Company
Price: $92.50
24" Length and 1 in 9 twist.

Kit: AR-15/M-16 Match Barrel
Manufacturer: Quality Parts Company
Price: $99.95
24" Length.

Kit: AR-15/M-16 Match Barrel
Manufacturer: Quality Parts Company
Price: $89.95
20" Length.

Kit: AR-15/M-16 Standard Barrel
Manufacturer: Quality Parts Company
Price: $74.95
20" Length.

Kit: CAR-15 Shorty Barrel Kit
Manufacturer: Quality Parts Company
Price: $ 89.95
Complete and ready to install.

Kit: CAR-15 Shorty Heavy Barrel Kit
Manufacturer: Quality Parts Company
Price: $ 99.95
Complete and ready to install.

Kit: National Match Heavy Barrel
Manufacturer: Small Arms Weaponry
Price: $ 84.95
Length: 20"; 1-in-9 twist.

Kit: National Match Heavy Barrel
Manufacturer: Small Arms Weaponry
Price: $ 94.95
Length: 24"; heavy barrel with 1-in-9 twist.

Kit: Shorty CAR Kit - Front Group
Manufacturer: NESARD
Price: $ 75.00

Kit: Standard Weight Barrel
Manufacturer: Small Arms Weaponry
Price: $ 60.95
Length: 20" — standard barrel.

Kit: XM Barrel
Manufacturer: Small Arms Weaponry
Price: $ 84.95
Ready to install.

Kit: XM Heavy Barrel
Manufacturer: Small Arms Weaponry
Price: $ 94.95
Ready to install on upper receiver.

Kit: XM(CAR)-15 Barrel Unit
Manufacturer: Texas Armament Company
Price: $ 84.95
Ready to install on upper receiver.

Kit: XM-177 10" Barrel Assembly
Manufacturer: Frankford Arsenal
Price: $ 149.95
Includes heat shields/liners, gas tube & sling guard.

Kit: XM-177 16″ Barrel Assembly
Manufacturer: Frankford Arsenal
Price: $ 99.95
11-1/2″ Barrel with permanently attached flash hider.

M1911 Barrels

Kit: Colt National Match Barrel
Manufacturer: Texas Armament Company
Price: $ 47.50
MK-IV Series 70 with bushing, barrel link & barrel link pin.

Kit: Threaded Barrel
Manufacturer: Military Accessories Company
Price: $ 67.50
Complete with pre-fitted bushing and integral muzzle threads.

MAC 10/MAC 11 Barrels

Kit: MAC 10/MAC 11 Barrel
Manufacturer: Catawba Enterprises
Price: $ 38.30

UZI Barrels

Kit: 10-1/4″ SMG Type UZI Barrel
Manufacturer: Small Arms Weaponry
Price: $ 54.95
Threaded for silencer adapter.

Kit: 16″ UZI Barrel
Manufacturer: Small Arms Weaponry
Price: $ 56.95

Kit: 10-1/4″ SMG Type UZI Barrel
Manufacturer: Small Arms Weaponry
Price: $ 48.95
Requires prior ATF approval

Kit: UZI Barrel
Manufacturer: Texas Armament Company
Price: $ 42.50
Length: 10-1/4″

Kit: UZI Barrel
Manufacturer: SCHERER
Price: $ 30.00
Plain barrel. Lengths: 10-1/4″ & 16-1/4″

Kit: UZI Barrel
Manufacturer: Texas Armament Company
Price: $ 47.50
Length: 16-1/4″

Kit: UZI Barrel
Manufacturer: SCHERER
Price: $ 30.00
Barrel threaded for 9mm MAC silencer. Lengths: 9-1/4″ & 16-1/4″

Kit: UZI Short Barrel
Manufacturer: RGS
Price: $ 39.95
Barrel Length: 10″.

AR-15/M-16 Bolts

Kit: Bolt Carrier
Manufacturer: Quality Parts Company
Price: $ 79.95
Comes with forward assist notches; new chrome-lined Colt part; bolt carrier key installed.

Kit: M-16A1 Bolt Carrier
Manufacturer: NESARD
Price: $ 59.00
Forward-assist type bolt carrier

Kit: M-16 Bolt Carrier
Manufacturer: Small Arms Weaponry
Price: $ 62.00
Stainless steel bolt carrier.

Kit: M-16 Bolt Carrier
Manufacturer: Small Arms Weaponry
Price: $ 55.00
Chrome plated bolt carrier.

Kit: M-16 Bolt Carrier
Manufacturer: Small Arms Weaponry
Price: $ 47.00

UZI   # Bolts

Kit: UZI Open Bolt (SMG)
Manufacturer: Quality Parts Company
Price: $ 89.95
Open bolt for Semi Auto.

Kit: Full-Auto Bolt
Manufacturer: Group Industries
Price: $ 59.95

Kit: UZI Replacement SMG Bolt
Manufacturer: RGS
Price: $ 79.95

AR-15/M-16   # Conversions - Miscellaneous

Kit: Belt-Feed Conversion
Manufacturer: Jonathan Arthur Ciener
Price: $ 475.00
Commercialization of a Colt SAWS design.

Kit: Gas/Mechanical Conversion
Manufacturer: Rhino International
Price: $ 180.00
Converts AR15/M16 direct gas action to gas/mechanical action.

Kit: 3-Round Burst Conversion
Manufacturer: SWD
Price: $ 99.00

Kit: AR-15 Bolt Carrier Conversion
Manufacturer: Sgt. Sandy's Parts & Surplus
Price: $ 21.97
Installs directly onto your AR-15 bolt carrier.

Complete Weapons Kits

Kit: .45 Automatic Builder's Kit
Manufacturer: SARCO
Price: $ 165.96
Everything you need except the receiver.

Kit: AR-15 Rifle Kit
Manufacturer: SARCO
Price: $ 295.96
Contains all the parts necessary to assemble an AR-15, except the lower receiver.

Kit: AR-15 Rifle Kit
Manufacturer: Quality Parts Company
Price: $ 469.95
FFL required. Available with 20″ heavy or standard barrel and 24″ heavy barrel. Kit includes sling, GI tech manual and 30 round magazine.

Kit: British STEN Submachinegun Kit
Manufacturer: SARCO
Price: $ 134.96
Contains everything you need except the receiver.

Kit: Browning 1917 Water-Cooled Machinegun
Manufacturer: SARCO
Price: $ 995.00
The side plates to this kit are missing and the water jacket has been cut in half.

Kit: Browning 1919-A4 Air-Cooled Machinegun
Manufacturer: SARCO
Price: $ 895.00.
30 Caliber machinegun; The side plates are missing and the top plate must be rebuilt. M2 tripod available.

Kit: Browning 1919-A6 Air-Cooled Machinegun
Manufacturer: SARCO
Price: $ 995.00.
30 Caliber machinegun; The side plates are missing and the top plate must be rebuilt. M2 tripod available.

Kit: Browning M-2 .50 Caliber Machinegun Kit
Manufacturer: SARCO
Price: $1465.00
The ultimate machine gun kit. Several receiver components require repair. SARCO will provide photos to interested parties. Also available in the aircraft configuration for $1245.00.

Kit: Browning M-37 Machinegun Kit
Manufacturer: SARCO
Price: $ 995.00
Side plates must be rebuilt, however the de-milled pieces are provided. Very similiar to 1919-A4.

Kit: M-1 Carbine Kit
Manufacturer: SARCO
Price: $ 79.96
All time favorite military weapon for most collectors and shooters. Kit includes all the parts necessary to build the M-1 Carbine except the receiver.

Kit: M-1 Garand MID Sniper Rifle Kit
Manufacturer: SARCO
Price: $ 625.96
Includes all the parts necessary to assemble an M-1 MID sniper rifle except the receiver and operating rod.

Kit: M-1 Garand Rifle Kit
Manufacturer: SARCO
Price: $ 175.96
Includes all the parts necessary to assemble the M-1 Garand except the receiver and operating rod.

Kit: M-3 Grease Gun Kit
Manufacturer: SARCO
Price: $ 175.00
M-3A1 also available for the same price as M-3. All original GI parts, no reproduction parts.

Kit: MAC 10/MAC 11 Parts Kit
Manufacturer: Catawba Enterprises
Price: $ 279.00
All the necessary parts except the receiver. Available in .45ACP, 9mm, and .380 ACP.

Kit: Model 2A-K Pengun Kit
Manufacturer: Covert Arms Manufacturing
Price: $ 57.35
Complete except outer tube. Comes with simple assembly instructions.

Kit: Springfield '03 Rifle Kit
Manufacturer: SARCO
Price: $ 69.96
The classic American bolt action military rifle. Kit contains all the parts necessary to assemble rifle except the receiver. Also available in the '03A3 configuration for an extra $10.

Kit: M-9 9mm Conversion Kit
Manufacturer: Frankford Arsenal
Price: $ 349.95
Adapts to all AR-15, M-16 or XM-177 type weapons. Easy assembly and disassembly allows caliber changes within a matter of seconds.

Kit: STEN Mk-II Kit
Manufacturer: York Arms Company
Price: $ 295.00
Authentic STEN Mk-II. Kit builder must restore de-milled receiver with tube supplied with kit. Requires some welding.

Kit: Thompson 1928-A1
Manufacturer: SARCO
Price: $ 238.96
Early style Thompson with detachable buttstock. Contains all the parts except the receiver and trigger frame.

Kit: Thompson M1-A1 Submachinegun Kit
Manufacturer: SARCO
Price: $ 154.96
The last version of the Thompson developed for mass production in WWII. Contains all the parts except the receiver and trigger frame.

Kit: XM-15 Shorty Kit
Manufacturer: Quality Parts Company
Price: $ 430.00
FFL required. Also available with heavy match barrel. Kit includes sling, GI tech manual and 30 round magazine.

Kit: .45 ACP Auto Parts Kit
Manufacturer: Dare Gun Room
Price: $ 189.95
All .45 Auto parts except frame.

Kit: AR/CAR-15 Rifle Kit
Manufacturer: SGW
Price: $ 375.00
Includes all parts necessary to build an AR-15 or CAR-15 rifle except for the lower receiver. Options available include 20″ or 24″ barrels, stainless steel barrels and choice of round or teardrop forward assist.

AR-15/M-16   Parts Kits

Kit: Complete Lower Receiver Parts
Manufacturer: NESARD
Price: $ 39.00
Includes all parts except receiver.

Kit: Lower Parts Kit
Manufacturer: Sparkey's Gun Tune
Price: $ 49.95

Kit: Lower Receiver Parts Set
Manufacturer: Small Arms Weaponry
Price: $ 39.00

Kit: M-16 Lower Receiver Parts Kit
Manufacturer: Quality Parts Company
Price: $ 36.95
Complete lower receiver parts kit except receiver.

Kit: M-16/AR-15 Lower Receiver Parts Kit
Manufacturer: Lone Star Ordnance
Price: $ 52.50
Complete parts set except receiver and pistol grip.

UZI   Parts Kits

Kit: Spring Kit
Manufacturer: Group Industries
Price: $ 14.95
Replacement springs for the semi-auto UZI.

Kit: .45 ACP Auto Frame & Slide Kit
Manufacturer: Dare Gun Room
Price: $ 139.95
All parts for the .45 except the frame and slide.

Kit: .45 ACP Auto Frame Parts Kit
Manufacturer: Dare Gun Room
Price: $ 85.95
All the frame parts except the frame itself.

Kit: .45 ACP Auto Slide Parts Kit
Manufacturer: Dare Gun Room
Price: $ 59.95
All the slide parts except the slide itself.

Kit: .45 ACP Frame Parts Kit
Manufacturer: Federal Ordnance
Price: $ 114.90
All parts except frame, ejector, grip bushings, & plunger tube.

Kit: .45 ACP Slide Parts Kit
Manufacturer: Federal Ordnance
Price: $ 54.90
Includes all parts except slide and sights.

Kit: .45 Auto Parts Kit
Manufacturer: Texas Armament Company
Price: $ 172.50
All .45 parts except frame. All parts are in new condition.

Kit: .45 Auto Spring Kit
Manufacturer: Dare Gun Room
Price: $ 2.45
All of the springs for the .45 auto.

M-1 Garand

Receivers

Kit: M-1 Garand Receiver
Manufacturer: Springfield Armory
Price: $ 215.00

M1911

Receivers

Kit: .45 Auto Frame
Manufacturer: J&G Sales
Price: $ 64.95
Blued steel.

Kit: .45 Auto Frame
Manufacturer: SARCO
Price: $ 49.50
Blued steel version.

Kit: .45 Auto Receiver
Manufacturer: Essex Arms Corporation
Price: $ 50.00
Investment cast in 4140 chrome-moly steel with stock screw bushings installed. Ejector and plunger tube installed for a nominal extra charge.

Kit: .45 Auto Receiver
Manufacturer: Essex Arms Corporation
Price: $ 60.00
Stainless steel investment casting with stock bushings installed. Ejector and plunger tube installed for a nominal extra cost.

Kit: .45 ACP Auto Steel Frame
Manufacturer: Texas Armament Company
Price: $ 57.50
Blued steel finish.

Kit: .45 ACP Frame
Manufacturer: Crown City Arms
Price: $ 64.95
Stainless steel model.

Kit: .45 ACP Frame
Manufacturer: Crown City Arms
Price: $ 57.50
Blued steel model.

Kit: .45 Auto Essex Arms Receiver
Manufacturer: Small Arms Weaponry
Price: $ 60.00
Investment cast frame with stock screw bushings installed. Available in either blued steel or stainless. Price shown is for blued steel version.

Kit: AMT Stainless .45 Frame
Manufacturer: J&G Sales
Price: $ 69.95
Stainless steel. Comes with grip bushings, ejector and plunger tube installed.

Kit: Light-Weight .45 ACP Frame
Manufacturer: Federal Ordnance
Price: $ 29.90
Made from 380 aluminum; 8 oz. lighter than standard frame.

Kit: Essex Arms .45 ACP Frame
Manufacturer: Ashland Shooting Supplies
Price: $ 49.25
Blued steel model.

Kit: Essex Arms .45 ACP Frame
Manufacturer: Ashland Shooting Supplies
Price: $ 56.00
Stainless steel model.

MAC 10/MAC 11   Receivers

Kit: MAC 10 Flat
Manufacturer: Catawba Enterprises
Price: $ 19.95

Kit: MAC 10 Lower Receiver Blanks
Manufacturer: Mike's Shooting Supplies
Price: $ 24.95

Kit: MAC 10 Frame
Manufacturer: H.Hsu
Price: $ 45.00
Cold-rolled, welded steel channel. Semi-finished, with plans.

Kit: MAC 10 Frame Blank
Manufacturer: Hard Times Armory
Price: $ 20.00

Kit: MAC 11 Frame Blanks
Manufacturer: Hard Times Armory
Price: $ 30.00

Kit: SM-10/SM-11 Frame Flat
Manufacturer: SWD
Price: $ 5.95

Kit: MAC 11 Flat
Manufacturer: Catawba Enterprises
Price: $ 29.95

Kit: MAC 10/MAC 11 Receiver Blank
Manufacturer: R&D Services
Price: $ 65.00
12 gauge steel with punched holes and finishing instructions.

STEN   Receivers

Kit: STEN Mk-II Receiver Blank
Manufacturer: CATCO
Price: $ 80.00
All ports & slots outlined on receiver tube with a paper overlay. Barrel nut, ejector & blueprints supplied with kit.

AR-15/M-16   Lower Receivers

Kit: AR-15 Lower Receiver
Manufacturer: Sparkey's Gun Tune
Price: $ 89.95
Machined.

Kit: AR-15/M-16 Lower Receiver
Manufacturer: L.L. Baston Company
Price: $ 87.50
Essential Arms Co. manufacture. Accepts Colt parts.

Kit: AR-15/M-16 Lower Receiver
Manufacturer: Quality Parts Company
Price: $ 123.95
Complete receiver assembled with AR-15 or M-16 parts.

Kit: SGW XM-15 Lower Receiver
Manufacturer: Small Arms Weaponry
Price: $ 79.00
Semi-auto lower receiver. Manufactured by SGW.

Kit: XM-15 Lower Receiver
Manufacturer: Quality Parts Company
Price: $ 87.00
No offset pin required.

Kit: XM-15 Lower Receiver
Manufacturer: SARCO
Price: $ 72.50
Raised rib to shield mag catch button.

Kit: XM-15 Lower Receiver
Manufacturer: Springfield Armory
Price: $ 49.00

Kit: XM-15A1 Semi-Auto Lower Receiver
Manufacturer: Texas Armament Company
Price: $ 74.50
This model accepts all AR-15/M-16 parts.

AR-15/M-16 Lower Receivers Cont.

Kit: Model 15 Lower Receiver
Manufacturer: DP LTD.
Price: $ 99.50
NuArmCo stainless steel receiver has optional black oxide finish.

Kit: XM-177E2 Lower Receiver
Manufacturer: Frankford Arsenal
Price: $ 82.00
For carbine. Also available machined to Class 3 specifications.

Kit: XM-16 Lower Receiver
Manufacturer: Frankford Arsenal
Price: $ 82.00
For rifle; standard, or heavy barrel. Also available machined to Class 3 specifications.

Kit: M-15A1 Lower Receiver
Manufacturer: SENDRA CORP.
Price: $ 65.00

AR-15/M-16   Upper Receivers

Kit: AR-15 Upper Receiver
Manufacturer: MAC
Price: $ 130.00
Upper receiver with custom installed Buehler sight base.

Kit: Colt M-16 Upper Receiver
Manufacturer: Small Arms Weaponry
Price: $ 65.00

Kit: Colt Top Receiver - Forward Assist Model
Manufacturer: Euclid Sales Company
Price: $ 89.95
Receiver has forward assist.

Kit: M-16A1 Upper Receiver
Manufacturer: NESARD
Price: $ 59.00

Kit: M-16A1 Upper Receiver
Manufacturer: Sparkey's Gun Tune
Price: $ 64.95
Drop forged.

Kit: Upper Receiver (old style)
Manufacturer: Texas Armament Company
Price: $ 49.50
Old style upper receiver.

Kit: M-16/XM-15 Upper Receiver
Manufacturer: Springfield Armory
Price: $ 57.00
With forward assist.

Kit: Upper Receiver
Manufacturer: Crown City Arms
Price: $ 54.50

Kit: Upper Receiver
Manufacturer: Quality Parts Company
Price: $ 72.95
Forward assist model.

Kit: Upper Receiver
Manufacturer: SGW
Price: $ 59.00

Kit: Upper Receiver (New Style)
Manufacturer: Texas Armament Company
Price: $ 67.50
New style upper receiver.

.22 Caliber   Silencer Kits

Kit: .22 Silencer Parts Pack
Manufacturer: CIONEC
Price: $ 95.00
Pack includes 14 page book, spare parts, schematic & instructions.

Kit: .22 Suppressor Kit
Manufacturer: SIONAC
Price: $ 95.00
25 Page manual included.

Kit: Silencer Outer Tube
Manufacturer: Sub-Sonic Engineering
Price: $ 30.00
Outer tube made from sound absorbing nylon. For .22 caliber.

Kit: MAXIM Silencer Rebuild Kit
Manufacturer: DAQ
Price: $ 50.00
For .22 caliber, with 17 baffles, front cap & rear bushing.

.380, 9mm, .45 cal Silencer Kits

Kit: Silencer Outer Tube
Manufacturer: Sub-Sonic Engineering
Price: $ 35.00
Outer tube made from sound absorbing nylon. For .380,
9mm, .45 calibers.

AR-7 Silencer Kits

Kit: AR-7 .22 Suppressor Kit
Manufacturer: RFP
Price: $ 100.00

Kit: Sionics Type Suppressor Parts
Manufacturer: Don Floyd
Price: $ 90.00

Kit: AR-7 Suppressor
Manufacturer: S & H Arms
Price: $ 90.00
Comes with installation instructions and 2 extra end wipes.

AR-15/M-16 Silencer Kits

Kit: AR-15/M-16 Suppressor
Manufacturer: S & H ARMS
Price: $ 110.00
Comes with installation instructions and 2 extra end wipes.

Kit: AR-15/M-16 Suppressor
Manufacturer: Frankford Arsenal
Price: $ 189.95
Standard thread — 1/2″ X 28″.

Kit: Sionics Type Suppressor Parts
Manufacturer: Don Floyd
Price: $ 150.00

HK-91 Silencer Kits

Kit: Sionics Type Suppressor Parts
Manufacturer: Don Floyd
Price: $ 150.00

HK-93 Silencer Kits

Kit: Sionics Type Suppressor Parts
Manufacturer: Don Floyd
Price: $ 150.00

MAC 10 Silencer Kits

Kit: MAC 10 Suppressor Kit
Manufacturer: RFP
Price: $ 100.00

MAC 10/MAC 11 Silencer Kits

Kit: .380, .45 & 9mm Suppressor Kit
Manufacturer: SIONAC
Price: $ 175.00
Comes with 25 page manual.

Kit: MAC 10/MAC 11 Suppressor
Manufacturer: S & H ARMS
Price: $ 90.00
Comes with instructions and 2 extra end wipes.

Kit: MAC 10/MAC 11 Sionic type Suppressor
Manufacturer: Frankford Arsenal
Price: $ 169.95
Complete.

Kit: RPB MAC Suppressor
Manufacturer: Big John's Weapons
Price: $ 180.00

Kit: Sionic type Suppressor Parts
Manufacturer: Don Floyd
Price: $ 90.00

Kit: Suppressor Parts Kit
Manufacturer: Silence is Golden
Price: $ 49.95
Includes all parts except outer tube.

MAC 11 Silencer Kits

Kit: MAC 11 Suppressor Kit
Manufacturer: RFP
Price: $ 100.00

Ruger 10/22 Silencer Kits

Kit: Ruger 10/22 Suppressor
Manufacturer: S & W ARMS
Price: $ 110.00
Comes with installation instructions and 2 extra end wipes.

Kit: Ruger 10/22 .22 Silencer Kit
Manufacturer: RFP
Price: $ 100.00

Ruger Mini-14 Silencer Kits

Kit: Ruger Mini-14 Suppressor
Manufacturer: S & H ARMS
Price: $ 110.00
Comes with installation instructions and 2 extra end wipes.

UZI Silencer Kits

Kit: Suppressor Parts Kit
Manufacturer: Silence is Golden
Price: $ 49.95
Includes all parts except outer tube.

Kit: UZI Suppressor Kit
Manufacturer: RFP
Price: $ 150.00
Slides over barrel and replaces barrel nut.

M1911 Slides

Kit: .45 ACP Slide
Manufacturer: Crown City Arms
Price: $ 78.95
Features a barrel rib and is ported.

Kit: .45 ACP Slide
Manufacturer: Crown City Arms
Price: $ 87.95
Stainless steel. With barrel rib and ported.

Kit: .45 Auto Ribbed Slide
Manufacturer: Essex Arms Corporation
Price: $ 66.00
Rib with or without 5 serrations. With or without GI sight cuts.

Kit: .45 Auto Slide
Manufacturer: Essex Arms Corporation
Price: $ 58.00
Investment castings.

Kit: .45 Auto Slide
Manufacturer: Essex Arms Corporation
Price: $ 65.00
Investment casting.

Kit: GM Steel .45 ACP Slide
Manufacturer: Crown City Arms
Price: $ 64.95

Kit: Ribbed .45 Auto Slide
Manufacturer: Small Arms Weaponry
Price: $ 75.00
Investment casting.

Kit: Ribbed .45 Auto Slide
Manufacturer: Small Arms Weaponry
Price: $ 85.00
Investment casting.

Kit: Short .45 ACP Slide
Manufacturer: Crown City Arms
Price: $ 68.95

Kit: .45 Auto Ribbed Slide
Manufacturer: Essex Arms Corporation
Price: $ 75.00
Rib comes with or without serrations or GI sight cuts.

Kit: Short .45 ACP Slide
Manufacturer: Crown City Arms
Price: $ 89.95
Stainless, short, ribbed and ported.

Kit: Short .45 ACP Slide
Manufacturer: Crown City Arms
Price: $ 78.95
Short, ribbed and ported.

Kit: Short Stainless .45 ACP Slide
Manufacturer: Crown City Arms
Price: $ 76.95

Kit: Stainless GM .45 ACP Slide
Manufacturer: Crown City Arms
Price: $ 76.95

Kit: Standard GI Slide
Manufacturer: Small Arms Weaponry
Price: $ 63.00
Investment casting.

Kit: Standard GI Slide
Manufacturer: Small Arms Weaponry
Price: $ 68.00
Investment casting.

ATTENTION GUN WRITERS

If you're like us, you like guns. You enjoy owning, building and shooting them. You may also enjoy writing about them — sharing your knowledge and experience with others. *KIT GUNS & HOBBY GUNSMITHING* is looking for interesting, accurate and well-written articles.

Our editorial scope includes all aspects of kit gun building, gun design and gunsmithing techniques that are suitable for the amateur or home-workshop enthusiast. We will also consider special construction articles; historical perspectives; articles on shooting, collecting, and craftsmanship; or problem-solving articles which pertain to blackpowder firearms, modern firearms, and exotica.

Being published identifies you as an expert in the field, and is almost as much fun as shooting. If this appeals to you, and you want to learn more, we'll send you a free Author's Information Kit. Write to us at:

KIT GUNS & HOBBY GUNSMITHING
Attn: Editorial Department
P. O. Box 2204
Dayton, Ohio 45429

If you've already got a great idea for an article, write a letter and tell us about it. We like single-page queries that contain a good definition of your subject and your point of view (as well as a sense of your writing style). Include your name, address, and daytime phone number.

We don't guarantee instant fame and fortune; however, we do promise prompt consideration of your idea. If we accept your proposal for an article, we can also promise encouragement and the professional help needed to complete your project. Fees will be negotiated on an individual basis. *KIT GUNS AND HOBBY GUNSMITHING* will not be responsible for any unsolicited material. We will not return any material that does not include a SASE.

Are You Reading Someone Else's KG&HG?

If so, we know that you'll probably want to have your very own copy. Or, maybe you have a friend who would appreciate one as a gift. Now that you've had a chance to see *KIT GUNS & HOBBY GUNSMITHING* first hand, we know that you'll agree that this is the most unique new gun publication in years. In addition to the detailed construction articles and factual information, the comprehensive *Directory* section makes this book a useful reference work for years to come — a valuable addition to every gun enthusiast's library.

KIT GUNS & HOBBY GUNSMITHING is only published once a year, and quantities are limited. So, if you need additional copies of the *FIRST EDITION*, order now. Use the Reader Service Card and enclose your check or money order for the correct amount, or use your credit card if you wish. Also, be sure to check the proper box to be notified when the *SECOND EDITION* comes off the press. It's sure to be even bigger and better than the first, and we know you won't want to miss out.

Manufacturers and Suppliers

Use the convenient Reader Service Card at right to obtain product information from these sources.

1	3-Way
2	AG Supply
3	ARM-TEC
4	Allen Fire Arms
5	Alpha Armament Ltd.
6	Armsport
7	Ashland Shooting Supplies
8	Big John's Weapons
9	Bro-Caliber International
10	C&C Tubing
11	CATCO
12	CIONEC
13	Catawba Enterprises
14	**Classic Arms Ltd.**
15	**Connecticut Valley Arms**
16	Covert Arms Manufacturing
17	Crown City Arms
18	DAQ
19	DP Ltd.
20	Dare Gun Room
21	**Dixie Gun Works**
22	Don Floyd
23	EMF Company
24	**Electroless Specialities**
25	**Essex Arms Corporation**
26	Euclid Sales Company
27	**Euroarms of America**
28	FKF
29	Federal Ordnance
30	**Frankford Arsenal**
31	**Green River Barrel Company**
32	Group Industries
33	H. Hsu
34	H.N. Company
35	Hard Times Armory
36	**Hopkins & Allen**
37	J&G Sales
38	J. Miniard
39	Jonathan Arthur Ciener
40	L.L. Baston Company
41	Light Enterprises
42	Lone Star Ordnance
43	**Lyman Products**
44	Lynn & Betty Fletcher
45	Mike's Shooting Supplies
46	Military Accessories Corp.
47	Mowrey Gun Works
48	NESARD
49	**Navy Arms Company**
50	**Quality Parts Company**
51	R&D Services
52	RFP
53	**Rhino International**
54	S&H Arms
55	**SARCO**
56	SCHERER
57	Sendra Corporation
58	**SGW**
59	**SIONAC**
60	SWD
61	Sgt. Sandy's Parts & Surplus
62	Silence is Golden
63	Small Arms Weaponry
64	Sparkey's Gun Tune
65	Springfield Armory
66	Springs Import & Export
67	Sub-Sonic Engineering
68	**Survival Consultants**
69	Texas Armament Company
70	The Postal Armorer
71	Thompson/Center Arms
72	**York Arms Company**